MOKU O LO'E

A HISTORY *of* COCONUT ISLAND

MOKU O LO'E

A HISTORY *of* COCONUT ISLAND

P. CHRISTIAAN KLIEGER

WITH CONTRIBUTIONS BY PHILIP HELFRICH AND JO-ANN C. LEONG

I hope you enjoy this! Mahalo for all your help

Jo Ann

BISHOP MUSEUM
PRESS

The publication of this book was made possible by funding from the Edwin W. Pauley Foundation.

Bishop Museum Press
1525 Bernice Street
Honolulu, Hawai'i 96817

Cloth ISBN-10: 1-58178-072-9
Cloth ISBN-13: 978-1-58178-072-7

Paper ISBN-10: 1-58178-048-6
Paper ISBN-13: 978-1-58178-048-2

Cover photo by Douglas Peebles

Design by Nancy Watanabe

Printed in Korea

Klieger, P. Christiaan.
    Moku o Lo'e : a history of Coconut Island / by P. Christiaan
Klieger ; with contributions by Philip Helfrich and Jo-Ann Leong.
        p. cm.
    Includes bibliographical references and index.
    ISBN 1-58178-048-6 (pbk. : alk. paper)
  1. Coconut Island (Hawaii)--History. 2. Coconut Island (Hawaii)--
Social life and customs. 3. Coconut Island (Hawaii)--Biography. I.
Helfrich, Philip. II. Leong, Jo-Ann. III. Title.

    DU628.C63K58 2007
    996.9'3--dc22
                              2007008585

To the Memory of Bobbe Pauley Pagen

CONTENTS

ORTHOGRAPHIC NOTES

When the Hawaiian language was first written down, neither the emically-occuring glottal stop (*'okina*) nor the macron (*kahakō*) representing vowel lengthening entered the Roman orthography. Since these linguistic sounds are integral components of the Hawaiian language, recent efforts have begun to apply these marks to common Hawaiian terms and most place names. Over the past few years, many institutions have begun to adopt the use of these marks, but the practice is by no means complete or consistent. One difficulty is the temptation to apply the marks to historic periods when the marks were not used. For example, there never was a "Territory of Hawai'i." However, for the sake of continuity in this work, names of institutions that currently utilize the *'okina* and *kahakō* will be represented with the diacritics throughout (e.g. Hawai'i Institute of Marine Biology).

ACKNOWLEDGMENTS

One exciting aspect of writing a book is the creation of "something out of nothing," which no doubt must be some of the same emotion felt when Christian Holmes set out to build a palace on a tiny, rat-infested island in Kāneʻohe Bay. However, the stories and recollections shared with me by dozens of individuals have great substance on their own and it is to this process of sharing that fuels enthusiasm for the publication of a moʻoleo o Moku o Loʻe.

I first remember hearing about Coconut Island and its famous marine biology institute when I was in high school and considering colleges and college majors. Having been a fan of Flipper, I fancied myself living the life of Luke Halpin's character Sandy, frolicking with the dolphins on a tropical island, of course all the while studying for a career in marine biology. Well, it was several more years before I finally arrived at the University of Hawaiʻi, as a graduate student—and by then my interests had shifted to anthropology. But I'll never forget that crystalline dream of the turquoise seas, the coral reefs, and the sun-bleached hair that for me represented my first image of Coconut Island. It has been a great pleasure to get back to Coconut Island, in a manner totally unexpected.

First and foremost I thank Dr. Philip Helfrich, director emeritus of the Hawaiʻi Institute of Marine Biology, for originally dreaming up the idea of a history of Moku o Loʻe, finding funding, requesting proposals, and championing the work through numerous phases leading to eventual publication. Thanks also to Kathleen Helfrich for her work with her father in these efforts.

A big part of the creation of this book must be credited to the Edwin W. Pauley Foundation of Los Angeles, in the 1990s under the direction of the late Bobbe Pauley Pagen (née Barbara "Bobbe" Jean McHenry), for providing financial support to begin to write a history of the remarkable little island that the Pauley family once owned. I acknowledge with thanks Dr. Stephen and Marylyn Pauley for their support and patience in this process, as well as other family members, the late Robert "Buzz" Pauley, Susan Pauley Hillyer French, Kevin Hillyer, and Foundation executive secretary Tanya Hendrix. Ten years after the original report was written, the Pauley Foundation came forth again to provide a grant to Bishop Museum Press for the publication of this book. I am grateful for this constant support.

Of great inspiration has been the warm friendship of the Fleischmann and Holmes families. I would like to acknowledge Christian Holmes II's daughter Ann Holmes Terrell, her son Bruce Spaulding, and her husband Don; Carole Holmes, Michael and Genta Holmes, and Michael's brother Christian Holmes IV, who always helped me maintain a clear vision of his grandfather. All have been most generous in sharing information about Moku o Loʻe, the Queen's Surf estate, or other aspects of their family. Thanks also to Charles Fleischmann III of Cincinnati for his particular insight into his family's place in history and his spirited letters, and to Monte Schulz.

In this passage of twelve years, some individuals with intimate knowledge of Moku o Loʻe have passed on. These include Dr. Robert Hiatt, Charles Nakamoto, Dr. Frederick Reppun, Lester Zukeran, Tom

Beyer, and Bobbe Pauley Pagen. To these individuals and their families go special thanks for helping to document a portion of their lives that might have been lost.

The Anderson family, Dolores Mokuoloe Beyer Berengue, Col. A. R. Brashear, W. Dudley Childs, Jr., Mary Clark, Helen S. Davis, Rose Deang, Bill Drake, Charles Forquer, Steve Gates, Anita Gouveia, George and Fumiko Harada, Julia Ing, Sen. Daniel Inouye, Pamela Larson, Charles Lucas, Jr., Richard Miller, Steve Miranda, Harry Myer, Gary Nakamoto, Antonio Pagliotti, Grieg Porter, Samuel Price, Rick Rainalter, Sydney Schwartz, Barbara Shanahan, G. W. Sumner, Doug Uyehara, Ethel Taka-hashi Uyehara, Henry Walker, Jr., Brenda Yette, and Ruth Youngren—I thank for their gracious permission to participate in the gathering of oral histories. My conversations with Paul Breese, first director of the Honolulu Zoo, were very insightful, explaining the extent of Christian Holmes's interest in collecting wild animals.

So much of the work in preparing this book was done not on the coral sands of Coconut Island, but in dark and dank shelves of libraries and archives. I thank Margaret M. Greenan, Ilene P. Karpf, and David R. Stivers of the Fleischmann archives of RJR-Nabisco at Parsippany, New York; Robert Boyle of the Field Library of Peekskill, New York; John Curran of the Peekskill Museum; Robert Blesse of the Special Collections Department, Library of the University of Nevada-Reno; Special Collections, Library of the University of California-Los Angeles; archivist Terri Sheridan of the Santa Barbara Natural History Museum; DeSoto Brown, Betty Kam, and Dr. Susan A. Lebo of the Bishop Museum, Honolulu; University of Hawai'i-Mānoa; Hawai'i State Archives; Cynthia Keller of the Cincinnati Museum Center; and Billie Broaddus of the University of Cincinnati Medical Heritage Center. I would also like to thank Christine Crawford, Keith Dierburg, James Parker, and Rob Trabert of the Fleischmann Company. Thanks to Dr. Gordon Grau and his staff for allowing me access to Coconut Island, and to current Hawai'i Institute of Marine Biology director Dr. Jo-Ann Leong and George Atta of Group 70 International for sharing their vision for the future of the island and its institute.

All hail Blair Collis, Ron Cox, and Lan Tu of Bishop Museum Press for being patient with a stubborn author throughout the long process of selection, editing, and production.

To Scot Parry I send special mahalo for all his help in the gathering of documents, interviews, and follow ups to construct this book. To all that have shared their own special encounters with Moku o Lo'e, a warm *aloha* to each!

P. Christiaan Klieger, Ph.D.
San Francisco, California, 2007

FOREWORD | BY STEPHEN M. PAULEY, M.D. | PRESIDENT, EDWIN W. PAULEY FOUNDATION

To spend vacation time as a youngster on a private island is, well, hard to explain to most people. Wanting to be like everybody else, I kept it pretty quiet. The reality is that between age five and fifteen, with a few summers off for boys camp and work, my parents would take me and my brother, sister, and grandmother to Coconut Island. Learning to go off a water ski jump, the first in Kāneʻohe Bay, combined with sailing, spearfishing, swimming with dolphins, and generally having the time of our lives, were the order of the day. But it was the exposure to science and scientists working on the island that really shaped my future.

My first memory on the island was at age five. I was sleeping with my brother and sister at the now-destroyed beach house on the north end of the island. On April 1, 1946, a 7.8 earthquake in the Aleutian Islands sent warnings of a tsunami throughout the islands. My parents came down and told us we needed to quickly move up to higher ground, up to the "Retreat" as it was called. I looked up to see them all leaving and shouted, "Can I come too?" Horrified, my mother came running back in the dark to carry me up the long concrete stairs. Sadly, the ensuing tsunami on the Big Island killed 122 people. North-facing Kāneʻohe Bay, with its barriers of multiple coral reefs, went untouched.

It took me awhile to figure out that not all kids spent their summers on a 28-acre island off Oʻahu. Fortunately, my father realized that if he didn't crack the whip once in a while, I'd become an insufferable brat. So as I grew older I was assigned work around the island, mostly in the form of cleanup projects for which I was paid 25 cents an hour.

My father resisted all my requests for a raise.

My father had made it possible for the late Dr. Bob Hiatt and the Hawaii Marine Laboratory in Waikīkī to construct a few buildings at the south end of the island. The association with our family and the marine biologists on the island later made it possible for me to have a summer job at the lab. Chipping rust off the wire screens separating the fish ponds allowed me to appreciate at least some of the ongoing science at the lab, and I quickly figured out that I didn't want to be a rust chipper when I grew up.

Marine biologist, and tropical fish expert, Dr. Jack Randall, who had sailed with his wife Helen to the islands in the 1950s, was hired to look after us kids. He taught me the names of the reef fish, took me spearfishing on Kāneʻohe Bay's coral reefs, and we snorkeled off the rocks at Makapuʻu Point. Others assigned to keep us kids out of big trouble were Tay Perry, now a master canoe builder, and Mike McCormick, now a prominent realtor in Hawaiʻi.

It was being around guys like Jack, Dr. Hiatt, and later Dr. Phil Helfrich, who became director of what is now called the Hawaiʻi Institute of Marine Biology (HIMB), that shaped my life-long interest in science and which greatly influenced me to become a physician and surgeon.

I cannot look back on those idyllic days without mentioning the kindness and the loving, gentle spirit of the *kamaʻaina* who cared for us and who worked on the island: Grace Oyama, our babysitter in the early years; island caretaker, the late Robert Miranda, and his wife

Rosita, and their children, some of whom they named after the Pauley kids; the late Rose Wailehua, a loving spirit and the best cook I've ever known; the late Lester Zukeran, the highly talented "Mr. Fix It" for HIMB and captain of the lab's vessel *Salpa* upon which I would hitch rides from time to time; the late Charles Nakamoto ("Naka") who took me with him to pull fish traps and showed me a little about fixing boat motors; and the late Andy Anderson, a wonderful man who had a constant toothless grin, and who could build anything. Their gift to me, my brother, and sister, was the Hawaiian virtue of genuine *aloha*—unconditional love with no strings attached.

There were also many at the marine lab who tolerated my just hanging around the various experiments for hours at a time asking questions. I didn't know it then, but those patient marine biologists were my first mentors in the world of science and medicine.

Under today's director Dr. Jo-Ann Leong, HIMB is achieving much notoriety. The lab's proximity to salt water and coral reefs makes it a coveted location for studies in marine sciences and the new lab has attracted some top molecular biologists.

As kids we were taught to swim properly by Hawai'i's distance swimming legend, Keo Nakama (didn't everyone have a swim coach like Keo?). Learning his easy stroke ("glide, Steve, glide") helped me with high school distance races and it has stayed with me to this day. I liked competitive swimming, but football and rugby became my main sports.

When I was 15 my father thought it would be nice if I worked out with the Hawaiian swim team under Coach Soichi Sakamoto. I was swimming in high school then, but of course the Hawaiian swimmers were in a league of their own. As all Hawai'i knows, Coach Sakamoto was a terrific human being and swimming coach. He tolerated my working out at the Waikiki Natatorium with the likes of Ford Konno, George Onokea, Evelyn Konno, Bill Woolsey, and Dick Cleveland. At that time Olympic diving champion Sammy Lee practiced off the highest platform at the Natatorium. Amazingly, years later we would become medical colleagues in otolaryngology—head and neck surgery—at a hospital in Anaheim, California.

Today I have the pleasure and privilege of being associated with the UH Sea Grant program as an affiliate professor. My contribution is to attempt to preserve Hawai'i's night skies from the ravages of light pollution (I am an amateur astronomer). Unfortunately, the stars over O'ahu, Maui, and the Big Island are slowly disappearing in the sky glow caused by bad outdoor lighting practices. The Sea Grant appointment was made possible by UH Sea Grant director and environmentalist, Dr. Gordon Grau. I first met Gordon on Coconut Island when he was a young scientist and we have become good friends. He later became acting director of HIMB. So returning to Hawai'i is always a rich experience for me, seeing old friends and making new ones, and I have the opportunity to make a small contribution to the quality of life in Hawai'i.

Because all of these people shaped my life to such a degree, and because they were such wonderful human beings, I treasure the time we had together, more so than island visits by presidents and other dignitaries whom Paul mentions in this book. (However, I do admit that short-sheeting President Truman was very cool as was his response—see Chapter 5.)

That I could play a role in shaping Coconut Island's final and best use as a research facility gives me great pleasure. The Edwin W. Pauley Foundation's grant to allow the UH Foundation to own the island and lease it back to UH for marine research will protect this wonderful place in perpetuity. The foundation also funded the Edwin W. Pauley Marine Lab, a state-of-the-art science facility designed to attract today's best scientists. I think that my father and the previous co-owners of the island, who at times toyed with developing the island in a number of different ways, would be pleased with this outcome. But it was my mother who was the island's real protector. She resisted every attempt at development, and my father would not override her on this issue. She loved the natural beauty of Coconut Island and thought it should not be spoiled in any way. I appreciate so much the great times and rich experiences on the island that my late parents made possible.

Much misinformation is floating out there regarding the island's history—I always like to eavesdrop on the tour bus speeches at the Pali Lookout. But now P. Christiaan Klieger's depth of research and detailed history sets the record straight. I hope you enjoy this book and may the spirit of *aloha* fill your hearts in the same way that this place with its memories and experiences have filled mine. The island is a special place, and I believe she has her own special *mana*. I hope we continue to treat her with the respect she deserves.

Mahalo nui,
Stephen M. Pauley, M.D.
Ketchum, Idaho, 2006

FOREWORD

by Christian R. Holmes IV | Rice University

I know this may be an unorthodox way to introduce P. Christiaan Klieger's impressive history of Coconut Island, but let me start with a story about a six-year-old boy, a lamp, some monkeys, orchids, an island, and my grandfather, Christian Holmes, my namesake who died three years before I was born.

As a small child living in San Francisco, I had heard that that my grandfather had monkeys. Many monkeys. I think it is fair to say I developed a six-year-old boy's obsession with my grandfather's monkeys. It began with my fixation on a lamp in our home from his living room on Coconut Island. The lamp displayed carved in relief, two furry monkeys, teeth bared, glaring at bees buzzing about a honeycomb held by one of the monkeys.

Again and again, I would ask my mother, "Where are my grandfather's monkeys from?"

"I just don't know for sure," she would sigh. "He had monkeys everywhere. He had a zoo in Santa Barbara with monkeys. He had a zoo in Hawai'i with monkeys, and he had two huge chimpanzees on Coconut Island. They roamed at will and terrorized your great aunt Bubbles Holmes *en dishabille* in her dressing room."

"And where are the monkeys now?" I would ask.

"Well, some of the monkeys are in the San Francisco Zoo. He gave them to the zoo."

"Are the monkeys from Coconut Island...the monkeys on this lamp?" I would persist.

After she ran out of information on the monkeys, I would return

to the lamp—gazing at it, running my fingers along the monkeys' brown lined fur, moving my hand to the sharp teeth, the wings of the bees, the mysterious red block *kanji* signature of the Japanese artisan at the base of the tusk. I was hooked on those monkeys.

And one day, age six, I took off on my Great Monkey Odyssey. I left home, convinced a bus conductor to take one dime and a nickel, got a transfer, and I made it all the way—to my mother's subsequent horror and chagrin—to the San Francisco Zoo.

"Where are the monkeys?" I asked the attendant.

"Monkey Island," he replied.

And there they were, dozens of monkeys jumping around a concrete island, enclosed by a moat.

"Do you know which monkeys are from Coconut Island?" I asked

"Nope. Why?" an attendant said.

"Well, my grandfather lived on Coconut Island; he had many monkeys and some of these were his."

"Where are your parents?" asked the attendant, worried about this seemingly delusional six year old.

The flowers, the orchids, became my second obsession.

Mr. Mike (Mike Pagliotti), my grandfather and father's gardener would tell me about the flowers on Cocunut Island. Beautiful flowers, strange flowers, thousands of them. Look in your father's library, look at your grandfather's books, he would say. And off I would go to the library, pulling down volumes until I found the books with the flowers. *The Orchid Albums. The Collection of Hawaiian Flowers.* And as I opened the first book to tumble to the floor from a shelf barely within reach, there was my grandfather's book plate with his name: "Ex libris Christian Holmes"; embossed on the bookplate were...monkeys on a ledge taunting a tiger.

Periodically, I would try to tell my childhood friends about Coconut Island, especially the monkeys and flowers, but no one would believe me. Too much of a fantasy.

Yet, with time, I met people, many, many people from different walks of life who lived and shared the stories of Coconut Island. I recall working for the State Department and testifying before the Senate Appropriations Subcommittee on Foreign Operations, chaired by Hawai'i's Senator Daniel Inouye. At the close of the hearing, he beckoned me to the dais, and asked, "Are you related to the Chris Holmes from Coconut Island?" "Yes," I said, and then a new story would begin, this time about my grandfather opening up his fishponds to the local population.

The island is shaped by not only natural and man-made physical forces, but also by its stories. Some of the stories may have given new definition to the term "partying hard." Others demonstrated that he played hard, but also cared deeply for the people who worked for and with him. Of all the stories, my favorite was my father's recollection of the help and protection he offered to the Japanese-American fishermen who worked on his tuna fishing fleet and who faced possible internment with their families during World War II.

My grandfather scripted and lived his Coconut Island life, regrettably burning out and dying young, never living long enough to see the impact of his life on his descendants, on the island itself. The stories of the monkeys and flowers, the island itself, are stories of commerce, distraction, and amusement. Fortunately, my grandfather's life went beyond sheer amusement.

My grandfather, like so many of our clan beginning with Dr. Christian Holmes and Charles Fleischmann, was fascinated by science and natural history; he was strongly influenced by his uncle, Maxmillian Fleischmann, who helped establish Santa Barbara's Museum of Natural History where my grandfather also maintained his private zoo, similar in size and diversity to his zoo on O'ahu. Coconut Island in many ways was a "living laboratory" for him, replete with fishponds which stocked bait for his tuna fleet, huge orchid collections, plantings of exotic trees, shrubs and other flowers, and a significant library of natural history books. It is wonderful that this living laboratory became the home of a major marine biology research laboratory.

And now P. Christiaan Klieger has painstakingly documented the story of Coconut Island, and I am pleased to note the emphasis that he gives to the island becoming, thanks to the Pauley family and University of Hawai'i, a major center of marine biology research.

I would like to express my family's deep appreciation for Dr. Klieger's thorough research on the social, economic, and natural history of Coconut Island and the role my grandfather played in the island's evolution.

As Dr. Klieger has noted, this "sawed-off volcanic plug" has indeed had a remarkable history, formed by volcanic action, a place of sustenance for the native peoples of Hawai'i, a place of commerce, discovery, and enjoyment for my grandfather, a place of enjoyment and scientific research for the Pauley family, and now the site of a major marine biology research center for the University of Hawai'i.

While my grandfather played a major role in the physical expansion and landscaping of the island, were it not for the Pauley family's care in protecting the island and transferring it to the University of Hawai'i, I doubt the island would have remotely retained the "stamp" which my grandfather placed on it. I admire the generosity and foresight of the Pauley family.

As I close this foreword, I reflect upon some pictures my grandfather commissioned of Coconut Island in the 1930s. The island and mountains across Kāne'ohe Bay are lush with deep green vegetation. The only structures on Coconut Island are my grandfather's "lookout" and the main house. I consider how remarkable it is that 80 years later, this volcanic plug is still so beautiful. That it has so endured may be the most remarkable story of all.

Christian R. Holmes IV
Houston, Texas, 2006

FOREWORD | BY PHILIP HELFRICH, PH.D. | DIRECTOR EMERITUS, HAWAI'I INSTITUTE OF MARINE BIOLOGY

Moku o Lo'e, or Coconut Island, often seems to fascinate and captivate those who visit this special place. My personal involvement began upon my arrival in Hawai'i, in September 1953. As a graduate student and an aspiring marine biologist, I was fascinated with this beautiful little island in Kāne'ohe Bay, with the rich coral reef community in the surrounding waters, and with the absorbing group of marine biologists at the Hawaii Marine Laboratory with whom I shared the experience. I became acquainted with the Pauley family who owned the island, and visited every summer with a variety of engaging guests. Gradually, I became aware of another dimension of my island experience—the colorful past history of Coconut Island.

The Pauleys were prominent in the world of business, politics, sports, and education, and they seemed to thoroughly enjoy entertaining a variety of interesting guests at their lovely island retreat. In the 1950s and '60s they hosted such notables as Harry Truman, Lyndon Johnson, governors John Burns of Hawai'i and Pat Brown of California (and on one occasion, the governors of all 50 states), senators Daniel Inouye and J. William Fullbright, as well as many other celebrated personalities in the fields of politics, education, sports, and entertainment. As an available young biologist-in-residence on Coconut Island, I was frequently invited by the Pauley family to represent the University of Hawai'i's Marine Laboratory at social gatherings. On numerous occasions, Ed Pauley asked me to accompany him and guests on a tour of "his" marine laboratory.

Soon after my arrival, I became intrigued by two individuals on Coconut Island, both of whom had worked for Christian Holmes during the 1930s–1940s. Andy Anderson, a loquacious part-Hawaiian, had been employed by Holmes, and now worked as a handyman for the Pauleys. Lester Zukeran, the soft-spoken son of an Okinawan farmer, was born and raised on the shores of Kāne'ohe Bay, and had worked for Holmes from 1936–1941. During World War II, he served with distinction in the famed 442nd Infantry Regiment of the U. S. Army in Europe. He returned to Coconut Island, and for more than four decades was a boat operator and overall maintenance supervisor for the Hawaii Marine Laboratory.

Upon completion of my degree in 1958, I was employed as a researcher on a project to study ciguatera fish poisoning. This required extensive travel to islands of the tropical Pacific in search of the elusive toxin causing this condition, to acquire specimens of toxic fish, and to investigate the cause of outbreaks in human populations. Lester Zukeran frequently accompanied me on expeditions to the Pacific Islands as a fisherman, boat handler, and a person with extensive knowledge of the marine environment. Long days in a fishing boat, and evenings at our field camp, brought Lester out of his usual reserve. He told me many fascinating stories of Coconut Island in the Christian Holmes era. Lester and Andy Anderson filled in details of the history of this enchanting place in the early part of the twentieth century and I was convinced that this was a story that had to be told.

As the 1950s became the 1960s, and then the 1970s, I continued to be invited to attend numerous social functions of the Pauley family and island co-owner, Troy Post. As I conversed with more of the "rich and famous" and shared the lore of the island in times past, these guests seemed entranced with the lore of Coconut Island, and conveyed an insatiable curiosity about its past history.

From a wealth of firsthand experience and the many more hours of thoughtful dialogue (what local Hawaiians refer to as "talk story") with Lester Zukeran, Andy Anderson, and other elders in the community, I saw a fascinating picture unfold and felt a responsibility to tell the complete Coconut Island saga.

Many storytellers visited the island over the years, and they wrote their own version (a mixture of fact and fiction) of the Coconut Island story. These tales lacked the breath, veracity, and scholarly authenticity that, influenced by my scientific background, I thought this story deserved. I was convinced that the story needed a professional historian, possibly one with a background in cultural anthropology, to accomplish the task of writing the history of Moku o Lo'e.

In 1995, I approached Edwin Pauley's widow, Bobbe Pauley Pagen, with a proposal for the production of a thorough, scholarly history of Coconut Island. She enthusiastically endorsed the project and generously offered to support the effort. I then convened a group of colleagues from the University of Hawai'i, and we prepared for the solicitation of proposals to produce a history of Coconut Island. Upon the receipt of several responses, we were unanimous in our choice of Dr. P. Christiaan Klieger, an accomplished author then working as an anthropologist at the Bishop Museum in Honolulu.

Dr. Klieger relates the early history of the island and the engaging individuals who have owned and cared for it over the decades. He researched the Pauley and Holmes eras with many interviews with Pauley, Holmes, and Fleischmann family members and friends. It was fortunate that he was able to interview persons like Bobbe Pauley Pagen, Robert Hiatt, Lester Zukeran, and others who have since passed away.

For my portion of the story, that of the University of Hawai'i's role in Coconut Island, I chose to emphasize the early history of the marine laboratory (through the term of Vernon Brock as HIMB Director). This is the story of a few pioneer marine biologists who labored under difficult conditions to make this little marine field station in the middle of the Pacific into the world-class Hawai'i Institute of Marine Biology that exists today. Central to this effort was the inspirational leadership of Robert W. Hiatt, and the vision and generosity of Pauley family. The later history (1970 to the present) is a cursory review that reflects the growth of HIMB, with a few highlights in research programs and areas of emphasis, but by no means is it a comprehensive consideration of the diverse programs or their accomplishments. The succession of leadership is presented, with a general indication of how the laboratory evolved to its current status. Dr. Jo-Ann Leong then summarizes progress since she assumed directorship of HIMB in 2002, with her goals and aspirations for the future.

I wish to acknowledge the assistance and insightful discussions on Coconut Island experiences involving Arlene Gilliland, Fred E. Trotter, Nancy Davis Pflueger, and Christian Holmes V. Additional assistance from the following collegues is gratefully acknowledged: Marlin Atkinson, Richard Brock, Jack Davidson, E. Gordon Grau, Kim Holland, Paul Jokiel, Robert Kinzie, George Losey, Paul Nachtigall, Wayne Nakamoto, Jack Randall, Ernst S. Reese, and Sidney J. Townsley. Special thanks to my wife, Maybelle Helfrich, daughter, Kathy, Joe O'Reilly, and the late Elizabeth Hiatt for their efforts and encouragement in the production of this book.

The story of Moku o Lo'e as it is revealed here is one of colossal importance to future generations who will visit Coconut Island. I hope that readers will be as excited and captivated by this story, and they will enjoy reading it as much as those of us who experienced it, and have been involved in the preparation of its fascinating history.

Philip Helfrich, Ph.D.
Kāne'ohe, Hawai'i, 2006

Western shoreline of Moku o Loʻe looking southward, ca. 1910s. Tai Sing Loo, Bishop Museum

A Concept of Paradise

It was just all that wonderful romantic music,
the idea of soft nights, guitars, water lapping,
and nothing to worry about.

Elvi Whittaker

The philanthropist, the environmentalist, the scientist—the three authors of the preceding forewords represent three of the major chapters in the life of the little island, Moku o Loʻe—Coconut Island. Pauley, Holmes, and Helfrich, and their predecessors represent three worlds inextricably linked through the passage of time on this tiny island in the Hawaiian chain. It is a story of high ideals and thoughtful change, all inspired by a dream of Arcadia.

One dreams of paradise, a physical place devoid of the paradoxes and conflicts that burden everyday life, of a place set apart. In Hilton's *Shangri-La*, a lush valley inhabited by wise sages serves as the focus of human delight, not the harsh, windswept Himalayan mountains that frame the real place and the hard-scrabble life of its inhabitants. For the lotus eaters of Hawaiʻi's 28-acre Moku o Loʻe, later known as Coconut Island, the paradox remains: Moku o Loʻe originally was but a potato-shaped, sawed-off volcanic plug in the middle of Kāneʻohe Bay on the North Shore of Oʻahu—a *moku*, a place set apart. Yet it was, as shaped by human agency throughout the years, considered by many individuals of international reputation to be the epitome of paradise. This story examines the cultural construction of a paradise from a very real place. It is the story of that rare Hawaiian locale that has managed to escape the ravages of over-development and misguided economic schemes, emerging as a pre-eminent and unique temple of learning as the Hawaiʻi Institute of Marine Biology.

Moku o Loʻe's spectacular setting lies at the heart of the emotion that has bound generations of powerful and talented individuals to this place. Set in a colorful coral sea, the visitor to Coconut Island is embraced by a 180° verdant curtain, a semi-circular amphitheater formed by the 2,000 ft. Koʻolau Range. Serrated cliffs rise precipitously behind the shorelines of Kāneʻohe and Heʻeia, from the high peak of Lanihuli to the sea walls of Kualoa to the north. It is memorable to all that visit. Gorham Gilman, an early nineteenth-century travel writer, described the setting of Moku o Loʻe as one of the prettiest sites he had

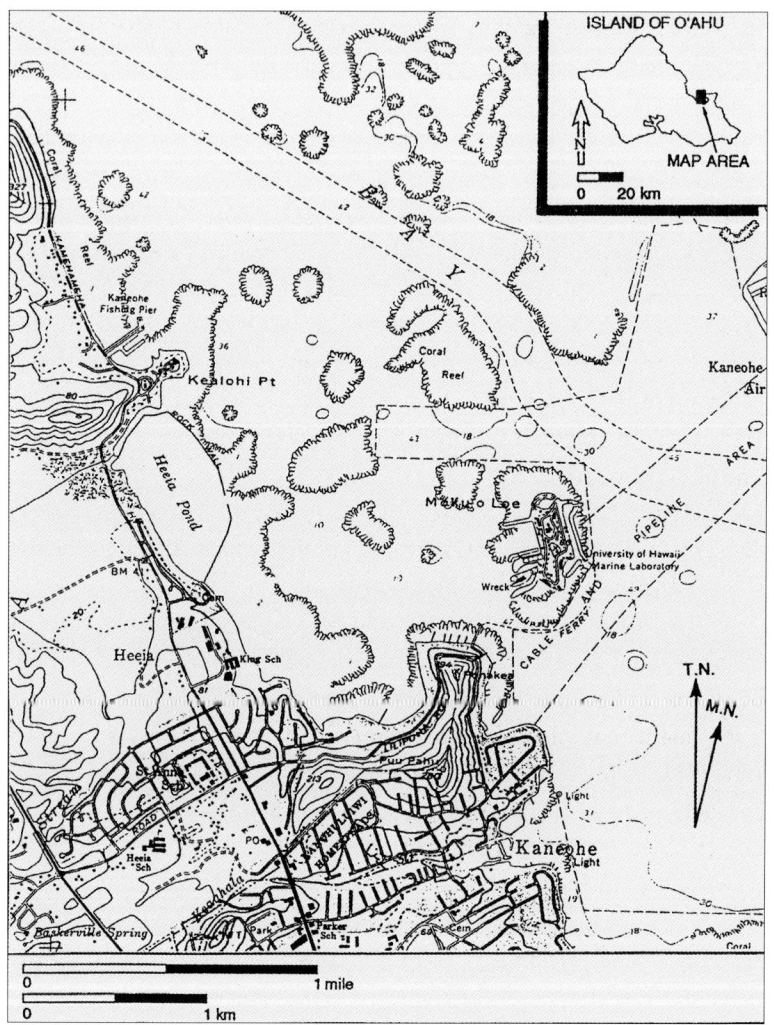

| *Modern topographic map of Moku o Loʻe, Oʻahu. USGS*

seen on his tour of Oʻahu in 1828.[1] To him it was a deep emerald set in a field of smooth turquoise. Such sentiments were to continually repeat themselves throughout the years.

For most of its existence with humanity, Moku o Loʻe was a fishing way station—a place where Native Hawaiian and later commercial fishing could mend their nets and repair their boats. Developed in the 1930s into a pleasure dome by Fleischmann Yeast heir Christian Holmes, it became a rest and relaxation center for war-weary servicemen by the 1940s. A cadre of oilmen and airline owners purchased the colorful islet and attempted to develop a hotel and country club on the island. Failing that, the center of the island was used as a summer retreat for Democratic strongman Edwin Pauley. He donated much of the shoreline of Moku o Loʻe to the University of Hawaiʻi to develop laboratories for the study of marine biology. In the 1990s, the private sector was given by the Pauley Foundation to the university to further develop the Hawaiʻi Institute of Marine Biology.

The story of Moku o Loʻe, and its transformation to Coconut Island, is another example of the reinvention of Hawaiʻi from a place of prosaic indigenous associations to that of exotic Western illusion— a sentiment that still dominates popularized, commodified, and appropriated Hawaiian culture. It is the image of Hawaiʻi that is so successfully promoted by the Hawaii Visitors Bureau, a viewpoint not without its critics. In referring to mainlanders' comments on finding paradise in Hawaiʻi, social commentator Elvi Whittaker notes that:

the very core of romantic philosophy is woven into these descriptions, a familiar Western view of the South Sea. The Islands suggest a seductive nostalgia and hold out a promise for a life of simplicity, immediacy, license, sensuality, warmth, mysticism, and unabashed sentiment. The mainland, in inevitable contrast, becomes lacking in magic and romance, anxiety-ridden...[2]

| *Dr. Christian Holmes, Sr. (left) and family explore remote corners of the world. Univ. of Nevada, Wheeler Collection*

Over the 230 years of Western contact in the Hawaiian Islands, Moku o Loʻe evolved from a place of utility for the Native Hawaiian pursuit of fish to a multifaceted "Coconut Island," a place of grand *lūʻau* and elaborate parties, peaceful family retreats, informal political summits, and now to the disciplined study of marine biology. In its later guise, Coconut Island matches the ideal image of the "desert island"—one ripe to be transformed by Western civilization to a garden of earthly delights and an incubator for positivist ideals. It was logical that the islet served as a stage for the prototypical paradise in the 1932 film *Bird of Paradise* and the 1960s television series *Gilligan's Island*. Within this paradigm, it is entirely logical that it would become a Xanadu for the super rich of their generations, and eventually become one of the world's most exotic laboratories for advanced graduate education. This book traces that transformation.

In Chapter 1, we examine the origins of Moku o Loʻe from the flanks of great Mt. Koʻolau, and its subsidence into a coral sea. Thousands of years later, fisherfolk from Polynesia found respite here from their nighttime hunting of octopus in the broad lagoon. From Moku o Loʻe's summit, schools of fish could be spotted darting among the coral heads—no grand *ahu* or temple for the gods, little Moku o Loʻe served quotidian interests.

With the arrival of the rule of the Kamehameha dynasty, discussed in Chapter 2, Moku o Loʻe, as a part of the *ahupuaʻa* of Heʻeia, was granted to Chief Abner Pākī. The tiny island passed to his daughter, Bernice Pauahi, and then to the Bishop Estate in the late nineteenth century. Despite the island's grand setting, there are only a handful of clues that the rock was used at all during this era.

In Chapter 3, an heir to the Fleischmann Yeast fortune moves to Oʻahu and acquires not only a famous Waikīkī property, and Hawaiian Tuna Packers canning company, but purchases Moku o Loʻe from the Bishop Estate to serve as a repair shop for his fishing boats and as a personal retreat. Construction of the facilities on the little island became somewhat of an obsession for Holmes, dredging nearby sandbars and filling the fringing reef surrounding the island. Thousands of palms were planted as "Coconut Island" rose from the lagoon. A sizable portion of the vast Fleischmann fortune had been plowed into the creation of this pleasure dome. Indeed, few private resorts were as grand as Coconut Island. Hollywood stars and the powerful and celebrated of their day flocked to Holmes's hideaway.

The long party ended on December 7, 1941, when Oʻahu was attacked by the Japanese Airforce. The island, near the Kaneohe Marine Corps Base, was itself strafed. Worn out from excess and dismayed at the turn of events, Holmes turned Coconut Island over to the U.S. military for use as a recreation center for servicemen before dying in 1944.

In Chapter 4, the post-war era saw Coconut Island on the auction block as a broad array of real estate speculators and entrepreneurs thought of turning the site into a nuclear power station, a hotel, a cult headquarters, or a nudist camp. Cooler heads prevailed when oilman Edwin Pauley of Los Angeles purchased the island, in increments, for a summer home for his family. A powerful Democratic fundraiser, Pauley also used the island to entertain presidents Truman and Johnson, royalty, and the moguls of a thousand realms (Chapter 5). In the 1960s, Coconut Island became identified with the television comedy *Gilligan's Island*, although the association was purely accidental.

The Hawaiʻi Institute of Marine Biology had an early start on Coconut Island with Christian Holmes's interest in science and fisheries. In the 1950s, Edwin Pauley let the University of Hawaiʻi establish a permanent marine laboratory on the island. With additional support from Pauley, this grew to be the Hawaiʻi Institute of Marine Biology, a major component of the university's School of Ocean and Earth Science and Technology (SOEST). In the mid-1990s, Ed Pauley's widow donated the remainder of her island to the University of Hawaiʻi Foundation, and provided funds for the reconstruction of new laboratories. The institution is now one of the great centers of learning in the field, a gem of the state's educational system, and a resource for all.

Little Coconut Island has seen much.

Mōkapu Peninsula across Kāneʻohe Bay from Moku o Loʻe. HIMB Collection

CHAPTER ONE

Traditional Life on Moku o Lo'e

Back in the days of prehistory, a rocky plug of solidified basalt formed in the center of the caldera of the massive Ko'olau volcano on O'ahu in the Hawaiian Islands.

Over the eons, with its fires extinguished the great Koʻolau mountain and its caldera began to sink. Simultaneously, vigorous trade winds and torrential rains eroded the windward flank of the enormous shield volcano. Finally, the crater rim was breached and the caldera floor was flooded by the Pacific Ocean, creating a shallow, semi-circular lagoon.[3] Pastel-colored coral soon began to flourish.[4] Weathering this remarkable transformation was the tough little basalt dike.

During the last Ice Age, as the sea level fluctuated with the repeated freezing and melting of the continental ice caps, the coral reef around the tiny island was periodically exposed and flooded, leaving terraces of white coral limestone above the current shoreline composed of eroding coral sand.[5]

Thousands of years after the island's creation, the Polynesians arrived from the south. The wet, expansive windward side of Oʻahu was an ideal place to settle and to raise the Polynesians' staple, taro, in flooded pondfields called *loʻi*. Kāneʻohe Bay, what remained of the old crater, provided abundant fish to complement the diet. In the center of the bay stood the old rock, which the new Hawaiians named "Moku o Loʻe."

In order to understand the importance of the little island in the bay, it is necessary to examine the social context within which the island was framed—the traditional Hawaiian land tenure system. Kailua, Kāneʻohe, and Heʻeia, of which Moku o Loʻe was considered a part of, were three traditional mountain-to-ocean land sections, or *ahupuaʻa*, surrounding the Bay and comprising Koʻolau District. These wedge-shaped zones, extending from the mountains to the coastal fisheries, were designed to provide a maximum of diversified resources for human subsistence and other utility. With such a resource base, each of these units might seem to be able to function autonomously, but in later pre-Contact times each *ahupuaʻa* was ruled by a chief who held allegiance to the district paramount chief (*aliʻi nui ʻai moku*) or king (*mōʻi*).

Kailua, Kāneʻohe, and Heʻeia are landscapes rich in Hawaiian legend. This is indicative of a long and populous human habitation in the region. A growing body of archaeological evidence suggests that this fertile, densely populated area of Windward Oʻahu was continually inhabited for 1,500 to 2,000 years; it may, in fact, be one of the first colonizing centers of the Hawaiian chain.[6]

The lowlands of Heʻeia were once vast salt marshes that extended towards the mountains (*mauka*) from the muddy shoreline incised with a large, artificial fishpond. The expansion of human population inland is reflected in the development of irrigated *loʻi*, especially evident in the extensive terraced pondfields and dryland fields along the sides of Heʻeia Stream—an intensification that occurred between AD 1000–1200.[7]

Heʻeia itself literally means "land of the octopus" (H. *heʻe*), but while it also may refer to a number of myths, Moku o Loʻe is most especially noted, however, in a story of banished siblings as recorded by Sterling and Summers:

There were brothers and a sister from Moku-ʻumeʻume and Kahuaʻiki at ʻEwa, who were expelled for constantly fighting with their parents. The four who were sent away were Kahoe (m.)[8], Kahua-nui who was also known as Kahua-uli (m.), Pahu or Puʻu Pahu (m.) and Loʻe (f.). Kahoe was a farmer who lived on the Haʻiku side of Keaʻahala and so was Kahua-uli a farmer at Kaʻakau-wai at Luluku. Pahu was a fisherman living on the Heʻeia side of that hill now known today as Puʻu Pahu (Pahu Hill). Their sister lived at the place that is still known as Moku-o-Loʻe (Loʻe's island).... It was said that where Loʻe's tears fell, they formed a spring in front of the cliff of Ke-ahi-a-Kahoe, facing Paʻu and there it is to this day.[9]

| *(opposite) Moku o Loʻe seen from Puʻu Pahu, ca. 1935. Bishop Museum*

| *Taro fields (loʻi) under cultivation in Heʻeia. Bishop Museum*

The name of Kahuauli lives on as an *ʻili*, or small land division, of Kāneʻohe adjacent to Luluku *ʻili*. Puʻu Pahu ("Knuckle Point") is the hill on the point of land nearest Moku o Loʻe. It marks the traditional border between Heʻeia and Kāneʻohe. Keahiakahoe ("Akahoe's fire") is a major peak in the Koʻolau Range. The Loʻe story reflects the daily subsistence technology of the area, with its sociopolitical concerns and frictions.

| TRADITIONAL FISHING RESOURCES OF KĀNEʻOHE BAY

The fishery is an integral component of the traditional district of Koʻolau Poko. Kāneʻohe Bay, the large lagoon formed behind a barrier reef that extends far out to sea,[10] was first described by Nathaniel Portlock in 1780:

The bay all round has a very beautiful appearance, the low land and valleys being in high state of cultivation, and crowded with plantations of taro, sweet potatoes, sugar-cane, etc., interspersed with a great number of coconut trees.[11]

The earliest Western chart of the bay and Moku o Loʻe is that surveyed by the U.S. Exploring Expedition of 1840 led by Lieutenant Charles Wilkes. It shows a small, ovoid island lying just off "Knuckle Point" (Puʻu Pahu) that is without a doubt Moku o Loʻe.

Kekepa and Kapapa islands (referred to as "Nohinohi" and "Kimoa" on the Wilkes map) are exposed regions of the Kāneʻohe Bay barrier reef capped with lithified sand dunes.[12] The fisheries of Kāneʻohe and Heʻeia were a particularly rich source of high-quality protein to Native Hawaiian inhabitants, very useful in supplementing a diet of starchy tubers that were cultivated in pondfields and terraces on land.

Due to the absence of substantial wave action within the lagoon and the large amounts of alluvial discharge from the streams of Heʻeia and Kāneʻohe, the shoreline of Kāneʻohe Bay is predominately muddy.

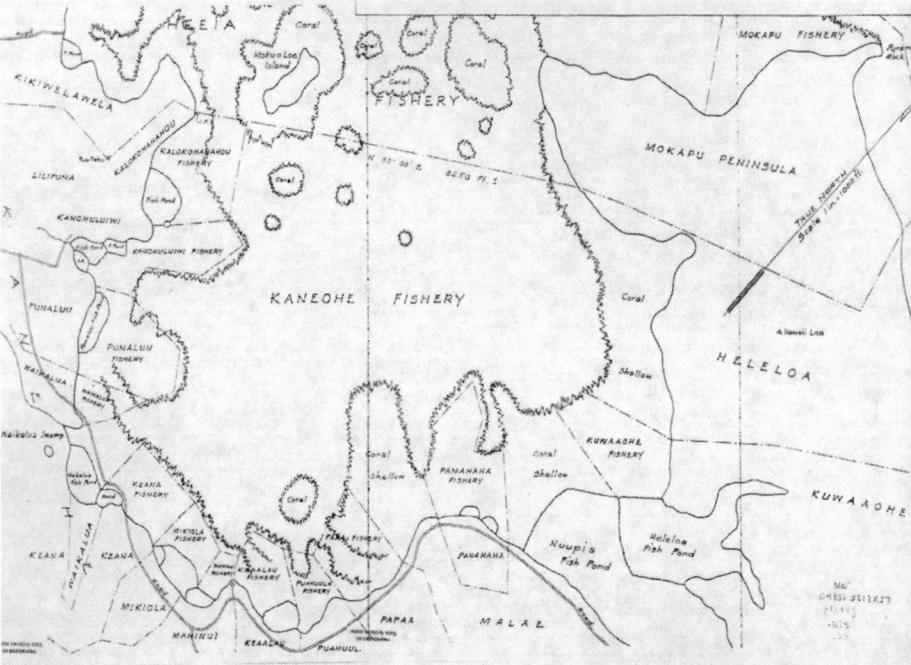

| *Early chart of south end of Kāneʻohe Bay showing reefs and numerous shoreside fishponds. McKeague*

The original leeward beach of Moku o Loʻe appears to have been silty as well. Easton states "the margin of Coconut Island is of dual origins—erosion and deposition. The depositional portion is a splendid example of a fringing coral reef growing seaward while it concurrently disintegrates to form limey sediments that accumulate in the back-reef area."[13]

Coralline sandy beaches with large dunes persist on the windward side of the Mōkapu Peninsula, at about the same distance as the reef is to the Kāneʻohe and Heʻeia shoreline. Once adjacent to Mōkapu was a sandbar known as Sand Island.

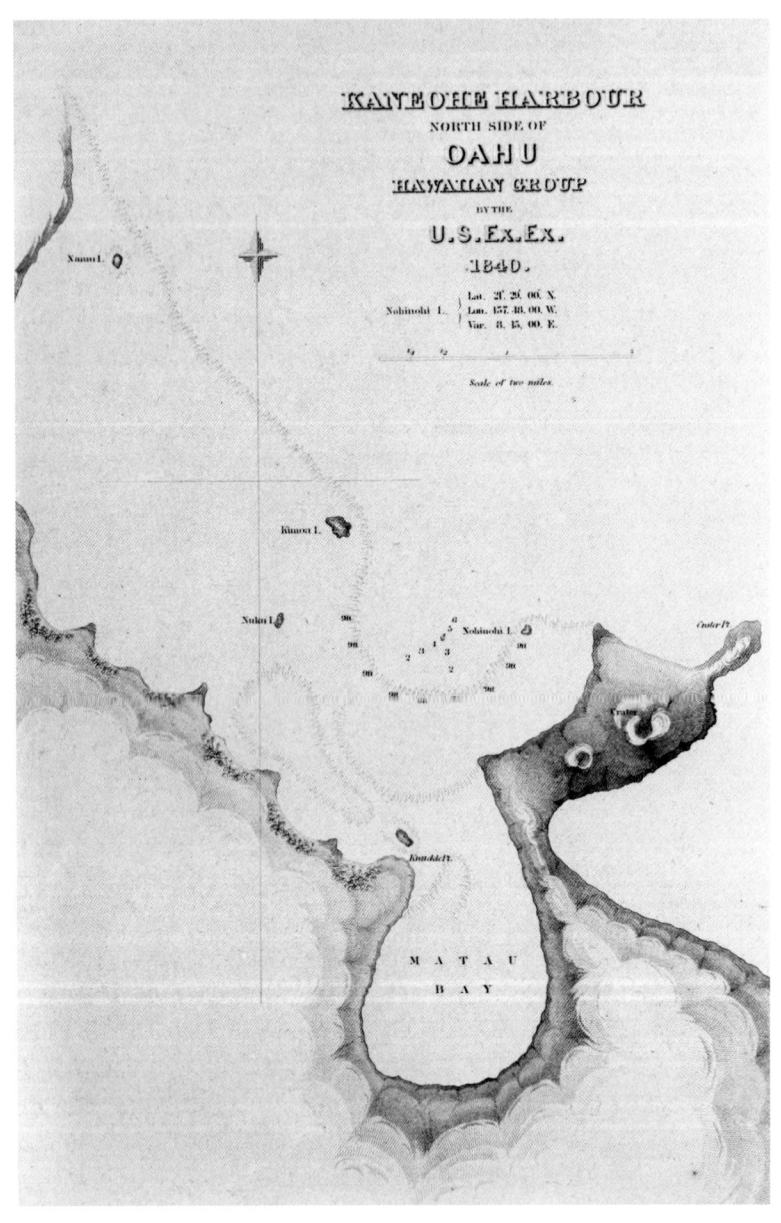

| Sustainable Aquatic Resources

Despite the mud, a large number of artificially created fishponds once studded the Kāne'ohe and He'eia shorelines. Most of these ponds, or *loko 'ia*, were of the *kuapā* type. *Kuapā* were basalt boulder or coral block-walled fishponds built out into the reef between two points of land. Streams draining into the ponds lowered the natural salinity of the water, which encouraged the growth of particular algae that were favored by the young of selected fish species, especially mullet (*'anae*).[14] Fish were carried in on the high tides and trapped in the ponds. Gates (*mākāhā*) helped regulate the flow of seawater.

Many of the Hawaiian fishponds were of great size (as much as 500 acres), the results of elaborate public projects initiated and managed by high-level chiefs. The construction of fishponds necessitated the cooperation of large numbers of people; their existence is a reflection of a high level of sociopolitical complexity. The large fishpond at He'eia, close to Moku o Lo'e, has the largest stonework wall of all fishponds in Hawai'i, some 5,000 feet in length.[15] On the Kāne'ohe side of Pu'u Pahu Hill near Moku o Lo'e was the 7-acre fishpond Kalokohanahou (also known as Kohanahou); there were two watch-houses but no outlet gates to this pond.[16] Other fishponds in the Moku o Lo'e region included Loko o Kanahuluiwi and Loko o Waikapoki. The ponds frequently were rich with many species of fish including *'ama'ama* (striped mullet), *'anae* (full-sized *'ama'ama*), *'āholehole* (Hawaiian flagtail), Samoan crabs, tilapia, *'ōpae huna* (freshwater shrimp), and *'o'opu nākea* (goby). The ponds' aquatic life attracted birds such as *'alae 'ula* (Hawaiian mudhen), *'auku'u* (black-crowned night heron), and the *'alae ke'oke'o* (Hawaiian coot).[17]

| (left) Wilke's map of Kāne'ohe Bay, 1840. Bishop Museum
| (opposite) Loko o O'ohope in foreground, Loko o He'eia in background. Bishop Museum

| *Fishponds of Kāneʻohe Bay: (left to right) Kanahuluiwi, Waikapoki, and Puanaluʻu, ca. 1930. Bishop Museum*

| *Kalokohanahou, immediately south of Moku o Loʻe. Bishop Museum*

While Kāneʻohe, Heʻeia, and other *ahupuaʻa* of Koʻolau Poko were teaming with the rich bounty of taro and sweet potatoes, the fisheries of Kāneʻohe Bay provided abundant fish, edible seaweed, and shellfish. The name of the nearby cliff on Mōkapu Peninsula, Palikilo, is suggestive of observation lookouts (*kilo*), which were an important part of the fishing routine in Kāneʻohe Bay. Moku o Loʻe was probably also used in traditional times as a *kilo* for fishermen.[18]

The activities at the various *kilo* in Kāneʻohe Bay have been remembered in oral histories. The head of a fishing party was usually one well versed in the habits of the fish. From a high vantage point, he watched for large schools of fish. When these were spotted, he signaled the fishermen at sea with his hands, a stick, or a strip of cloth. If he signaled in a semicircular manner, the men in their canoes knew the time was right to surround the school of fish. Once the fish were caught, the head fisherman normally received the largest share.[19]

Around Moku o Loʻe and the Heʻeia fishponds, many types of fishing techniques were practiced. Spearfishing from rocks was popular, as was collecting mollusks and seaweed along the shoreline by hand. On occasion, large groups of people were used in a traditional *hukilau* to reel in gigantic nets cast near the shoreline. Fishing the reefs and deeper waters was often accomplished with wooden outrigger canoes.

Fishing around Moku o Loʻe was remembered by Anita Gouveia, whose family has resided in Heʻeia for more than 150 years. This grand lady spent summers catching and drying fish on the island.

If you use your imagination and go back [to] 1900 and picture standing on a high hill of Moku o Loʻe and surrounding you completely [are] the most beautiful coral gardens—the colors, the spectacular fish around it. Kāneʻohe Bay was so beautiful, it was a treasure.

The principal fish species caught during the spring at Moku o Loʻe were *ʻōhua*, the young of such fish varieties as *humuhumu, manini, uhu,*

| *Hukilau fishing, Maui, 1936. Harold T. Stearns, Bishop Museum*

relation to Christian), visited Moku o Loʻe and apparently interrupted the blessing of a fishing canoe by a *kahuna*. The interloper was promptly locked in a shack until the ceremony was over. In the style of the times, the author of the article implies that Holmes felt he was to be made the main course at the accompanying *lūʻau*![33]

Two named individuals, Ueneaiku and Kawika, are mentioned in the oral traditions as having been buried at Moku o Loʻe. In addition, two other young men may have been interred on the island (see below). Lester Zukeran, a caretaker of the island, remembers that Christian Holmes's landscaping crew often encountered human bones. But these were probably secondary deposits brought with sand from the Mōkapu region and Sand Island in Kāneʻohe Bay, which was used to build up the beach and lagoons at Moku o Loʻe. These remains were blessed by a Hawaiian priest and reburied around Holmes's main house, according to Zukeran. One legend Zukeran relates is a tradition that the bodies of those who died in Kāneʻohe and even beyond were brought to Moku o Loʻe for shallow burial.[34]

The islands of the bay at Heʻeia are mentioned in a myth about the Pele family of gods. From the "He Moolele No Ka Ohelo,"[35] two women from the Pele family brought the decomposing body of Malulani, Pele's sister, to Oʻahu, where they scattered her body parts to form the islets of Heʻeia:

After some days Waialani made up small bundles of the body of Malulani which she scattered outside of Heeia, a hill here and a hill there until the place held many hills which are standing even unto this day. And because of the Flood, all these hills were submerged, and appeared as islets, and that is why it is called the sharp coral of Heeia; and it is there even to the present time.[36]

In the same story, Heʻeia, grandson of ʻOlopana, marries another of Pele's sisters, Hiʻiaka.

Heʻeia is also recalled as an important place where the souls of the dead leap to the underworld. There were many such places (*leina a ka ʻuhane*) throughout the Hawaiian Islands, including Kaimalolo, Leilono, and Kaʻena Point on Oʻahu. Usually *leina a ka ʻuhane* are on bluffs or cliffs overlooking the sea or on valley walls. Often a branching tree serves as a "roadway by which the soul takes departure."[37] One branch is a pathway to the peaceful realm of the guardian deities (*ʻaumākua*), the other leads to the dark afterworld (*Pō*) of Milu. The dualism is evident in the soul leap at Heʻeia:

There were, and are,
Two place-names, Heeia
One is Heeia-uli, the Dark Heeia;
The other, Heeia-kea, Fair Heeia.
There is all the difference
Between these two
Heeia-uli and Heeia-kea,
As is the difference
Of night and Day
Men Died in Old Hawaii
They entered places
Where dead men dwell.
But the difference here,
At Heeia,
The dead men entered
The Depths of Seas.

Their lives were judged,
Their Fate decreed,
With some judged white
And some called black.

The black souls leaped
From the left-hand shore;
The white souls jumped
From the right-hand shore.
Heeia, here, the Dividing Line.[38]

"Dark Heʻeia" is the section of land immediately north of the Heʻeia/Kāneʻohe *ahupuaʻa* boundary, adjacent to Moku o Loʻe. "Fair Heʻeia" is the section on the northern side of Kealohi Point, the place of soul leaping. The *heiau* Kalaeʻulaʻula (probably meaning "the very sacred point") once stood at Kealohi Point. McAllister found nothing remaining at Kealohi to indicate a temple, and suggested that it was destroyed by the sugarcane plantation.[39] A state park now marks the site.

The mythic dualism of Heʻeia may have been recognized by Hawaiian scholar Frederick W. Beckley, who testified in Land Court in 1937 that Moku o Loʻe really means "land of the split" (actually, the "split of Loʻe"). If you stand on the Kāneʻohe shoreline and look toward the ocean, he explained, the view is split (*moku*) by the islet.[40]

Pukui and Elbert's dictionary of the Hawaiian language[41] defines *loʻe* as the curve of a fishhook, which provides yet another interpretation of the place name of Moku o Loʻe. The original shape of the island was indeed configured like some of the smaller shell fishhooks common to traditional Native Hawaiian fishing assemblages. It is characteristic of the poetics of the Hawaiian language that many traditional place names can have multiple interpretations and meanings.[42]

| OCTOPUS AND SHARK TALES OF MOKU O LOʻE

The region around Moku o Loʻe was noted for its *heʻe*, or octopus. Some of these creatures terrorized mankind, while others served as a favored delicacy. Informant Mrs. Gouveia, emphasizing the association between the name Heʻeia and *heʻe ʻia*, recalled that her mother saw the

| *Heʻe fishing. Henry E. Knapp, Bishop Museum*

delicious mollusk hanging to dry on Moku o Loʻe as a child—indeed, strung along on clotheslines. The drying of *heʻe* on the island was also remembered by the Olevides family in the early twentieth century.

The theme of octopi continues into more recent times with the recollections of Andy Anderson (1904–1975), a carpenter at Moku o Loʻe from the 1930s to 1960s. He had known Kila, the old caretaker of the island during the period when it was leased to Marcus R. Coburn (1889–1894). Kila was still living on Moku o Loʻe in 1913 when ten-year-old Andy visited him, bringing the old man water and helping him catch crabs to feed his octopi:

[Kila's] hobby was raising octopus, but he didn't eat octopus. He had an octopus right in front of the Seth Parker *[an old schooner moored on Moku o Loʻe from the 1930s]. A great big octopus weighing about 200 pounds. His tentacles were 40 feet long and 8 to 9 inches in diameter, biggest octopus I had ever seen.... The octopus could kill a man. Now there were two Hawaiians, taro planters who lived in the mountains. They used to come down here to keep the old man company and he would drink ʻawa root with these two young fellows, then went over and sat on a chair and pretended he was drunk and falling asleep. Then he heard one fellow say, "Let's go out and get the octopus." They went on their little canoe, which was about eight feet long.... They had to dive into the water to get at the squid. The octopus got hold of this man and he never came up. The other fellow...dived in and the octopus got him also and grabbed the canoe.... The old man saw that the canoe was near the octopus's hole where the old man used to feed the octopus every day...he walked out to the end of the reef.... When the octopus came up...he lassoed the octopus and guided it to shore. All the while the octopus was hanging*

onto the two bodies.... Of course, the old man killed the octopus, his pet. The old man buried the two young Hawaiians and the following day he died. I don't know whether it was from worry or sorrow.

Robert Miranda, Jr., a caretaker's son who lived on Moku o Loʻe from 1954 to 1989, remembers a worker who had a house on the leeward side of the tiny island. One day he discovered that his octopi traps were missing. After searching for the traps for some time, he eventually realized that they had been taken by a gigantic octopus. It had its arms around his traps. On another occasion, a tuna sampan cruised past the island fishing for bait. Miranda was watching as the boat suddenly stalled in the water. Men dove off the boat yelling that a huge octopus had seized the propeller. The fishermen then killed the creature. Judging from the size of the pieces of octopus they brought out of the water, the animal may have weighed 60–80 pounds.

Tales of predatory marine life in the Moku o Loʻe region were not limited to octopi. Just west of Moku o Loʻe was the Koʻamano Reef, inhabited by legendary man-eating sharks. McAllister described this small reef as oval in shape and containing many caves where numerous sharks lived. His informant told him that Makanui, the keeper of the sharks, lived in Heʻeia to the northwest of Loko o Heʻeia (Kealohi Point) and spent most of his time feeding the sharks. People's curiosities were aroused when it was noticed that the bodies of the dead were disappearing. They finally discovered that the sharks of Koʻamano were carrying the bodies from Heʻeia to their caves. Makanui was killed by the angered populace, and his own body was fed to the sharks.[43]

Throughout its entire history, Moku o Loʻe was a pervious membrane between the marine world and the earthly realm, of human activity and imagination. This is seen in myth, in Native Hawaiian oral history, and in the construction of future memories for the present era.

| *(opposite) Hawaiian net fishermen at Kekepa and Kapapa islands adjacent to Moku o Loʻe. Mōkapu Peninsula is seen in the background. Tai Sing Loo, Bishop Museum*

Battle of Nuʻuanu.
Herb Kane

CHAPTER TWO

Changing Land Tenure

Protect and take good care of the
cocoanut trees.

C. R. Bishop

The early history of Moku o Lo'e is inextricably linked to that of its *ahupua'a* He'eia and to that land segment's relationship to other parts of the district of Ko'olau Poko. Oral histories of the pre-Contact Hawaiian past are clearest at that point where living memory overlaps the threshold of written documentation. For He'eia and its child Moku o Lo'e, the unification of O'ahu under a single ruler in the late sixteenth century seems to have been particularly distinct and memorable.

| UNIFICATION OF O'AHU

The reign of the paramount chiefess Kalaimanuia of O'ahu in the early seventeenth century was a time of rapid population growth and agricultural intensification throughout the Hawaiian Islands, a period referred to as the Late Expansion period by Kirch.[44] At this time, the classical wedge-shaped *ahupua'a* probably became the primary units of political control in the Islands; He'eia as a political unit probably reached final form during this time. Distant landlords, many related to the ruling chiefs rather than to the people of the land (*maka'āinana*), replaced the ancient, local kin-based system of rule. In short, a state-level society, with socially distanced ruling classes, was forming on O'ahu during the reign of the Ali'i Wahine Kalaimanuia.[45]

The unification of the island under a single strong ruler, however, was not yet a completely stable system. Upon the death of Kalaimanuia around 1650, O'ahu was partitioned into four quarters, but her three sons and daughter fought for dominance over the island. As a result, Kū-a-Manuia, the eldest son, was killed. His brother Kaihikapu-a-Manuia succeeded in asserting his dominance over the eastern half of O'ahu, including Ko'olau Poko. He was succeeded by a son, Kākuhihewa, who set out to reunify O'ahu and reestablish a government similar to that in the well-remembered days of his grandmother, Kalaimanuia.

Ko'olau Poko rose to political supremacy over O'ahu during the

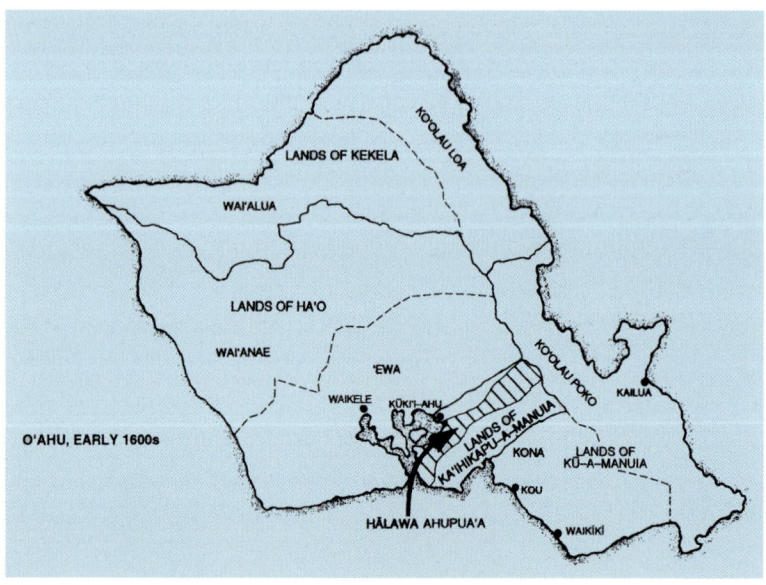

| The four kingdoms of O'ahu, 17th century. Bishop Museum

rule of this king Kākuhihewa in the mid-seventeenth century, since he preferred to stay in his residence of Pāmoa in Kailua, Ko'olau Poko. The oral histories of Kākuhihewa speak of a golden age in Ko'olau Poko. Kākuhihewa's immediate successors, however, were faced with the same sort of usurpations and political fissionings that occurred at the death of Kalaimanuia. It was not until the reign of Kūali'i, a great-great-grandson of Kākuhihewa, that the island was again unified, bringing us to the late seventeenth century.[46]

| INTERISLAND UNITY

Like his ancestor Kākuhihewa, Kūali'i's home and power base was at Ko'olau Poko, one of the wealthiest and most populous areas of the island. One by one, Kūali'i suppressed the chiefs of other O'ahu districts. With O'ahu unified, Kūali'i set his sights on other islands of the archipelago. By the time he died, Kūali'i had also been ruling a portion of the island of Kaua'i, and had great influence over Moloka'i.

Continuing the political trend to unify the islands, the Maui king Kahekili II added O'ahu to his domain by the 1780s. Following precedent established by the descendents of Kalaimanuia, Kahekili also ruled from Kailua in Ko'olau Poko. Thus for centuries, the tiny island of Moku o Lo'e was near the political center of the kingdom of O'ahu, not on the periphery as it subsequently became by the nineteenth century. With the coming of foreigners after 1778, the center of power shifted to the leeward side of the island. Large European and American ships could be berthed in the natural harbor at the village of Kou, soon to be called Honolulu—Kāne'ohe Bay was much too shallow.

King Kahekili II was succeeded in 1794 by Kalanikūpule, who was defeated by Kamehameha I of the island of Hawai'i at the Battle of Nu'uanu, O'ahu, in 1795. At this famous battle, Kalanikūpule's warriors were thrown off the *pali*, the high cliffs above Kāne'ohe. With the defeat of Kalanikūpule, Kamehameha became ruler of all the islands save Kaua'i, which was peacefully ceded to the unified Kingdom of the Hawaiian Islands in 1810.[47]

As was traditional with a change in paramount rule, Kamehameha ordered a redistribution (*kālai'āina*) of lands among himself and his chiefs. Much of Ko'olau Poko, in addition to vast tracts of land elsewhere on O'ahu and throughout the unified archipelago, was reserved by the king as his private land under his direct control. But, unlike Kahekili of Maui and the native O'ahu rulers, King Kamehameha I did not make Ko'olau Poko his principal residence. Rather, he preferred to monitor the foreign trade activity being established around the deep port of Honolulu.

According to the testimony of one of Kamehameha's granddaughters, the Ko'olau Poko lands held directly by the king included the large

| *Ka Mō'ī – King Kamehameha III. Wilkes Expedition watercolor*

| *Queen Kalama, wife of Kamehameha III, ca. 1850. Bishop Museum*

ahupua'a of Waimānalo, Kailua, Kāne'ohe, He'eia, Ka'alaea, Waiāhole, Kahalu'u, and Kualoa.[48] He'eia, the sacred lands of Kualoa, and the vastly productive *ahupua'a* of Kāne'ohe are consistently mentioned as having been set aside by the king. But despite the continuing productivity of the land and sea of the district, Ko'olau Poko would never again be prominent in Hawaiian history.

Governor Boki of O'ahu appointed Keaniani (Keanini) as district chief (*ali'i nui 'ai moku*) of Ko'olau Poko in 1825.[49] Keaniani is remembered for his important role in the building of Kawaiaha'o Church in Honolulu, the first major missionary church in the town. For this task, Keaniani expedited the delivery of logs cut in Ko'olau Loa. They were transported by canoe to Kāne'ohe and then transferred over the *pali* to Honolulu. Boki had improved the Pali Road through Nu'uanu Valley for that purpose.[50]

When Governor Boki, heavily in debt, disappeared on a sandalwood collecting trip to the New Hebrides in 1829, his wife Liliha took over as governor of O'ahu. She resented the powerful rule of Queen Regent Ka'ahumanu and ignited a *coup d'etat* known in history as the Palikaua (the Sword) in 1831. Learning of the planned sabotage, however, crafty Ka'ahumanu spoiled the plot. In her rage, she had Liliha deposed and took away her lands and chiefs. Boki's associate, Keaniani of Ko'olau Poko, was replaced by her chief Ka'iakoili.[51]

Fifty years after Kamehameha I had redistributed lands to his favorite chiefs and retainers, his son Kamehameha III decided to replicate that action. During Kamehameha III's Great Mahele of 1848, Ko'olau Poko, including Kāne'ohe and Kailua, were awarded as a block to Queen Kalama as a gift from her husband. The difference, however, was that in the Mahele of 1848, the chiefs would henceforth own the land outright.

| Abner Pākī

A close associate of Governors Boki and Liliha, Abner Ka‘ehu Kūho‘oheiheipahu Pākī (ca. 1808–1855) was a man who dominated He‘eia and Moku o Lo‘e throughout the first half of the nineteenth century. He was the first individual known to history directly associated with Moku o Lo‘e. Pākī was the son of Kalanihelemai‘iluna Pākī and a grandson of Maui king Kamehamehanui.[52] He was physically gigantic, even for an *ali‘i nui*. It was a standard joke at court that no chair in the palace was safe should Pākī desire to sit.

The lordship of He‘eia and Moku o Lo‘e under Abner Pākī dates from the times of King Kamehameha II (1819–1824). Pākī was mentioned as the *konohiki* or landlord of He‘eia by most of the tenants living in the various *‘ili* or subdivisions of He‘eia in the Mahele testimonies.[53] For his many years of service as traditional *konohiki* of He‘eia under the district chief of Ko‘olau Poko, Keali‘i Nui Abner Pākī was awarded the entire *ahupua‘a*, less any smaller tenants' claims, as private property during the Great Mahele of 1848. The Land Commission Award and subsequent Royal Patent for He‘eia also recorded the tiny island of Moku o Lo‘e as part of He‘eia.

Pākī married a granddaughter of Kamehameha I, Laura Konia. They had one daughter, Bernice Pauahi, and adopted (*hānai*) Lydia Kamaka‘eha, daughter of Keali‘i Wahine Analea Keohokālole and Keali‘i Kaisara Kapa‘akea of the island of Hawai‘i. A mature Lydia Pākī Kamaka‘eha would reign as Queen Lili‘uokalani, the last sovereign monarch of the Hawaiian Islands.

Before the Great Mahele, Pākī controlled six lands on O‘ahu and one each on Maui, Moloka‘i, and Kaua‘i.[54] No commoner tenant (*kama‘āina*) claimed Moku o Lo‘e as their parcel, or *kuleana*, during the Great Mahele. After the land tenure reform, Pākī's O‘ahu lands included the *ahupua‘a* of Mākaha and He‘eia, the *‘ili* of Hanaloa in Waipi‘o, ‘Ewa, and Wai‘alae Iki in Waikīkī.[55] He was required to commute only one-third

| *Keali‘i Nui Abner Pākī, ca. 1850. Having ruled He‘eia and Moku o Lo‘e since the days of Kamehameha II, he received title to the land during the Great Mahele of 1848–1853. Bishop Museum*

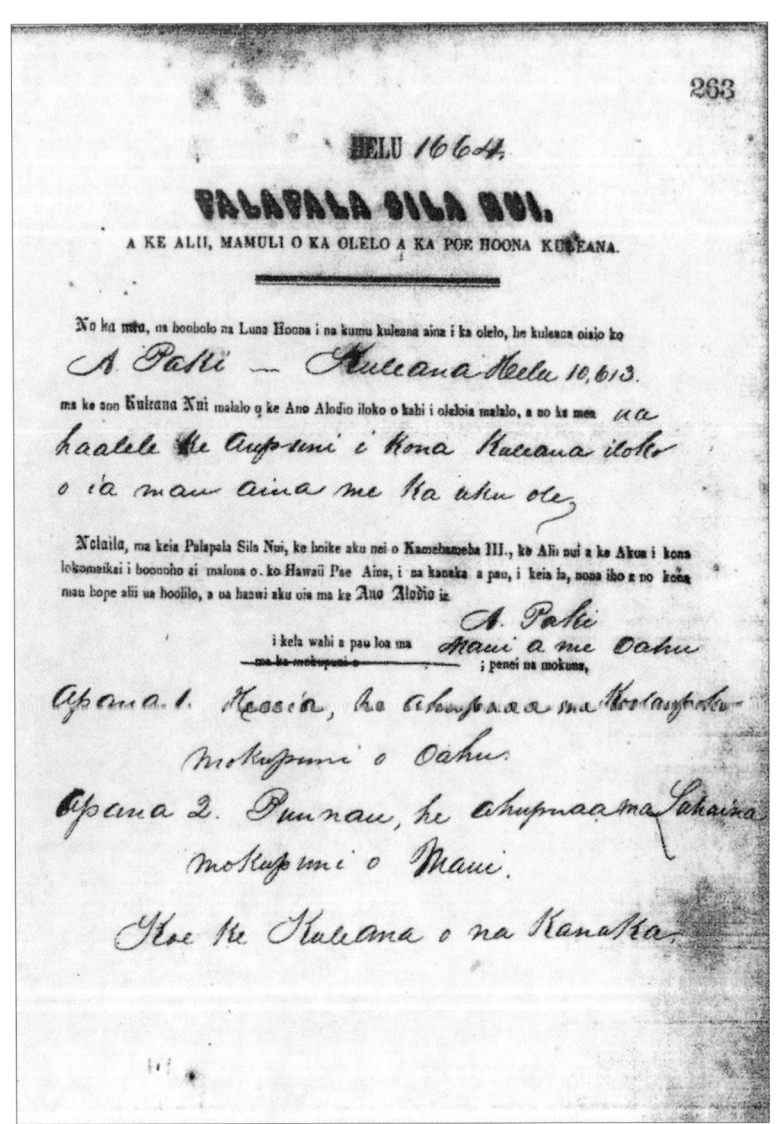

| *Royal Patent 1664 to Pākī. McKeague*

| *Pākī's Heʻeia fishery. LCA 10163 Survey Map*

| Keali'i Nui Wahine Laura Konia. M. Dickson, Bishop Museum

| Princess Bernice Pauahi Bishop, ca. 1880. She inherited Moku o Lo'e from her mother. Upon Bernice's death, the island passed to her estate, the Bishop Estate. Bishop Museum

of his lands back to the king, who subsequently issued a royal patent awarding the remaining land in fee simple to him.

Cash rather than taro being in demand in a changing Hawaiian economy, Pākī leased 2,000 acres of Heʻeia in 1850 to George Lathrop so the latter could erect a sugar mill.[56]

Catholic Diocese of Honolulu history tells of Pākī's grant of land for St. Ann's Church and school at Kikiwelawela, Heʻeia: One night in the early 1840s, Pākī was in need of kerosene for his lamps. He sent out his servant, who happened upon Father Martial. The Catholic priest readily gave the servant the needed fuel. A grateful Pākī in turn visited Father Martial and bestowed upon him a large parcel of land in Kiki-welawela.[57] Pākī considered Moku o Loʻe a part of his retained *kuleana*, for in 1851 he had the island surveyed with the rest of his lands for submission to the government as part of the registration requirements of the Great Mahele.

Rather than live on their income-producing lands, the Pākī family resided primarily in a house known as Haleakalā[58] in downtown Honolulu. Pākī perhaps never visited Moku o Loʻe. Indeed, St. Ann's aside, there are only fleeting records of his visits to Heʻeia itself. These agricultural lands owned by the *aliʻi*, especially after monetization of the economy, were used primarily for generating cash revenue, not necessarily for residence.[59] The court of the early-nineteenth century now displayed its power through the manifestation of imported Western goods, a flourish of silks, embroidered uniforms, jewels, and costly household furnishings.[60] The archaic mounds of tribute of taro and fish from the *ahupuaʻa* were no longer sufficient to maintain status at court. Boki and other chiefs ruined themselves through conspicuous consumption—Pākī almost did.

The king, Kamehameha III visited the Catholic priests at ʻĀhuimanu and Kikiwelawela in Heʻeia near the end of his life. The monarch himself stayed at the Roman Catholic rectory at St. Ann's for a month just before he died of chronic alcoholism in 1854.[61] No doubt he must have gazed at the lovely island of Moku o Loʻe from time to time.

Abner Pākī himself died in 1855; much of his estate was sold to pay off his enormous debts. Most of Heʻeia, however, as well as smaller houselots in Honolulu, Lahaina, and elsewhere were reserved as dower for his widow, Laura Konia. This land was assessed at $8,000 at the time. While Moku o Loʻe remained under family control, the 434 acres of Heʻeia on the Mōkapu Peninsula were sold to William and James Sumner for $870 in 1856.

Devastating disease brought about through Western contact decimated the Hawaiian population, and Heʻeia was no exception. According to a Mission report of 1849, while there were 51 births in Heʻeia that year, there were 368 deaths. Smallpox killed over 600 people by 1854 in the district.[62] The lands were being sold at bargain rates, an ominous portend of a radical transformation of the old ways of Heʻeia and the district.

CHANGING LAND TENURE OF HEʻEIA AND MOKU O LOʻE

Princess Bernice Pauahi, having married Charles Reed Bishop, inherited the ancestral lands of Heʻeia in 1858. Heʻeia then encompassed 4,712 acres and included the large Heʻeia fishpond (*loko iʻa*) and the little Moku o Loʻe as part of the fishery. Bernice continued to lease Heʻeia, however, and there is no documentary evidence that she ever maintained a permanent residence in the *ahupuaʻa*. However, she did visit:

A beautiful place, Heeia, on the windward side of Oahu, a feature of which was its extensive fishpond well stocked with mullet. She [Bernice] was accustomed to invite parties of her friends, entertaining them in the delightful informal manner in which she herself took pleasure.[63]

Charles Reed Bishop in later life. He held vast properties, including Moku o Lo'e, in trust from his wife's estate. Bishop Museum

In 1856, Bernice Pauahi, among the last legal[64] descendants of the conqueror King Kamehameha I, signed an agreement to lease segments of the *ahupua'a* to 97 individuals, most of whom were probably *kuleana* holders and other old tenants in He'eia.[65] In 1864 she sold another 772 acres of He'eia to Roman Catholic bishop Maigret for $970.[66] In 1866, John McKeague leased 2,500 acres of He'eia from Bernice to establish a sugar plantation. Three years later he deeded half-interest in the lease to his partner, Alexander Kennedy. Together they founded the Heeia Sugar Plantation Company.

The land use change occurring in He'eia and elsewhere in the Hawaiian Islands during the mid-nineteenth century was initially stimulated by the land tenure reassessments of the Great Mahele of 1848. In the conversion of land to cash after the Great Mahele, wealthy foreign entrepreneurs were able to purchase large tracts of land from the *ali'i* for transformation to ranches and plantations (See Appendix Table 1, which summarizes the changing land tenure of Moku o Lo'e from traditional, Native Hawaiian times to the present).

The commoners, the *maka'āinana*, also began to leave the land during the Great Mahele. This was due to their need to earn cash to pay taxes, the breakdown of traditional tenant/landlord relationships, and disease. Although many commoners now owned their own small parcels, they no longer had a practical right of commons, access to other regions of the *ahupua'a* for the collection of forest products and fish from the *loko*. Deprived of a substantial portion of their traditional subsistence activities, Native Hawaiians left the land (and the fisheries) and entered wage labor.

By 1871, the mass exodus of Hawaiians from their ancestral *kuleana* in He'eia left the once-extensive taro pondfields largely abandoned. Chinese immigrants, who were being brought in to supply additional labor for the developing plantation industries, began to lease these surplus *lo'i* for conversion to rice paddies.[67] By 1892 over 200 acres of He'eia and Kāne'ohe were reconfigured for rice production. The local demand for Heʻeia rice continued until cheap California rice became available in the early twentieth century.[68]

While many Native Hawaiians left their lands and the cultivation of taro, a few continued to fish, exclusively, for a livelihood. The large fishpond at Heʻeia was leased by Charles and Bernice Pauahi Bishop in 1878 to Kaʻale, who paid a rent of $120 per annum. In 1881 the lease was extended for another 13 years, but the yearly rent jumped to $2,000. Most likely Moku o Loʻe was still used as a way station and lookout for fishing in the Bay.

Throughout this time, the major Heʻeia lessee John McKeague struggled to retain control over Heeia Sugar Plantation Company— there were charges of mismanagement that had apparently brought the

company to the point of bankruptcy. In 1882 he sold all interest in his lease to the company for $1.00.[69] The following year a lease was executed directly between the Bishops and Heeia Sugar Plantation Company. Its provisions granted the company all traditional *konohiki* rights to the fisheries and seas around Heʻeia, and it threw in Moku o Loʻe for good measure. It was during this time, in 1883, when Bernice Pauahi planted the namesake grove of coconut palms on Moku o Loʻe.[70]

As the "last" of the Kamehameha dynasty,[71] Bernice Pauahi Bishop rapidly accrued lands and estates during her later years.[72] The death of her cousin, Princess Ruth Keʻelikolani, made Bernice the wealthiest woman in the Islands and its largest private landowner. Sadly, she was not long to enjoy this distinction—she was diagnosed with cancer in

| *Coconut grove along the western shoreline of Moku o Loʻe, 19th–early 20th century. J. A. Gonsalves, Bishop Museum*

1883. The princess immediately set about putting her affairs, the legacy of the Kamehamehas, in order. She wrote a will that placed most of her lands in trust (Bishop Estate) under her husband for the establishment and maintenance of schools for Native Hawaiian children (known as the Kamehameha Schools). She left the dynasty's material treasures to found the Bishop Museum, and endowed it with the *ahupua'a* of Waipi'o on Hawai'i. Bernice Pauhi died in 1884, leaving the lands of He'eia, her patrimonial estate, to her husband Charles Reed Bishop.

In 1885 the ailing Heeia Sugar Plantation Company was foreclosed upon and sold to M. Louisson for $125,000. Joseph Mendonça and M. S. Grinbaum Company subsequently bought the outstanding Bishop lease and other assets from Louisson and formed Heeia Agricultural Company.[73] Marcus Colburn leased Moku o Lo'e from Charles Bishop from 1889 to 1894 for $20.00 a year with the condition that "he . . . protect and take good care of the cocoanut trees now growing on said Island."[74] Colburn placed the island under the care of Kila (of giant octopus fame) and his wife, Kealoha. Heeia Agricultural apparently purchased the lease from Colburn and leased Moku o Lo'e and other properties in He'eia in its own name from 1893 to 1929. The rent for the *ahupua'a* was $3,500 per year for a period of 30 years.[75] In 1890, Charles Bishop deeded the title to He'eia, with its leases, to the trustees of the Bishop Estate. In the meantime, the sugar industry in the region faded away. In 1890, pineapple was introduced to the region. By 1912, over 1,000 acres had been leased to Libby, McNeill & Libby, which quickly became 2,500 acres. Parcels were often farmed by Japanese and Chinese families who had finished their sugar contracts. Pineapple canneries perfumed the tropical breezes of the Ko'olau Poko District until 1923, when rising production costs made this operation unprofitable as well.

A CHALLENGE TO BISHOP ESTATE TITLE

In 1937, a year following the island's purchase by Christian Holmes, the Bishop Estate was challenged in Territorial Land Court over its previous title to the island.

Malika Kekipi Silva testified that she was born on Moku o Lo'e in 1879. Her father, she said, had been sent there by Queen Kalama to care for chickens, turkeys, and pigs. Historian Frederick Beckley testified that he attended a *lū'au* on the island in 1884 in honor of Dowager Queen Emma. This is the first mention of a social occasion on the island.

In the 1937 testimonies, William Kekoa claimed a line of inheritance from Queen Kalama, who died in 1870, through Charles Kana'ina (father of King William Lunalilo), who died in 1878. Kana'ina's heir was Kukuilo, who died in 1893, giving the land to Charles Keawe. By means of a warranty deed, Moku o Lo'e was claimed to have transferred to William Kekoa.

However, even if Moku o Lo'e was part of Kāne'ohe, Queen Kalama eventually sold all her holdings there to her business partner, Charles Coffin Harris. The Harris property was passed in a fairly intact state to Nanny Rice Brewer and subsequently to rancher and planter Harold Castle. Although James Castle once leased Moku o Lo'e, he never owned it as part of Harold Castle's Kāne'ohe ranch.

Another claim to Moku o Lo'e was that of the Kamaka family. The petition is based on a posthumous adverse possession claim of Kila, who was a resident employee of Colburn on the island. It was claimed that Ueneaiku had title to the island from 1860 to at least 1911. Kila, the caretaker, was a son of Ueneaiku. A great-grandson of Ueneaiku, Frank Kaleimamahu, and the widow and children of another, John Kamaka, testified.[76] According to their recollections, Ueneaiku is buried on the island.

The last claim for Moku o Lo'e in the suit against Bishop Estate was that of James Holanikukana Keawehaku, who testified that he was the sole heir of a Ioane Nahu, a.k.a. Hanahua, who at the time of his death in 1889 claimed to have owned Coconut Island in fee simple. This was also recognized as an adverse possession claim due to Keawehaku's testimony that he lived on the island in 1889–1890.

In the end, Land Court decreed that Bishop Estate had indeed showed evidence of uninterrupted possession of Moku o Lo'e from the time of the Great Mahele. Bishop Estate had proved that Moku o Lo'e was a part of the *ahupua'a* of He'eia and that an unbroken title to the islet had existed since the days of Abner Pākī. With a secure land title, Bishop Estate could proceed with selling the island to Christian Holmes.

| Early Twentieth Century

After the expiration of Marcus Colburn's lease to Moku o Lo'e in 1893, several people appear to have utilized the island. C. Bolte, president of Heeia Agricultural Company, used his company's leased island as a fishing retreat for himself and his two sons from 1899 to 1904. The terms of the lease were $20.00 per year for 24 years. Lantana and guava were noted as growing on the island in the lease, and Bolte was required to erect and maintain a fence around the island.[77] John K. Sumner subleased Moku o Lo'e in 1904 from Heeia Agricultural Company for 10 years at $240.00 per annum.[78] Sumner surrendered the sublease in 1906. Heeia Agricultural Company returned Moku o Lo'e to the Bishop Estate in 1908.[79]

Rancher James Bicknell Castle, son of Castle and Cooke founder Samuel Castle, took over the property in 1908. He was granted a 40-year lease to He'eia, which included Moku o Lo'e and "the Ili Aina of Kikiwelawela," for an initial $3,500 per year and a percentage of the gross sales of any produce.[80] According to Castle's ranch manager, 50–60 sheep were brought to the island in an attempt to clear it of lantana shrubs. However, "rats attacked the sheep and the flock jumped into the sea and swam to Heeia."[81] It appears that Castle did not hold Moku o Lo'e long after that event, and he returned the island to Bishop Estate.

When James Castle's rancher son Harold became the major land owner in Kāne'ohe and Kailua in the years to come, Heeia Agricultural again leased Moku o Lo'e from Bishop Estate.

Not too much is known about the period from 1908 to the late 1910s, but the oral record provides some information: Leonard Kea, an uncle of Anita Gouveia, lived in He'eia for 26 years and visited Moku o Lo'e frequently in the 1920s. He recalled that his grandmother, Kahanu Paoa, lived on the island before that time. Kea was told by his grandmother that "there were people buried on the top of the island," one of whom was named Kawika. A fire control map of 1908–1922 shows a cluster of three structures on the northwestern portion of Moku o Lo'e, indicating habitation during this period.

It is also known that a family of Filipino immigrants lived on the island in the late 1910s to early 1920s—Faustino Olavides, his wife Portenciana, and their daughters Ruth and Rose. Brought to the Territory under contract, Faustino and his wife first lived on the Big Island of Hawai'i. Preferring the life of a fisherman to that of a sugarcane plantation worker, however, the Olavides moved to Moku o Lo'e, where Faustino was employed by Wally Davis, the sheriff of Kane'ohe.

Rose Olavides Deang, granddaughter of Faustino Olavides through her mother Ruth, states that her family was the only one on the island until near the end of their residency. Then, "a Caucasian couple moved to the island." The Olavides lived in a small plantation-style house on the windward side of the island, facing the open sea. The "Caucasian couple" apparently lived on the other side, facing Kāne'ohe and He'eia. Large thickets of *hau* grew right over the water in some regions of Moku o Lo'e. Ms. Deang recalled that *hau* and the thorny mesquite *kiawe* covered the island in those days. Later, the Joe Calizar family also lived on Moku o Lo'e.

The "Caucasian couple" referred to by the Olavides family was Paul Beyer and his wife. Paul Beyer subleased Moku o Lo'e from 1921 to 1925 in connection with a fishing business that he co-owned. His son Tom

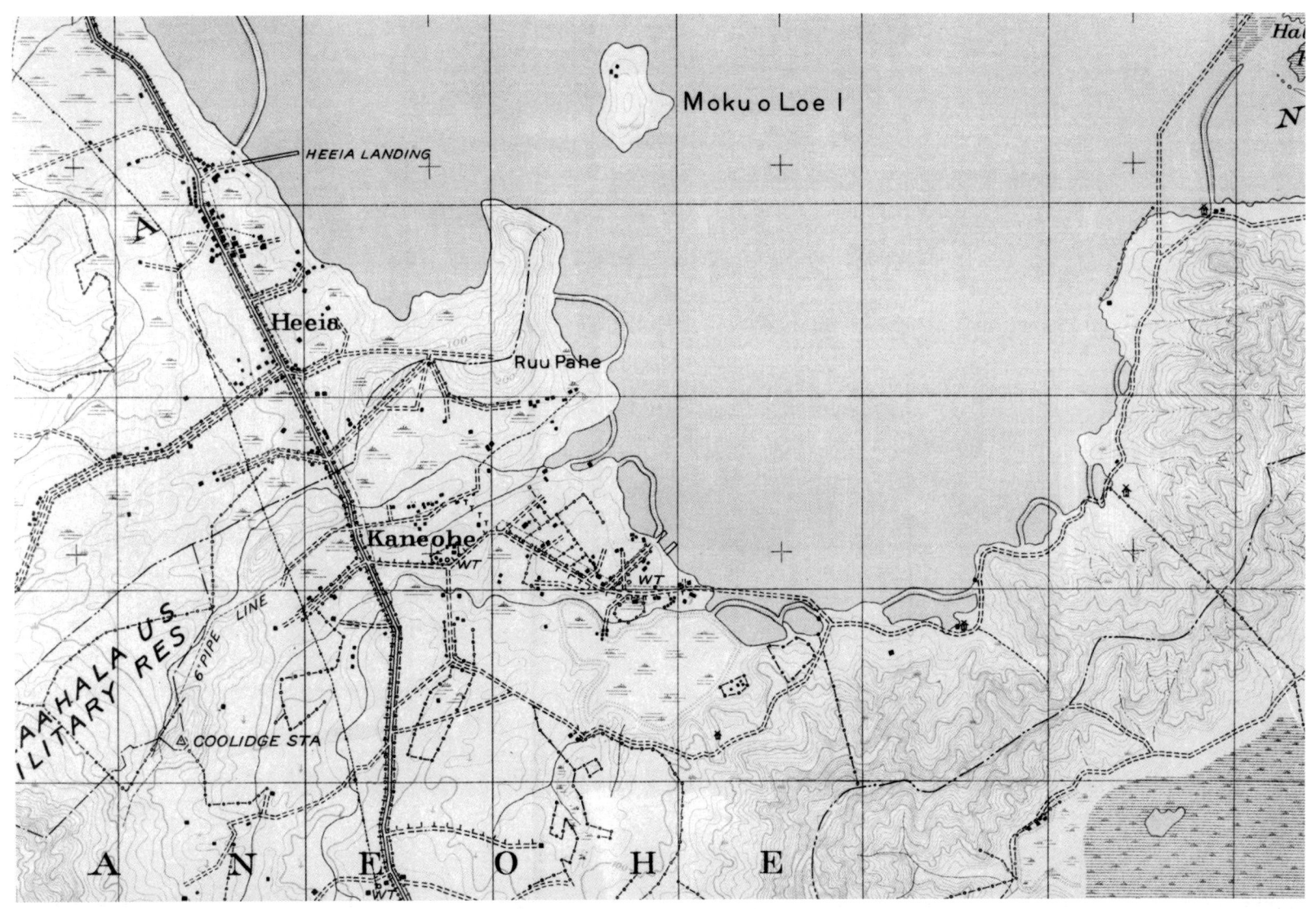

Moku o Loe I

HEEIA LANDING

A

Heeia

Ruu Pahe

Kaneohe

AAHALA U S
ILITARY RES

6" PIPE LINE

△ COOLIDGE STA

A   N   E   O   H   E

WT

| *Fire control map of 1908–1922 showing structures on Moku o Lo'e. Bishop Museum*

| *Western shoreline of Moku o Lo‘e looking southward, ca. 1910s. Tai Sing Loo, Bishop Museum*

Western shoreline of Moku o Lo'e looking northward, ca. 1910s. Tai Sing Loo, Bishop Museum

| *Paul Beyer and his homestead on Moku o Loʻe. Tom Beyer, Beyer Collection*

provided an oral history: Paul Beyer was a German immigrant from Stettin who in Hawai'i married Amelia Ernestberg, a part-Hawaiian woman from the prominent Saffrey family of Maui. Paul Beyer had jumped ship and settled in Honolulu, working first as a bouncer in a saloon along Nu'uanu Street in Chinatown just before its disastrous fire of 1900.

Tom's sister Dolores also retold vivid memories of growing up on Moku o Lo'e: One of seven children, Dolores Mokuoloe Beyer Berengue was born to Paul and Amelia on the tiny island on 24 August 1922. According to Mrs. Berengue, Paul Beyer spent most of his time in Kaka'ako, Honolulu, however, while her mother lived on the island with her brother, Henry Sorensen. On the island the family lived in a small plantation-style house with a tarp-covered lanai and raised chickens, ducks, and geese. The fishing boats offloaded their catch at Moku o Lo'e. The fish were subsequently transported to the shore, then trucked over the Nu'uanu Pali on ice to the cannery in Honolulu. Photographs of that time show a verdant landscape on the western side, with coconut, *kiawe*, date palm, and *hala* (pandanus) trees, and a rocky escarpment on the eastern, windward side. The family maintained a well on the island that was augmented by a rainwater catchment system.

The Beyer house was below the crest of the central hill, on the leeward side of Moku o Lo'e. This is also noted in the fire control map and photographs of the island at the time. Located on the southeast side of the island, a long causeway or pier extended from the house to an area beyond the reef, built to allow larger fishing vessels access to the island.

One of the most informative interviews done for this book was that of the late Kāne'ohe physician, Dr. Fred Reppun. He remembered an unoccupied Moku o Lo'e in the 1920s, which reflects the period immediately after the Beyer, Olavides, and Calizar families had left. The island was recalled as a jungle of coconut trees, guava, and lantana, "with thousands of rats." A similar impression was gathered by William

Paty, former chairman of the State of Hawai'i Department of Land and Natural Resources, when he was a boy.

On 1 November 1933, Heeia Company, successor to Heeia Agricultural Company, subleased Moku o Lo'e to Christian Rasmus Holmes II, an heir to the Fleischmann Company fortune. It was, in fact, Holmes's interest in purchasing Moku o Lo'e outright in 1936 that prompted owner Bishop Estate to seek clear title of the island through the Land Court in 1937. The agreement of sale of the island for $50,000 was contingent upon the Estate securing clear title. The dream of a multimillionaire from Cincinnati, Ohio, would soon manifest itself on the tiny Moku o Lo'e in the coral sea of Kāne'ohe Bay.

| *Amelia Beyer and her children, ca. 1924, looking west towards He'eia. The other men are probably Henry Sorensen, Faustino Olavides, and Joe Calizar, who also lived on the island. Tom Beyer, Beyer Collection*

| *A causeway once extended west across the reef to deeper channels. Tom Beyer, Beyer Collection*

Main living room,
Queen's Surf.
Ann Holmes
Terrell Collection

CHAPTER THREE

Christian Holmes and Coconut Island

To some men who inherit or acquire great
wealth is given the added responsibility
and the imagination to invest in things
of enduring value.

Santa Barbara News-Press[82]

Christian Rasmus Holmes II was to transform the fishing islet of Moku o Lo'e into one of the world's most spectacular private residences. His Coconut Island would become the casual Hawaiian equivalent of one of the great summer homes of wealthy industrialists built along the shores of Newport, Rhode Island, or Palm Beach, Florida. But unlike the fortunes of the old money of the East, built upon steel, railroads, and oil, Holmes's wealth literally arose from the humble household needs of rural American women. The family fortune was founded on baker's yeast, introduced to this country by Holmes's maternal grandfather, Charles Fleischmann, a brilliant inventor, an immigrant from the Austro-Hungarian Empire.

The story of the Fleischmann family, Christian Holmes, and Holmes's transformation of Moku o Lo'e to an ecological treasure known as Coconut Island is a tale of gifted, imaginative individuals with clear visions of the future, deep aesthetic sensibilities, and the desire to benefit humanity. The chronicle of Fleischmann and Holmes is a tale full of irony and essential to help understand the compelling mystique of Coconut Island.

| THE FLEISCHMANN STORY

While fermentation had been known for thousands of years, Charles Fleischmann and his brothers would take their advanced family knowledge of fermentation, yeast production, and distillation to America. By applying just-invented technology and scientific discoveries, they would proceed to make one of the largest business fortunes of its time.

While Charles Fleischmann is usually credited for the invention of commercially produced compressed yeast, credit must be given to German inventors Tebbenhof and Reiminghaus in the early nineteenth century. Charles and his partners' particular genius was to take the newly refined "Viennese Process" of compressed yeast production to America, create a powerful demand for the product, and satisfy that demand with a very efficient marketing and distribution system.

Charles Louis Fleischmann was born on 3 November 1834 in Jagerndorf, in the mountains of Silesia, between Moravia and Prussia, then part of the Austrian Empire. He was the son of Abraham (Alois) and Babette Fleischmann, the second of seven children. Charles left school at 13 for Prague and Vienna, where he learned the trade of a distiller under the tutelage of a Hungarian nobleman.[83] Around 1843 he became yeast production superintendent of his employer's large estate.[84]

Emigration to the United States was clearly on the mind of the Fleischmann children, especially as the Austro-Prussian War was raging and the American Civil War had just ended. When sister Josephine married in early 1866 in New York City, Max and Charles attended the wedding and decided to stay. Max took out naturalization papers in May of that year. In November 1866 Charles married Henriette Robertson, and applied for U.S. naturalization in August 1867.[85]

It is apocryphal that Charles Fleischmann was aghast at the poor quality of baked goods in America when he first attended his sister's wedding and immediately decided to do something about it. But Fleischmann did recognize that America was far behind Europe in fermentation technology. Prior to the producing of Fleischmann Yeast, most American home bakers had struggled on with various sourdough starters, liquid concoctions of sugar, malt, flour, and potatoes, the foamy brewer's yeast skimmed from fermenting ale, or other such potions.[86]

After moving to Cincinnati, Charles and his brother Julius formed a partnership with a local distiller, James Gaff. By 1868 they were manufacturing America's first standardized yeast in a plant in Riverside, Ohio, and were delivering yeast cakes hand-wrapped in paper door to door. In two years the Fleischmanns had expanded their work in controlled fermentation to produce America's first distilled gin under the Fleischmann Distilling Company name.[87] The business grew slowly at

| (above) Bread baked with Fleischmann's yeast was touted as being so superior that even hobos would reject a competitor's product! Author's Collection
| (left) Henriette and Charles Fleischmann, ca. 1875. Univ. of Nevada, Special Collections

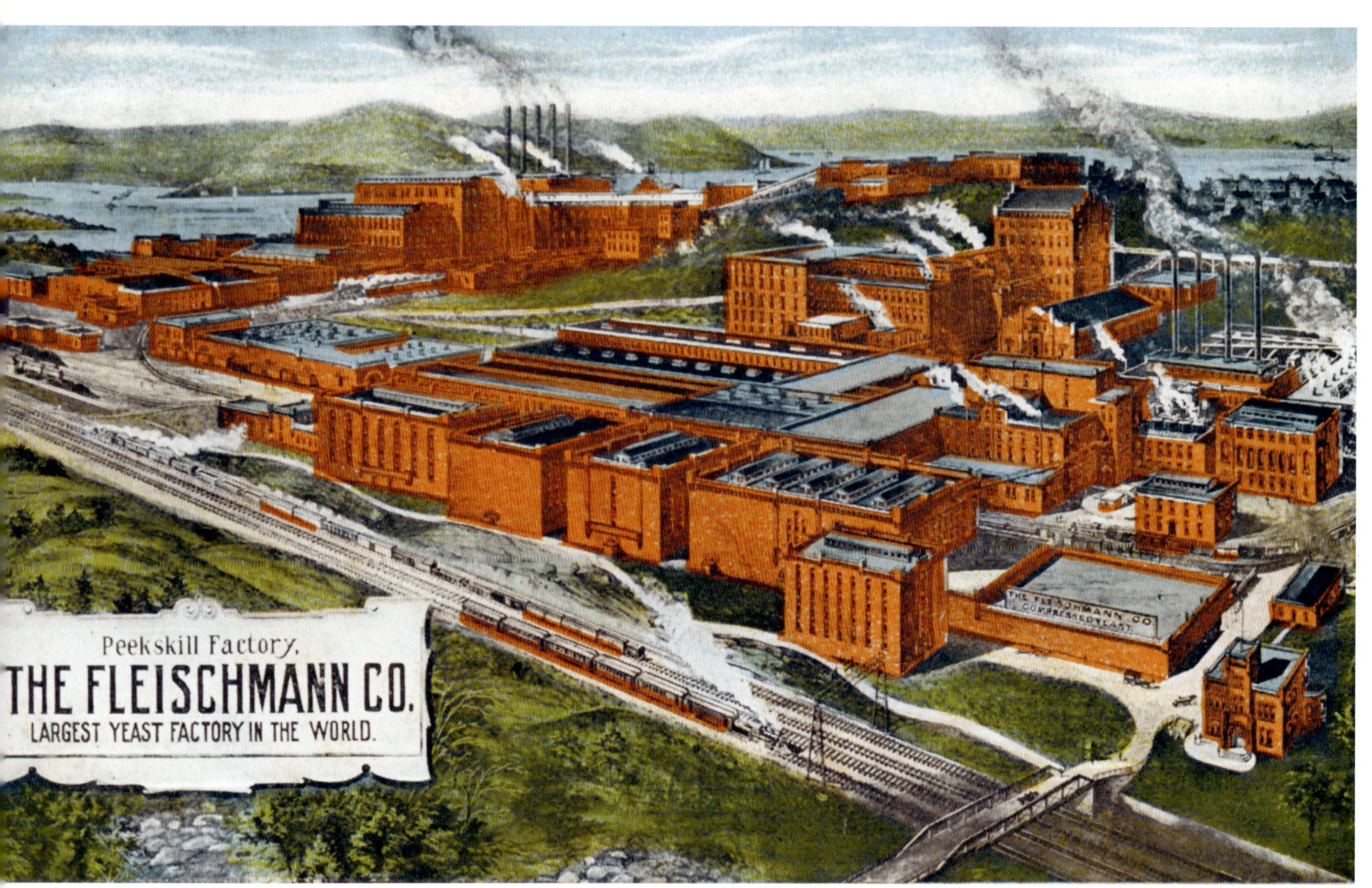

The ultimate Fleischmann factory at Peekskill, New York. Author's Collection

first, but in 1871 the company opened its second plant, at Blissville, Long Island, New York to be near that major market.[88]

At the Centennial Exposition in Philadelphia in 1876, the Fleischmann brothers demonstrated the benefits of their product at the "Vienna Bakery" booth. The Fleischmann genius could be seen in the development of a remarkable system of distribution that quickly brought the perishable product to consumers around the country.

Charles and Henriette Fleischmann had a daughter Bettie (b. 1871) and two sons, Julius (b. 1872) and Max (b. 1877). By the 1890s Charles Fleischmann had four production plants. When still a teen, Julius began to take over top management of the company, while Max, with his great love of travel and exploration, took just a symbolic vice-presidency.

| CHRISTIAN AND BETTIE FLEISCHMANN HOLMES

When Papa Fleischmann caught pneumonia in 1891, he summoned a young doctor named Christian Holmes. When the physician began to visit his patient daily at the Fleischmann's Avondale home, his devotion made a big impression on Charles's spirited daughter Bettie. Christian Holmes was the son of the miller Holm Christiansen and Karen Mikkelsen of Engom, Denmark. The names were transposed by immigration agents.[89]

Bettie married the devoted doctor the next year. In due time Carl Holmes was born. On 13 June 1896, Bettie Fleischmann Holmes gave birth to their second son, Christian.

In 1897, the patriarch Charles Fleischmann died and his eldest son Julius took over the reigns of the company. Driven to succeed in every realm, Julius was also elected mayor of Cincinnati in 1900 at the age of 28.

Christian Sr. and Bettie first operated a small, private hospital in downtown Cincinnati. Bettie saw to the operation of the hospital furnishings, meals, and general housekeeping. Christian was greatly

| *Dr. Christian Rasmus Holmes was born in Engom, Denmark. He met Bettie while attending to her father. Martin Fischer*

| (above) Bettie Fleischmann Holmes and her two eldest children, Carl and Christian (far right). Ann Holmes Terrell
| (far left) Bettie, Charles and Henriette Fleischmann's eldest child, on her wedding day in 1892. Cincinnati Museum Center
| (left) Julius Fleischmann, an early automobile enthusiast, was elected mayor of Cincinnati at age 28. Bushnell cartoon, 1900. Cincinnati Museum Center

| *The Great Gadsbys on an outing: (left to right) Lily, Max, and Sarah Fleischmann, chauffer Joe Bridges, Julius Fleischmann. Cincinnati Museum Center*

innovative in the procedures and post-operative care that he gave patients, and his fame grew. He was quickly appointed a professor of otology at the Miami Medical College in Cincinnati.[90] In the dawning years of the twentieth century, a third son, Julius, known as Jay, was born.

In 1914, Dr. Holmes became Dean of the College at the University of Cincinnati. With his brother-in-law Julius as mayor and the substantial financial backing of his wife and brother-in-law, Holmes lobbied the state legislature for support on various projects benefiting their city. Dr. Holmes, Bettie, and Julius Fleischmann can be credited with founding the University of Cincinnati Medical School.[91]

| *(above) Christian Holmes II as a cadet at Culver Military Academy, Ohio. Ann Holmes Terrell*
| *(above left) The first Holmes hospital in Cincinnati. Martin Fischer*

Both Carl and Christian II received military educations, and together with their father served in World War I. Christian Sr. established an otolaryngology clinic at Fort Sherman in Ohio, while Bettie built a recreation center for officers at Chillicothe.

Carl was wounded with shrapnel and mustard gassed, but recovered. Christian became a hero—for his bravery, he received the French Croix de Guerre and the Distinguished Service Award from the United States military. Christian was shipped home in September 1918, and was discharged as a captain in February 1919. Carl lingered on in Paris after the armistice, attending Pasteur Institut lectures on yeast, malting, and vinegar.

Holmes Sr. worked himself to death—in 1919 he developed cancer and passed away in January 1920. Now a young widow, Bettie continued her charitable work. In 1925 she established the Christian R. Holmes Hospital at the University of Cincinnati. Mrs. Holmes left Cincinnati for good soon after having donated her father's mansion on Washington Street in Avondale to the city, which today is Fleischmann Gardens Park.

| A Changing Market

New York had become the primary focus of Fleischmann's operations in 1900 when Julius built the gigantic Peekskill factory at Charles Point on the Hudson River.

In 1919, Julius Fleischmann decided to move corporate headquarters to New York. His son, Charles II, had died in WWI, and Julius felt the move would be best for all. The core of Julius's operating philosophy was that, "There can be no such thing as too much real service in business."[92] Fleischmann's "yeast men" would personally visit bakeries, in the middle of the night if necessary.

When Julius died of a heart attack in 1925, his brother Max assumed the leadership of the Fleischmann Company. Max enlisted the

| (top) Theodore Roosevelt, Jr. (left) and Christian Holmes II (center) with the Croix de Guerre. Christian Holmes IV

| (bottom) Christian R. Holmes Hospital, University of Cincinnati. Author's Collection

aid of Carl and Christian Holmes II, who served as directors "for a season."[93] By the 1920s, however, the pioneering days of home baking were drawing to a close. America was becoming more urbanized, and one's God-given daily bread could be easily purchased at the local market—demand for yeast for home sales plummeted. An even more devastating blow to the company, Prohibition (1919) closed down the less divine Fleischmann distilleries and breweries.

The company concentrated on twin market strategies to reclaim its profitability. First, Fleischmann developed strong traffic for its one-pound yeast cakes, which were sold to commercial bakers.[94] Second, the company signed with the J. Walter Thompson advertising agency, which began to experiment with the marketing of smaller foil-wrapped packets of yeast for home medicinal purposes. This highly successful tactic became an advertising legend.[95] Within a few years, however, with the market flooded with competing vitamin products, the Thompson agency had to modify its medicinal marketing approach for Fleischmann. Using the imposing prescriptions of European doctors, the Thompson agency began to tout its client's product as the world's most natural laxative.

With the founder's sons Julius, then Max at the helm, assisted by Jay and Chris Holmes, and the power of a health-restoring ad campaign,

| (left) Chopping the kegs in Chicago. Author's Collection

| (opposite) The yeast packaging line. At its peak, the Peekskill plant had nearly 1,000 employees and produced gin, vinegar, and other products in addition to yeast. Author's Collection

| As in microbiology, early 20th-century European medicine was considered advanced. Freud-like physicans lectured the American public on the benefits of yeast in ads like these. Author's Collection

| From the 1900s (left) to the 1960s (right), Fleischmann's recipes kept up with the times. Author's Collection

Fleischmann sales skyrocketed in the early post-World War I years. By 1925, the company had 12 plants and 2,500 sales agents, including women, a progressive achievement for the time. By 1926 the Fleischmann Company was in the top ten of American magazine advertising purchasers.[96] The Thompson agency's physician-touted "purification by yeast" treatment ultimately outraged the American Medical Association to the extent of banning testimony by its members. Unfazed, the Thompson agency simply turned toward the vast pool of European doctors with impressive scowls and exotic names to endorse their product. Eventually, the Federal Trade Commission stepped in and banned most of the more blatant health claims of Fleischmann's yeast.

It is one of many Fleischmann ironies that the company would be at odds with the medical community, which in Cincinnati was prominently represented by the Fleischmann-Holmes's legacy. Yet the "Yeast for Health" campaign continued well into the 1930s, boosting sales of the small foil-wrapped yeast packets from less than $1 million in the early 1920s to about $10 million by 1937.[97] Fleischmann give-away recipe books helped reintroduce the art of home baking throughout the twentieth century.

In June 1929, near the peak of its wealth and market share, the Fleischmann Company absorbed Royal Baking Powder Company, E.W. Gillette Co., Widlar Food Products, and Chase & Sanborn, becoming the

| The "deal" of 1929. One of Max Fleischmann's certificates traded for Standard Brands stock. Author's Collection

| The Chimneys, Bettie Fleischmann Holmes's estate on Long Island. P. Christiaan Klieger, Author's Collection

great Standard Brands corporation. Brokered by J.P. Morgan Company, Fleischmann stock was exchanged for the Standard Brands issue. Max Fleischmann alone received $20,000,000 in the new stock.[98] After the merger, a Royal Gelatin plant was added to the Peekskill complex, a brand line from the Royal Baking Powder Company.

| THE CHIMNEYS

Bettie became committed to beautiful Sands Point, Long Island by 1927. Her brothers Max and Julius had also built estates there. The second original Fleischmann factory was nearby and the flagship factory at Peekskill (built in 1900) was only about an hour's drive. Enchanted by

Sands Point and its relative convenience to New York City, Bettie brought together 24.5 acres with the purchase of 17 parcels.[99]

While there are hundreds of great mansions along Long Island's magnificent Gold Coast, few were built like Bettie Fleischmann Holmes's "Chimneys." The mansion was the prototype for her son Christian's two homes on O'ahu in distant Hawai'i—Queen's Surf and Coconut Island. In typical Fleischmann manner, she built her 42-room palace to last.

Construction of the Edgar Williams designed Chimneys began in 1929, the year the Fleischmann family formed Standard Brands. Outlying buildings included houses for gardeners and other staff and a large guesthouse that would qualify as a substantial residence in this neighborhood in its own right. Every major room in the main, three-story

of ancient Chinese bronzes anywhere—much of it ending up in the Avery Brundage Collection of the Asian Art Museum in San Francisco.

While most of the mansion's furnishings were French or English 16th–17th century, much of the woodcarving was done by contemporary English craftsmen utilizing American hardwoods. The centerpiece of the entrance hall was a carved mast from a clipper ship built in 1772 that supported a spiral stairway leading upstairs. The nautical theme, yachting being the paramount Fleischmann passion, was carried through on the stained glass windows around the entrance.

The main hall of the Chimneys featured a carved mantlepiece and an aeolian pipe organ. The original furniture made of dark woods and the heirloom tapestries are gone now, but in many places, the original wallpaper can be found.

In the basement, which is itself a historic site, is one of the country's first private recreation centers. It had a bowling alley, steam baths, a huge indoor pool, a racquet ball court, a bar, a shooting gallery, and Art Deco mirrored dressing rooms. Although now in disuse, many of the mural paintings of exotic tropical jungle scenes and most of the fixtures are still intact. Christian Holmes was to reproduce much of this ambiance on Coconut Island a few years later.

| Fleischmann's and Standard Brands

The merger of the privately-held Fleischmann Company and other food concerns in 1929, forming Standard Brands, symbolized the effective end of family operations and allowed heirs such as Christian Holmes II an unbridled lifestyle.

After his stint at Fleischmann Company, Carl Holmes moved to England; Christian II moved to Santa Barbara, California, where his Uncle Max and Aunt Sarah had established an avocado and citrus ranch in 1921. Despite the distance, Max usually directed the Fleischmann Company from his Edgewood Ranch in Santa Barbara, periodically

| *A mirrored Art Deco dressing room serviced the Chimney's indoor pool. P. Christiaan Klieger, Author's Collection*

mansion had a fireplace, hence the name. The residence costs over $3 million in Depression dollars, and had unheard of new technology: central air conditioning and vacuum systems, and built-in fire hoses.[100]

Bettie spent passionate years collecting furnishings abroad with which to fill her mansion. She had amassed one of the greatest collections

travelling to New York in his private rail car.[101] He continued as chairman until 1935, then served as a director until retirement in 1942. He stayed on as chair of the board's Finance Committee until his death in 1951.[102]

Prohibition in the United States was a severe blow to the great distilleries of the Fleischmann Company, which survived largely through Herculean efforts of a superb management team, superior distribution, the "Yeast for Health" ad campaign, and Bettie Fleischmann Holmes. As a social activist and a promoter of Fleischmann Company interests, Mrs. Holmes helped pioneer the repeal of the 18th Amendment in 1934, and Fleischmanns were again in the distilling business.

After moving to New York, Mrs. Holmes continued her prominent philanthropy and active life in social and musical circles there. She became a director of the New York Philharmonic Symphony Society, founded the Christian R. Holmes Foundation, and served on the board of the Metropolitan Opera Guild.

The last family member in the business, Gustav Fleischmann, was vice president of Standard Brands and managed the Peekskill plant until his retirement in the 1950s. While Jay Holmes administered much of the family holdings from New York in later years,[103] Christian II had other plans.

| CHRISTIAN HOLMES II IN HAWAI'I

Christian Rasmus Holmes II, the "father" of the tropical fantasy of Coconut Island, was thus raised in an environment of extraordinary personal achievement—and he lived up to that tradition. Most remember him vividly and fondly. Henry Walker, Jr. of Honolulu, with great tongue-in-cheek candor, remarked that Holmes was an "interesting man...he doesn't fit most of the usual descriptions." With Holmes, youthful brilliance and adventure gave way to middle-aged eccentricity and self-destruction.

| *Stills fired up again in 1934. Fleischmann's launched a hunt theme in its advertising. Author's Collection*

| *Trophies line the walls of Max Fleischmann's study at the Santa Barbara Museum of Natural History. Santa Barbara Museum of Natural History*

On Holmes's mother's side, great wealth had been accumulated through the innovations and business savvy of Charles Fleischmann. Christian Holmes's father, Dr. Christian Holmes, was one of the outstanding men in American medicine. Holmes's uncle Julius was the youngest mayor of Cincinnati and owner of the Red Socks baseball team. His other uncle, Major Max, was a compassionate philanthropist who established the Santa Barbara Foundation, developed both the Nevada State Museum and the Santa Barbara Museum of Natural History, and created the Max Fleischmann Foundation, a major donor of the University of Nevada-Reno. Young Christian had a great family heritage to live up to.

Not much is known of the early life of Christian II, although the photograph of a boy of five exists—a boy dressed in skirts with the first of the many monkeys in his life. Years later his father recalled Christian's youth in a letter to his son on the Western Front: "The other day in our garden, I happened to glance at the weather vane over the stable and it brought sad thoughts to me; at the same time, I could not help smiling because the old horse is certainly full of holes which you put there as a boy when you first got your .22 rifle."[104]

Christian II attended Culver Military Academy in Ohio and was on its varsity football team. Although he may have spent some time at Yale, he graduated from Culver in 1917. Very soon after he returned to the States after the war, he went west, most likely encouraged by his Uncle Max and Aunt Sarah, who had relocated to California in 1919. Max commanded the U.S. Army Balloon School at Arcadia during WWI. No doubt the Major had a strong influence on Christian. The Major loved safaris, world travel, and natural history. He accumulated a large collection of trophy heads and Native American artifacts and inherited the Fleischmann passion for yachting (he amassed 22 yachts in his lifetime)—all interests that Christian would share with his uncle. Whereas the Major would found two natural history museums (Santa Barbara, California and Carson City, Nevada), Christian would establish private menageries on his properties that later became the nucleuses of several zoos.

In 1919 Holmes bought a ranch in beautiful Montecito to establish a chicken farm. He named the place, appropriately, Feather Hill. But the family business still had some appeal, and in 1923, Holmes became a vice president of the Fleischmann Company. At this time, however, he married his first of three wives, Albertine Osborne Peck of New England, who had a short career as a stage actress. They had two sons, Christian Holmes III (1923–1999) and William Dayton Holmes (1926–2000).

In 1923 Holmes built Linden Lodge as a hideaway in the Santa Ynez Mountains at San Marcos Pass, 1,700 feet above Santa Barbara. He purchased it from the Ruiz brothers. The property was planted in apple,

| (above) Grounds of Linden Lodge on San Marcos Pass near Santa Barbara, California. P. Christiaan Klieger, Author's Collection
| (left) Christian Holmes II (center) at his Santa Barbara ranch. Ann Holmes Terrell Collection

| *Katherine MacDonald, Holmes's second wife. Bruce Spaulding Collection*

peach, and grapevine, and had a large lodge and comfortable guest house. Several dams along the adjacent San Jose Creek created delightful swimming holes for Holmes, his family, and guests. At Feather Hill, Holmes installed the largest private zoological gardens in the United States.[105] His love of animals was perhaps the single most memorable characteristic of his complex personality. At the Montecito ranch were bears and an elephant—the chimps always caused a stir. On one occasion, the mischievous Holmes escorted an ape to mass at All Saints Church—a feat, like many others of his, that would be remembered in local legend to this day.

Like his mother, Holmes was musically inclined and frequently played the piano for friends. Occasionally he was accompanied by his pet boa constrictor, which oftened wrapped itself around either the piano or Holmes's leg. Instead of fetching a wrap for a departing guest, he placed the snake across the shoulders of a young woman. "Why Christian, that's the nicest gesture," said the lady. When he kept a suite at the St. Francis Hotel in San Francisco, he took the boa along. Every now and then the serpent would get loose and cause an uproar. Since the snake was inclined to climb and move up the stairwells, the hotel management finally made Holmes take over the entire top floor, where he was welcome to collect his constrictors from the roof!

Even before coming to Hawai'i, Christian Holmes had developed a reputation as an athlete, aesthete, and an eccentric—a fun-loving playboy with nearly unlimited resources. In character he was nearly a twin of movie legend Errol Flynn, who eventually befriended him. Holmes and Albertine Peck divorced. He then married the beautiful Katherine MacDonald, a Hollywood actress known as the "American Beauty." MacDonald's career began with silent films in the late 1910s and continued to 1925. She had a popular following, however, and was promoted by B. P. Schulberg, one of the originators of United Artists.[106] She also worked on silent films produced by First National.[107] Christian and his new wife had one daughter, Ann (b. 1930). Like Christian Holmes II, Katherine MacDonald also would have three spouses in her life.

During the Santa Barbara years, Holmes, like his mother, traveled extensively to collect artifacts. Unlike his Uncle Max who collected trophy heads, Christian brought back botanical specimens and live animals from around the world. His reputation and notoriety grew by great leaps during the Santa Barbara years. (He once shot Katherine during a domestic tiff. Then there was the incident of the gelatin swimsuits he handed out to the starlettes on his yacht moored at Catalina.)

HOLLYWOOD DISCOVERS MOKU O LOʻE

Christian Holmes's junkets often took him to Hawaiʻi, where he was as awestruck by its beauty as he had been with Santa Barbara. He was intrigued with the idea of its great isolation.

Even though the Hawaiian Islands are the most secluded archipelago on earth, nothing occurs in the kind of utopian remoteness described by generations of occidental dreamers. In the Western imagination, a vision of the prototypical island paradise had slowly arisen from the times of the great Age of Exploration. It was a fantasy notably stimulated by the epic Pacific voyages of Cook, Vancouver, La Pérouse, and Kotzebue. The Hawaiian Islands fit well within that paradigm. Even after the American annexation of the islands in 1898, Hawaiʻi remained largely unknown, exotic, and isolated the minds of the public. And isolation, at least a warm and breezy one, signified paradise.

It was really the New York stage and Hollywood screen that created the popular image of the Hawaiian paradise that is so well known today. Long before television's *Magnum P.I.*, *Hawaii 5-0*, *Gilligan's Island*, and Elvis' *Blue Hawaii* there was a fable of pagan love that can be credited with introducing, if not inventing, many of the paradisiacal elements of Hawaiʻi into American pop culture.[108] Opening in 1912, *Bird of Paradise* had been a very successful play on Broadway. So popular was this tale of

forbidden love, the desirable "exotic other," that it helped launched the craze for Hawaiian music that lasted for many years.

In 1932, Joel McCrea and Delores del Rio starred in the film version of *Bird of Paradise*, partly shot on location at Moku o Loʻe. The movie was directed by no less than King Vidor and was produced by the legendary David O. Selznick. The plot of *Bird of Paradise* is a fairly saccharine, sentimental love tale between an American sailor and a native princess:

The idyll of forbidden passion—Bird of Paradise *was a genre prototype. Author's Collection*

A yacht appears from America with a group of millionaire playboys who discover an uncharted tropical island. Johnny, the young sailor, meets Kalua, a beautiful but taboo daughter of the island chief. Inevitably the sailor and the princess fall in love. An evil *kahuna* takes offense at the relationship, however, and makes Kalua test her resolve by walking on a bed of hot coals. Unsatisfied by her success in the ordeal, the priest nevertheless decides that she must be sacrificed to the angry volcano that is menacing the tiny island village. Although the couple ran off and enjoyed a few days of bliss, the young woman eventually tears herself away from Johnny to placate the volcano and is presumably consumed. Johnny sadly leaves the natural paradise without his love and sails off into the sunset.

The story, as clichéd as it now seems, touched the fires of fantasy in an entire generation of Western romantics. Tourism would boom in Hawai'i, and many a coconut-struck mainlander would take the radical gambit and move to the Islands. If not a causal agent, *Bird of Paradise* was at least symptomatic of the Hawai'i-as-Paradise craze that swept popular American culture in the post-WWI years. It is still with us to a large extent. For 28-year-old war hero Holmes it must have had a strong appeal.

Another idea that impacted Hawai'i originated in New York during the overheated 1920s. This lively vision of paradise suggested a synthesis of jazz-age progress and manifest destiny, "pushing ever westward to a frontier which offered both paradise and opportunity."[109] The message was carried in the popular media, in song, and in films. As Whittaker recalled in *The Mainland Haole*:

Well, I think you'd classify this under romance, perhaps, or something. Something in Hawaiian music completely entranced me, and I knew that this was my destiny. At fourteen, I didn't put it in those words, but I had that feeling, and it began right there. My intent was always to come to, or go to, Hawaii.[110]

HOLMES MOVES TO HAWAI'I

The same sort of frontier impetus that drove Charles Fleischmann to the American Midwest, and Easterners westward onto the Great Plains and California, drove Christian Holmes across the Pacific to Hawai'i. After the war, Holmes was restless and not content to be a Fleischmann executive any more than his Uncle Max. Both nephew and uncle put great emphasis on adventure and travel in their lives—making an impact, being monumental.

The Hollywood lifestyle and the escapist images of *Bird of Paradise* resonated deeply with Holmes, as it did with countless other Americans and Europeans with dreams of tropical paradise and rejuvenation. To create a new life in a new world, Christian undoubtedly had much in common with his grandfather Charles Fleischmann and his uncles Max and Julius.

Holmes and MacDonald ended their marriage in 1932. The following year Holmes had decided to establish a home on O'ahu. He purchased the C. F. Case Deering estate in Waikīkī from the widow, Mary Deering, for $76,000. The mansion, adjacent to Kapi'olani Park, was a fabulous, three-story masterpiece of whitewashed stucco that was later named "Queen's Surf" after the beach house of Queen Lili'uokalani that once stood nearby.[111] The elegant Arts & Crafts-style mansion was designed by Chicago architects Holabird and Roche and built in 1916. The house, which stood about 100 feet back from the beach, had a tall central portion containing bedrooms and a lanai on the second floor, and an informal, Hawaiian-style penthouse on the third floor. One-story wings flanked both sides of the center portion of the mansion. The west wing contained a suite of two rooms and bath for Holmes. The east wing contained a dining room and kitchen. Bungalows for guests, servants' quarters, and other outbuildings completed the estate, which enclosed more than 100,000 square feet of prime Waikīkī real estate. Considerably smaller than his mother's Chimneys, it nevertheless took

| (above) The Arts & Crafts masterpiece, beach side. Hawai'i State Archives
| (top left) The grand entrance to Queen's Surf on Kapi'olani Boulevard, Honolulu. Ann Holmes Terrell Collection
| (bottom left) Acres of rugs. At the end of WWII, most of the furnishings of Queen's Surf were auctioned. Hawai'i State Archives

| Lūʻau *at Queen's Surf. Wayne Harada Collection*

ubiquitous of American luncheon fare, is pure Fleischmann.

Bettie Fleischmann Holmes, fulfilling a maternal need to occupy her son productively in Hawaiʻi, purchased a small fishing fleet and cannery, Hawaiian Tuna Packers—a fairly new company quick on adopting innovation. It was established by F. W. MacFarlane in 1920 with W. P. English as manager. Paul Beyer, a Honolulu engineer interested in refrigeration, was also involved. They located their office on the corner of Cooke and First (Auahi) Streets in downtown Honolulu. In 1921, R. W. Shingle replaced MacFarlane, and R. W. Rodgers became the new manager of the fledgling firm. Initially the local market was characterized by a demand for the smaller reef fish popular with Native Hawaiians. These had been sold at the fish market in downtown Honolulu for generations.

Beyer had originally subleased Moku o Loʻe from Heeia Agricultural and maintained his family on the island. He had about a dozen Filipino fishermen plus his brother-in-law supplying the smaller reef fish to the local market. Beyer's operation was originally known as Lanikai Fishing Company after the schooner *Lanikai* that he had used in the fishing business. Eventually demand increased for the larger pelagic fish, especially tuna, which could be canned and sold on the mainland United States. Beyer's expertise as a refrigeration engineer was right for the moment.

The business continued to grow. In 1926, E. C. Wilson became president, and Paul Beyer became manager of the new Hawaiian Tuna Packers. Before the cannery was built, Beyer had established the Service Cold Storage Company near the downtown fishmarket on Kekaulike Street. Ice from this plant was used to transport reef fish from Moku o Loʻe directly to the Honolulu market.[113] At Service Cold Storage, entrepreneuring Beyer rented space to an ice cream firm and also began to manufacture potato chips. As the market shifted away from small reef varieties, fishing operations at Moku o Loʻe were transformed into catching tuna on baited poles from sampans, the boats being serviced on the island.

18 servants to staff the Queen's Surf estate.[112]

Following the tradition he had started at his ranch in Santa Barbara, Holmes was soon throwing lavish parties, often large *lūʻau*, for his friends at his Waikīkī mansion. It remained his principal residence even after he created Coconut Island retreat to his specifications.

| Hawaiian Tuna Packers

Inasmuch as Moku o Loʻe was traditionally associated with fishing, it seems logical that the first modern commercial enterprise related to the island was associated with the tuna industry of Kāneʻohe Bay. It's hard to image now, but at one time the territory was one of the nation's primary sources of tuna. It would be a Fleischmann, Christian Holmes, who would help commodify this food product and help assure its wide appeal to the American consumer. The tuna salad sandwich, that most

| *Hawaiian Tuna Packers wharf at Kewalo Basin, Honolulu. Camera Hawaii, Bishop Museum*

| *Kewalo Basin cannery with Dolores Mokuoloe and her father Paul Beyer (left at truck). Lester Zukeran*

In 1928–1929, offices of Hawaiian Tuna Packers were moved to 919 Kekaulike, next to Service Cold Storage in downtown Honolulu. Tuna canning operations were established at nearby Kewalo Basin. The firm also managed a shipyard, Kewalo Marine Railway, which built sampans and tuna boats. The sleek, silver fish were cleaned, cooked, canned, and marketed as "Coral Hawaiian Brand Tuna."

In 1932 or 1933, Randolph Crossley replaced Wilson as president of the cannery. The following year, Robert McCorriston replaced Crossley as CEO.[114] A. C. Hagen was made the new secretary of the corporation, and Alan Davis was made vice president. Davis would become one of Holmes's greatest friends and partners.

Bettie Holmes bought Hawaiian Tuna Packers for her second son in 1935, in the words of Christian's stepson Charles Lucas, to "keep him occupied." The sentiment was restated by Helen Davis, Alan Davis's widow who inherited the company from Holmes: "Well, my understanding was that his mother was very anxious to find something for him to be involved in." Bored with the yeast business, and tired of ranching, Holmes at last found a passion with Hawaiian Tuna Packers. Holmes and the company would be applying the Fleischmann touch—creating and maintaining strong brand name identification with the consumer.

Island caretaker Andy Anderson recalled how Holmes acquired the tuna cannery. Originally Holmes owned the modest Coral Gardens in Kāneʻohe, and he maintained three sampans and twelve net fishermen in his employ. The operation was limited to the catch of turtles and sharks. However,

one morning [Holmes] was down at the Coral Garden pier and he saw these Japanese fishermen catching minnows, very tiny little fish, and that fish was used for bait to catch tuna. He watched them for a while, then jumped into the water with his suit on to help the fishermen pick up their nets. Of course they wondered why he did that. He just wanted to see the bait. The following week he bought the whole tuna packers.

(top) Fishermen and bait at Coconut Island. Lester Zukeran, HIMB Collection
(bottom) P. Christiaan Klieger, Author's Collection

| *Alan Davis. Nancy Davis Pflueger Collection*

Christian Holmes assumed the office of president of the company and was perpetually active in its management, research, and development.

Paul Beyer resigned as manager of Hawaiian Tuna Packers on 31 August 1935. Clarence White then became vice president and general manager of the company. Beyer continued with his Service Cold Storage Company[115] and in 1939 became general manager of American Brewing Company in Honolulu. He moved into a colonial style mansion, the former Knutson estate, just off of Judd Street in Nuʻuanu. Beyer, the humble German fisherman who raised his large family on Moku o Loʻe and helped create Hawaiian Tuna Packers, died in Hilo in the 1940s.

| THE CREATION OF COCONUT ISLAND

In November 1933, Christian Holmes subleased Moku o Loʻe from Heeia Company for the period ending in September 1957.[116] Rent was set at $1,000 per year. He had visited the island prior to leasing it, as noted from his Land Court testimony in 1937. Then he had found it deserted, covered in dense guava and lantana.[117] With the Fleischmann millions, Holmes immediately set out to transform the isle from a fisherman's lookout to a garden of tropical magnificence perhaps unequaled in the United States.

Since fresh water had been a limiting factor for the early development of Coconut Island, Holmes first extended a 4-inch pipe between the tiny island and Oʻahu. Pure drinking water was piped here from the Koʻolau Range through several cisterns in the nearby hills. In 1934, a submarine telephone cable was established between Heʻeia and Coconut Island.[118]

In 1937, after clearing title with the Bishop Estate, Holmes purchased the island outright and ultimately invested over $1 million in its development. With the addition of vast amounts of landfill and numerous landscaping and building improvements, Coconut Island was created from the core of Moku o Loʻe.

While the first coconut palms were planted by Charles and Bernice Pauahi Bishop around 1883, much of the extensive grove of coconut trees now seen on the island were established by Holmes—brought in by the barge load, as were all the other exotic plants and flowering trees. Andy Anderson, who sold Holmes coconut trees for $5.00 each, recalls that many of the plants were Tahitian coconut palms.

By August 1934, most of the island's structures had been built on the original nucleus. By far the most elaborate Holmes modification to Coconut Island would begin soon, however, with the addition of 16 acres to the isle's total area. In legal descriptions of this fill, about ten acres were normally above water, while approximately six acres of fill were directly below the water's surface (this is why modern descriptions of the island usually give an area between 22.5 to 28.5 acres). Much of the fill was sand poured directly on top of the reef platform encircling the natural basalt of Moku o Lo'e. The sand apparently was removed from a feature appropriately known as Sand Island in Kāne'ohe Bay, owned by the U.S. government. Anderson was in charge of the operation:

I was the skipper of a barge and I had ten men with me. We used to go to Sand Island. Sand was 34 a bag, cement bag size, about 60 lbs. We had to fill the bags three-quarters full so we could tie the top. If we made 300 bags, that was enough for a day's work. We used to work during the night.... We slept during the day...we kept hauling the sand until we had a mountain of it down here at Coral Garden.... I've been doing that a long time, for about three years. Sand Island disappeared.

In addition to building beaches and lagoons, sand mixed with cement created walls for fishponds and swimming pools. Holmes owned hoppers and cement mixers for this operation. Channels for ships and boats were carved into the living reef surrounding Coconut Island. During the height of construction, Holmes had more than 200 workmen and 30 laundry women. Although the higher elevations of the island had a

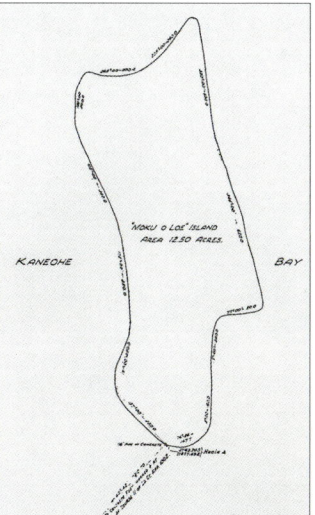

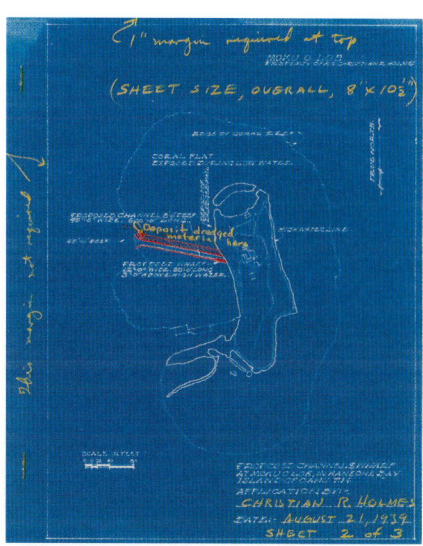

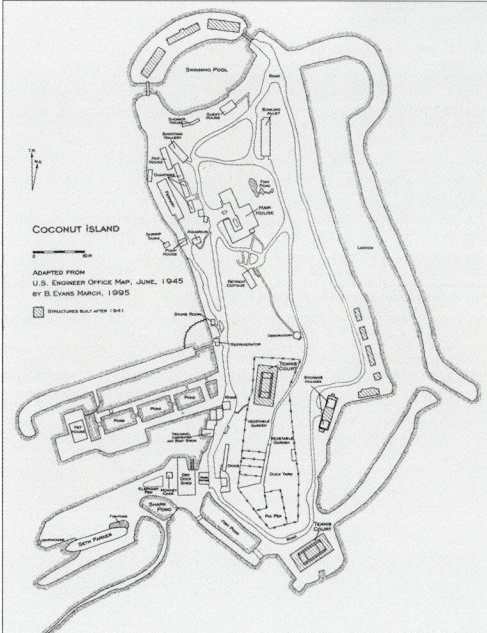

(top left) Before. Bishop Estate map of Moku o Lo'e prepared for Land Court Application #1134, 1936. Hawaii Land Court

(top right) During. Holmes's blueprint of proposed construction in 1939. Ann Holmes Terrell Collection

(left) After. Coconut Island at the end of the Holmes era, 1945. Bishop Museum

| (top) The great lagoon on the eastern shoreline. Christian Holmes IV Collection
| (bottom) Boat repair facilities, domestic animal pens, and shark pond. Christian Holmes IV Collection

certain amount of original soil, boatloads of rich volcanic topsoil were obtained from local Japanese gardeners and added to the accreting Coconut Island. A concrete wall was built completely around the island, a project that took about three years to complete.

Among the more ambitious enterprises at Coconut Island was the construction of a barrier shoal to protect the eastern side of the island, the region exposed to the open sea beyond the reefs. This sand bar had two boat-turning basins, excavated into the coral, with a single outlet to the south. Three lagoons or mooring areas were built on the southwestern side of the island to accommodate larger ships. A four-masted schooner, the *Seth Parker*, was placed in one of these slips. This region also contained a shark pond and a larger fishpond. A dry dock, complete with marine railway, was built here, as well as shops for carpentry, mechanics, and general boat repair. Just to the north of this region two jetties were built out onto the reef, facing the He'eia shoreline. Four separate fishponds were constructed here. A net house was built on the

| *(above and opposite top right) The one-acre saltwater pool on the far (north) end of the island. Christian Holmes IV Collection [opposite top right], Pauley Collection [above]*

western point of one of the jetties. On the north end of the island, a natural saltwater swimming pool was established by enclosing a portion of the shoreline with rock and sand fill and excavating another portion into the base rock of the island. This created a shallow lagoon. The large swimming pool opened to the bay in two places. The filled portions of the lagoon, containing out buildings, were attached to Coconut Island by bridges. Holmes procured from the U.S. Navy two giant searchlights to help illuminate the pool for nighttime swimming. The lagoon was also graced with water slides and a shower house. A beach house for guests was built adjacent to the pool.

Holmes built a perimeter road encircling the island. The portion of the route from the main wharf to the main house was paved and lined with beautiful trees and exotic plants. Other gardens supported rare cacti and other succulents. Along the west coast of the island Holmes constructed several servants' quarters, a hothouse for his orchids, and a fernery. Nearer the shore he had several aquaria installed for his tropical fish collection, and he raised shrimp in tanks for his own consumption. Clam and oyster beds were established near the shoreline on the west and south portions of the island. Holmes also raised eels. A pumphouse to bring seawater to the marine aquaria was set in the center of the island on the western shoreline. Adjacent buildings were used for storage and refrigeration. He kept a magnificent shell collection in the net house, an interest he shared with his cousin Julius Fleischmann II.[119]

The shark pond near the *Seth Parker* was a commercial enterprise. A dyed-in-the-wool Fleischmann, Holmes sold shark liver oil as a vitamin supplement in San Francisco and shark fin as a delicacy to chefs in Honolulu's Chinatown.

The main structure of Coconut Island was a fairly simple, straightforward ranch house. Constructed of hollow tile, the home consisted of an office and kitchen in the north wing, a large dining and living room in the center, and four bedrooms and bath in the south wing. The house was roughly C-shaped and erected around a central fountain and garden

| (above) Portent of things to come. Holmes maintained extensive tropical aquaria on the island, ca. 1938. Botanical Society, Bishop Museum
| (opposite) The exotic gardens of Coconut Island, 1938. Ray Jerome Baker, Bishop Museum

area. This courtyard was covered with an arching lattice roof hung with baskets of ferns. Orchids in pots were set out along the patio walls. The walls along the plaza contained 10 built-in aquaria filled with Holmes's exotic fish. There were six glass aquaria in the main house, and three in the private cottage.

The comfortable living room of the main house was decorated in a breezy, contemporary style, in contrast to the study, which was furnished in a formal theme. The adjacent lanai was furnished in Hawaiian style with *lauhala* mats and bamboo-covered walls. The lanai opened

| (above) Quiet and secure. Holmes's modest private Retreat.
  P. Christiann Klieger, Author's Collection
| (top left) The front lawn of the Main House led to the
  obseratory at the island's summit. Hawai'i State Archives
| (bottom left) Lily ponds on the lawn were home to ducks
  and carp, 1938. Ray Jerome Baker, Bishop Museum
opposite:
| (top left) Orchid-covered lanai in the Main House. HIMB
| (top right) Central atrium of the Main House on Coconut
  Island, ca. 1944. Steward Fern, Bishop Museum
| (bottom left) Living room of the Main House, as built in
  1934. Ann Holmes Terrell Collection
| (bottom right) Main House study, as built in 1934.
  Ann Holmes Terrell Collection

Not for swimming laps, the Retreat Orchid Pool was deeper than it was wide. It could be filled with heated salt water or fresh water. Pauley Collection

onto a lawn that afforded spectacular views. The lawn contained art-fully arrayed lily ponds filled with ornamental carp and ducks.

Holmes did not live in the main house, however, but in a cottage known later as the Retreat. Located up the hill and about 40 feet to the south of the main house, the Retreat cottage was a cozy place to get away from the endless stream of visitors Holmes was fond of entertaining. The bungalow contained a large living room with a high ceiling, a capacious bathroom, a comfortable bedroom, and a small but deep private swimming pool surrounded by walls of orchids. The Retreat was staffed with its own maid.

On the summit of the hill just south of the Retreat, Holmes built an observation lounge. This was a hexagonal building with large picture windows that provided a spectacular view of Kāneʻohe Bay and the Koʻolau Range. The interior of the lounge was arrayed with couch sections along the walls, with a service bar off to one side. A Dictaphone and telephone line linked the observatory with the kitchen so snacks could be ordered. On top of the observatory was a tower and searchlight and, nearby, a red beacon—reminding visitors and planes that this spot was just south of the glide path of the airbase main runway at Mōkapu.

One of the more lively funhouses on Coconut Island was Holmes's shooting gallery. Chris had visited the Playland shoreline amusement park in San Francisco on Fulton Avenue near Seal Rocks. Here he came upon a shooting gallery and fired a few shots. Not feeling well, he missed the birds completely. He then sent for the owner and asked how much he would sell the business for. The proprietor indicated the gallery was not for sale. Pressed, the owner said it had cost him $5,000 for equipment and $2,000 was invested in "good will." Holmes then offered him $10,000 and the owner accepted. "Sold!" chirped Holmes, "Pack it up and ship it to the island complete." Ethel Uyehara vividly recalled seeing the shooting gallery on Coconut Island: "When you flipped on the switches, everything would turn on. There was a player piano that played, and the ducks would be flying and swimming on a pond, and the

| *(top) Playland by the Sea, San Francisco. The amusement park was torn down in the 1970s. San Francisco Public Library.*
| *(bottom) Shooting gallery at Playland, reinstalled after Holmes's purchase. San Francisco Public Library*

rabbits would be hopping...the ducks would actually swim on real water." Guests were enchanted. Nancy Davis Pflueger remembers Holmes's favorite target was a tin baby that would cry if hit. Many of the features had been similar to those kept in the recreation rooms of his mother's estate on Long Island. When I visited the Chimneys in 2003, there, in the basement, was a Holmes shooting gallery.

In addition to the shooting gallery and nickelodeon, Coconut Island housed a portion of Holmes's extensive collection of artifacts and knickknacks from around the world. These included, according to one observer, "mummified Indian heads, hunting knives and guns of every description, mounted birds and giant lizards, bear rug trophies, shark heads, and grotesquely carved primitive figures."[120] Holmes possessed a jeweled Venetian dagger with the monogram "NB" that was attributed to Napoleon Bonaparte.[121]

| *(top left) The ducks and windmills haven't moved for 65 years. The Chimneys' shooting gallery, 2003. P. Christiaan Klieger*
| *(top right) The Venetian dagger attributed to Napoleon, one of Chris Holmes's prized possessions. P. Christiaan Klieger*
| *(bottom) Holmes contemplates a spare in the bowling alley on the island. Hawai'i State Archives*

| *Model airplanes grace the card tables in the bowling alley. Ann Holmes Terrell Collection*

Not satisfied with a single fun house, Holmes built a second recreation house on his island paradise. This long, log cabin was located on the north side of the island. It contained a two-lane, manual pin bowling alley and was furnished with rattan chairs. One could also play pool or ping-pong, get a soda from the Coke machine, or try one's luck with the slot machines. From the ceiling hung a superb model airplane collection, many of which were given to him by aviator Paul Mantz.

Coconut Island was designed to be nearly self-sufficient in farm produce. Extensive vegetable and flower gardens were established on the top of the island, just south of the observatory. Fruit trees were planted.

Visitors recall the rare spectacle of Hawaiian-grown raspberries thriving on Coconut Island. Holmes had banished the noisy chickens from MacFarlane's day from the island, but he built large duck yards and pigeon lofts. Lester Zukeran recalls that 30 to 40 turkeys were raised on the small island, and he remembers donkeys as well. Even a pigpen was built near the south point of the isle.

Consistent with his lifelong interest in zoology, Holmes again established a rather fabulous zoo at his island paradise. And by this circuitous path of association, Holmes provided the nuclei for two Hawaiian institutions: the Honolulu Zoo and Hawaiʻi Institute of Marine Biology.

It was an exceptionally entertaining place for a small child—a six-year-old boy visiting Holmes's island (George Sumner) recalled that it was filled "with strange animals." A kennel for about fifteen dogs was built on the island, complete with a dog food kitchen and dog bath. Lester Zukeran recalls that Holmes had as many as 30 or 40 dogs, including three gigantic Great Danes that used to frighten the guests. He also kept several dachshunds. One report mentions a zebra, another a camel.[122] A talented mynah reportedly sang "Isle of Capri" to amazed guests.[123] Andy Anderson credits Holmes with bringing over tigers, a giraffe, and "all kinds of monkeys." A large primate cage was built near the *Seth Parker*. Here Holmes kept Maryann, Butch, and Whoopee, his three chimpanzees. According to Zukeran, the mature female chimp Maryann could become quite dangerous during estrus, and a young George Sumner remembers the strong chimp nearly pulling his arm off. Among the various birds imported to the island, exotic peacocks and pheasants are vividly remembered. Holmes had a beautiful butterfly collection housed under glass in a room to itself.

In 1938, Holmes outdid himself and ordered a baby elephant for his private zoo. A two-year-old, 1400-pound female Indian elephant was obtained from Hagenbeck Zoo in Germany, brought through San Francisco, and transferred to a freighter for final shipment to Hawaiʻi. The pachyderm was named Beckel and was given a large, stone-walled

| (far left) Holmes and Beckel. *Charles Lucas*
| (left) A humorous moment for one of the more sedate chimps. *Lester Zukeran*
| (bottom) Trainer Junior Lee with Beckel the elephant. *Lester Zukeran*

opposite:
| (top) Animal pens and gardens provided much food for the island. *Christian Holmes IV Collection*
| (bottom) Junior Lee (left) and Jack Kim with Whoopee and Maryann. *Lester Zukeran*

| HAWAIIAN TUNA PACKERS EXPANDS

After Paul Beyer left Hawaiian Tuna Packers, A. G. Korol became manager under Holmes. From 1936 to 1939 Mona Hind's son, Charles Lucas, Jr., was in charge of marketing. The Hawaiian Tuna Packers eventually cornered the local market. Prior to Holmes's leadership of the Tuna Packers, White Star from the mainland United States was the sole supplier of canned tuna to the territory. When Hawaiian Tuna Packer's Coral Hawaiian Brand began to appear on the shelves, it quickly supplanted White Star in sales. During World War II, Coral Hawaiian Brand was the only tuna available in the local markets, according to Lucas.[130] It was difficult to obtain the fish, however, because the company's fishing boats were appropriated by the U.S. military during the war.[131]

As Holmes had observed, the bulk of the fish obtained for Hawaiian Tuna Packers was caught with live bait on poles immediately outside Kāneʻohe Bay. In general, most of the fishing in the vicinity of Moku o Loʻe had been done by individuals on private fishing boats, but Holmes purchased several sampans. A heavy harvest of fish for Hawaiian Packers would run 12–14 tons per day, mostly *aku* or skipjack tuna. The sampans of Holmes's day usually carried a crew of five to seven men. The going rate for the purchase of the catch at that time was about $80 per ton. Although it may have seemed small scale, the operations were ultimately unsustainable. Today, due to overfishing in the Hawaiian Islands, tuna are caught hundreds of miles off the islands.

Chris Holmes privately maintained one of the largest tuna boats in the territory, the *Yamato Maru*, which contributed substantially to the operation of the harvest. A smaller fishing boat, the *Mona H*, was also owned and operated by Holmes. The *Iguchi Maru*, named after its original skipper Jujiro Iguchi, took passengers to and from Coconut Island. Coconut Island became a secondary service facility for the company after the main Kewalo Bay pier in Honolulu. Holmes maintained a net house and a marine railway for minor repairs on-island. As Bettie

| *Chris and Mona, Mona's daughter Lamie (center), and fishermen pulling the boat in. Harada Collection*

opposite:
| *(top left)* Yamato Maru, *the largest sampan in the territory. Lester Zukeran*
| *(top right) The* Mona H, *Holmes's personal fishing boat, commanded by Captain Yagi. Lester Zukeran*
| *(bottom left)* Iguchi Maru, *used for passenger transport. Lester Zukeran*
| *(bottom right) Sharks' fins and marlin snouts grace the eaves of Holmes's net house. Lester Zukeran*

had hoped, Holmes took an avid interest in the operations of Hawaiian Tuna Packers, a further development of a long-term fascination with the study of marine biology.

| A Flotilla of Luminaries

With nearly unlimited wealth and his Hollywood network from his days at Santa Barbara with Katherine MacDonald, Christian Holmes now had perhaps the most spectacular island setting in America on which a glittering social life of parties, retreats, and festive celebrations could be held. The international "propeller" set of the late 1930s was incandescent. This was the streamlined era of Wallis Simpson and the Duke of Windsor, of a young Howard Hughes, and of King Carol II of Romania and his mistress Magda Lupescu. Amelia Earhart and Shirley Temple were setting their own records, and they were among the earliest guests of Holmes in Hawai'i. Nearly all the stories of the fabulous entertaining done by Holmes are recalled directly from guests who had attended. That gives one an idea, over 70 years later, how memorable such occasions were.

Amelia Earhart, her co-pilot Paul Mantz, and husband George Putnam were friends of Holmes. In late 1934, she had her Lockheed Vega shipped to Honolulu aboard the *Lurline*. The party were guests of Holmes at Queen's Surf and Coconut Island. On January 11, she took off from Wheeler Field and flew solo to Oakland, California, becoming the first person to do so. On January 20 she stayed with Holmes again at Linden Lodge on San Marcos Pass. The aviatrix returned to Honolulu in her new Lockheed 10E Electra in March 1937 on her first attempt to fly around the world at the equator. She gave Holmes a short spin in her new plane. Upon leaving Hawai'i at Hickam Field, O'ahu, her heavily-laden plane's tire blew and the landing gear collapsed. The plane spun around on the runway, bending the tips of one propeller. It was removed and given to Holmes as a souvenir while her airplane was shipped back to

| *An unusual catch-of-the-day, Holmes examines a great white shark. Bruce Spaulding Collection*

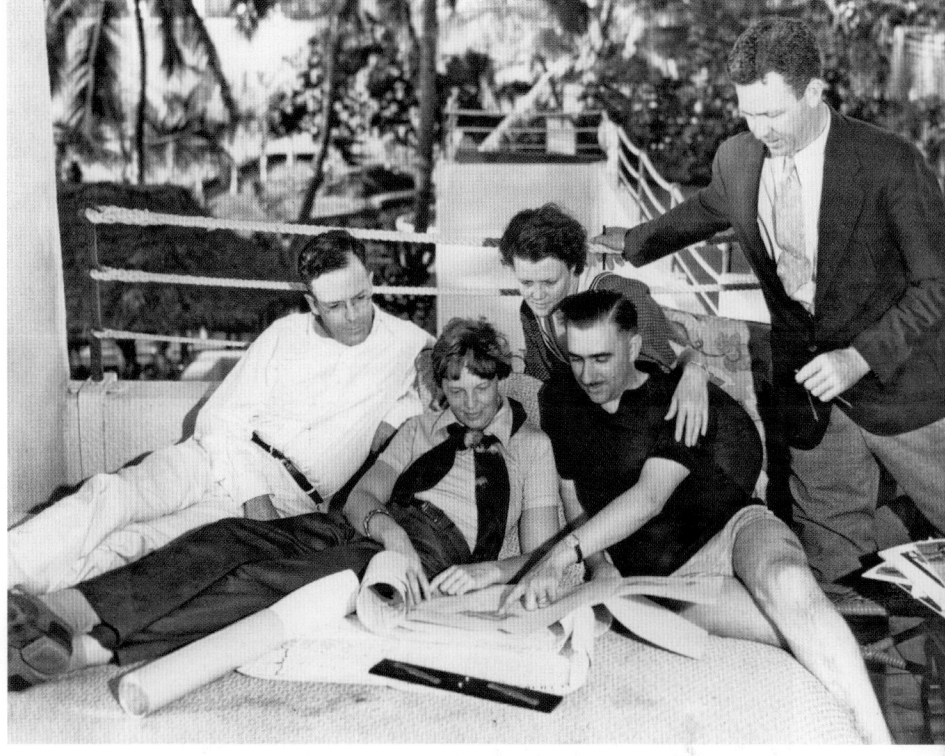

| *(above, left to right) George Putnam, Amelia Earhart, Paul Mantz, and other guests looking at charts, Queen's Surf. Bishop Museum*
| *(top left) Amelia Earhart's* Vega *being unloaded in Honolulu from the* Lurline *for her non-stop flight to Oakland. Library of Congress LC-USZ62-110858*
| *(bottom left) Amelia Earhart hiding among sofa pillows as Holmes (seated) talks with guests at Linden Lodge. Bruce Spaulding Collection*

| *Shirley Temple entertains children at her birthday party. Nancy Davis sits in the life ring. Bishop Museum*

California for repair. The propeller was enshrined in the Coconut Island shooting gallery/museum. Mantz gave Christian the splendid collection of model airplanes that were housed in Holmes's bowling alley. On her second attempt in June 1937, she headed east from Oakland with navigator Fred Noonan. She never made it back to Hawai'i—she crossed the Atlantic Ocean, Africa, and Asia, and was presumed lost at sea near Howland Island in the Western Pacific.

Shirley Temple, the little girl most likely to be given an elaborate birthday party, was hosted at Coconut Island around 1935. At this fête, all the children were given two live rabbits to take home. Nancy Davis Pflueger, daughter of Holmes's business partner Alan Davis, remembers the little star's party and how children loved Holmes: "He was awesome with kids, he would do things like putting his hands in his pockets and pulling out a newly hatched duckling for the children."

Duke Kahanamoku, Olympic gold medal swimmer, popularizer of the sport of surfing, and sheriff of Honolulu, was also making the social circuit with Holmes, with whom he became a lifelong friend. In 1936, Duke co-hosted a gala party on Coconut Island for the world's best yachtsmen. It wound up as a cabaret party on the *Seth Parker*.

Holmes did not neglect his family, however. Holmes's sons by Albertine Peck, Christian III and William Dayton, were frequent visitors to the island, as were Mona's daughter Lamie and son "Charlie-boy" Lucas. Ann Holmes, daughter by Katherine MacDonald, visited once. Bettie Fleischmann Holmes was a peripatetic visitor at her son's estates at Queen's Surf and Coconut Island. Holmes was particularly close to his

| *(top, left to right) Jujiro Iguchi, Christian Holmes III, Duke Kahanamoku, Dayton Holmes, and other guests. Ann Holmes Terrell Collection*

| *(bottom) Boat days in Honolulu. Mrs. Carl Holmes (Bubbles) (left) and Bettie Fleischmann Holmes being greeted on the* Lurline *by Duke Kahanamoku and Mona Hind. Christian Holmes IV Collection*

| *Bettie Fleischmann Holmes and guest, Queen's Surf* lūʻau. *George and Fumiko Harada*

| *Little Ann Holmes on the island. Ann Holmes Terrell Collection*

mother. Associating with characters as different as Leopold Stokowski to Duke Kahanamoku, she was a well-seasoned world traveler well into her golden years.

Christian Holmes II was considered by many a brilliant host, well-educated and cosmopolitan, a good conversationalist, widely read, and sharp in business. "I don't know of anybody who disliked him," remarked Robert Richardson, husband of housekeeper Katie Napier. He had been a highly decorated war hero. To his friends and employees, Christian Holmes seemed always a gentleman. Nancy Davis Pflueger said that he was "the most wonderful person I ever knew."

Although his behavior might at times be eccentric and outrageous, Holmes was always kind. Helen Davis said that, "He really was concerned about his people and his friends, and he had lots of them visit him. He was always wanting you to enjoy yourself and be relaxed about it all, and you know he didn't hover over you like some people do."

Holmes originally had a glass bottom ferry boat to shuttle friends and family between Kāne'ohe Pier and the island, but later he obtained the *Iguchi Maru*. A miniature concrete lighthouse marked the end of the artificial pier at Coconut Island. While the poky old glass bottom boat was replaced by a vessel marginally faster, Holmes acquired for himself something considerably more speedy. Its story has been handed down from Ralph Clark, Holmes's insurance man, to Rick Rainalter. Regarding the fateful purchase of Coconut Island's first Chris Craft speedboat:

Holmes ordered a Chris Craft, mid-engine, front and rear cockpit speedboat, which was a very sleek machine, with varnished mahogany and white lines between boards...with a flag up front and a flag in the rear...low-slung to the water and...basically built for high speed operation on lakes and flat water.

| *Jujiro Iguchi at the wheel of Holmes's replacement Chris Craft,* Auwe, *the fastest boat in the islands. Holmes ripped the engine through the floor boards of its predecessor. Lester Zukeran*

So Chris Holmes took delivery of this in Honolulu Harbor and he and some friends took the boat around from Honolulu...to Kāne'ohe Bay. And the weather kicked up. The only way that they could keep from being inundated by the waves was to go full power on the speedboat, and they were slamming from one wave into the next...Inevitably the motor in the boat broke through the floorboards and went right through the bottom of the boat right off Mōkapu'u. And the boat sank and the occupants swam to shore without event.

Holmes put in a claim to Ralph Clark for the boat. Clark called Holmes to ask him if he wanted the money or a new boat. Holmes wanted a new boat exactly like the first one, but he agreed to promise Clark to take it around in calm weather. The new vessel, appropriately called the *Auwe* (H. "lamentation"), survived for a time, then was destroyed when the throttle was floored in reverse, causing the boat to crash upon the dock and sink. No claim was submitted that time around.

Andy Anderson recalls the big parties on the island: "We...would watch the people, about 200 or 300 of them, all guests coming from Mōkapu base." Holmes brought a Hawaiian orchestra out to the island about three times a week, complete with singers and dancers. Holmes rarely got to bed before 5:00 a.m.!

Formal social gatherings were usually held at the Queen's Surf estate, but more intimate parties and *lū'au* were popular at Coconut Island. According to one guest:

Well, they were all very informal. Once in a while there would be about ten people at the table for some dinner or something. But [at times] they were bigger than that like when you had Bing Crosby and all these other people that came from Los Angeles and New York.... The [meals] were all very informal, just a buffet type meal, always very casual, very friendly, it was a relaxed sort of feeling that you got there. He wanted you to just come and enjoy the place like he did. He was a very nice host.

At midsummer, it was a tradition to throw a large party at Coconut Island. Barbara Silva Shanahan, daughter of Holmes's dentist friend, recalls one such occasion:

That was a Fourth of July party that took place sometime in late August or early September by convenience. He had some fireworks company on the Mainland make him some kind of banner out of fireworks that was going to be lit right at dinner time. [It] was strung between the masts [of the Seth Parker], I believe, or it could have been outside, I was quite young then. It had a heart on each end that went up in the fireworks and then it spelled out "Mona and Chris." It was very impressive because it was very large. He missed the Fourth of July for some reason and any other day was going to be just as good. The party was a gala affair that started early in the afternoon and went on until it was dark enough to light the fireworks. They served dinner. A very, very, beautiful place to have a party of that type!

George Sumner also remembers the fireworks display, which seemed to go on for two hours. Holmes reputably spent $7,000 for the pyrotechnics each Fourth of July.

Guests recollected Alice Faye visiting the island paradise, as well as prizefighter Jack Demsey. Johnny "Tarzan" Weismueller, John Wayne, and swashbuckler Errol Flynn dropped in, as did Bette Davis, Samuel Goldwyn, Hal Roach, Noël Coward, Spencer Tracy, and Janet Gaynor. Chris Holmes was friends with the Rockefeller family. Herbert Hoover, William Randolph Hearst, Jr., and Union Pacific Railroad chairman Averell Harriman all visited Coconut Island, according to Charles

Lucas. The cream of Honolulu society wore a path down Waikalua Pier. Some of the more frequent guests were local: Rose Davis, Walter MacFarlane, Harold Castle, Mr. and Mrs. Peter McLean, Mr. and Mrs. Rainalter, and SS *Lurline* Captain Berndtson. Tobacco heiress Doris Duke was also a visitor at Coconut Island.

The chimpanzees of the isle of dreams were the life of the party. Sumner recalls one of the chimps dressed in white tie and tails and seated next to an unescorted lady guest. Actually, the apes had quite their own wardrobe of dresses, tuxedos, hats, and shoes. Ethel Uyehara remembered that one ape used to mimic Mrs. Holmes on the phone. Sometimes the troglodytes were sent in to awaken guests in the morning, such as Bubbles Holmes's dawn visitor. Helen Davis recalls that "everybody loved the chimps. But you didn't dare get too close to the huge cage. They liked to spit and they had very good aim...everybody got a kick out of it...as long as they were under control."

Holmes allowed the Davis children and their friends to romp through the Retreat, with its gigantic tiled bathroom. Chris would hose down the floor to let the children run and slide. This room was adjacent to the outdoor Orchid Swimming Pool. On one occasion he stocked the pool with conger eels, floated in a few hundred-dollar bills, and dared anyone to jump in to retrieve them.

Once a year Christian Holmes invited family and friends of his employees to an open house on the island. On one such occasion, young senator-to-be Daniel Inouye observed that guests were given bamboo fishing poles and encouraged to fish in one of his fishponds. Holmes failed to tell his visitors, however, that he had fed the fish just before they arrived. Everyone was standing around looking at the fat fish, none of which were biting.

A perspective of "downstairs" life on Coconut Island under Holmes has also been preserved. Ethel Takahashi Uyehara worked as a domestic helper at Coconut Island from September 1941 to the outbreak of World War II on December 7:

| *(above) Mona Hind explains the art of reef fishing to one of the chimps. Frank Harada Collection*
| *(opposite) Holmes's friend and confrere in pranks, Errol Flynn. Author's Collection*

| *The Coconut Island china pattern. P. Christiaan Klieger, Ann Holmes Terrell Collection*

There were more servants on Coconut Island than there were people being served. Once a week we got all the silver out and polished it. The kitchen boy did the servant's dishes and the pots and pans. He never touched the guests' or the family's dishes. The pantry staff did all the dishes for the family. All the china, even the breakfast dishes, had the Coconut Island logo on them. Once a week we made butterballs.... The servant's cook prepared all our food. He made the best pies and Mrs. Holmes used to come and take what she wanted for the guests. This is where I learned to eat artichokes in drawn butter. I had never seen an artichoke before. Oh yes, the finger bowls with porcelain roses were on plates with doilies.... When it was time to serve meals, the butler would lead with the heavy dishes and then we would follow with other dishes. The hostess used her "magic eye," a signal that we were to come.

Hardly a Scrooge, Holmes presented each employee with a large turkey at Christmas. One of the most enduring and popular legends of the fabulous Chris Holmes, however, was the allegorical spending of $1,000 a day to maintain Coconut Island. The effects of wind and salt spray on the island's improvements were considerable and unending, and with a large staff of servants, the $1,000 overhead seems realistic.

SS *Seth Parker*

The landmark that would be most remembered by generations of visitors to Coconut Island and Kāneʻohe Bay is the moored sailing ship *Seth Parker*, which Holmes purchased in 1935. The four-masted schooner was originally obtained by Holmes for use as a bait ship for Hawaiian Tuna Packers. The ship, more than any other object, helps explain the complex personality of its owner. Its rise and decline is metaphorical to the life of Holmes himself.

Christian R. Holmes II came from a family passionate about sailing. Beginning with his grandfather's sleek yacht *Hiawatha*, his Uncle Max's huge *Haida* diesel ship, and his Uncle Julius's fabulous *Camargo* series of vessels, Holmes wished to add a noteworthy sailing ship to his fleet of humble fishing boats. Holmes found his own Fleischmann icon in the *Seth Parker*.

Built as the *Georgette* in 1918 as a lumber hauler at Columbia Yard in Portland, Oregon, the ship was 188 feet long and weighted 867 tons. It was initially operated by G. W. McNear of San Francisco and was placed on the New Zealand run. The schooner's agent in San Francisco was the Hind-Rolph Company,[132] co-owned by Holmes's future father-in-law, Robert Hind and "Sunny" Jim Rolph, future mayor of San Francisco and governor of California. In 1920 the ship worked the route from Alexandria, Egypt, to Seattle. It then was placed in Atlantic service until 1932. The schooner was purchased the next year by radio personality Phillips Lord, whose folksy character was known as Seth Parker, sort of an early, New England version of Garrison Keeler. After the installation of a diesel engine, the ship was rechristened after Lord's character.

Lord conceived an idea to sail his new ship to various exotic ports over two years, with a team of celebrities, to broadcast his radio programs on NBC. On its inaugural voyage, the *Seth Parker* sailed from New York, calling at various ports on the East Coast to broadcast the weekly show on its own shortwave station, KRNA.[133] A special song was ever written to commemorate the journey, and a booklet was published by the sponsor, Frigidaire. The company underwrote the trip as a promotion for its refrigerators, demonstrating their reliability in storing great quantities of food for a voyage around the world: "The Folks aboard the *Seth Parker* do not have to live on 'bully-beef' and 'hard-tack' as did the old-time sailors...they have *fresh* food, *kept* fresh by Frigidaire!"

The voyages were heavily marketed, in the armchair argot of radio in the 1930s:

'Frigidaire presents the cruise of the Seth Parker.*'*
On Tuesday nights, this announcement thrills millions of radio listeners as they sit back in their chairs and eagerly await another half-hour of the

| *Reflections of 19th-century New England aboard the* Seth Parker. *Author's Collection*

| Seth Parker *cover sent from Haiti en route. Author's Collection*

Phillips Lord
as "Seth Parker"

Phillips Lord

| (top) Phillips Lord and his character. Author's Collection
| (bottom left) "A bachelor's kitchenette or bar could easily achieve distinction, efficiency
and charm, by borrowing architectural details from the Seth Parker's galley."
Frigidaire booklet. Author's Collection
| (bottom right) Main cabin where broadcasts were made. Author's Collection
| (far right) Atop deck before the last voyage. Author's Collection

| *The* Seth Parker *in Pago Pago Harbor, Sāmoa, following its battle with Pacific typhoons, 1935. Bishop Museum*

world's most unusual radio entertainment—broadcast direct from an old sailing ship...what a setting for a modern radio broadcast to every nook and cranny of our huge country![134]

The ship, with a crew of 20, passed through the Panama Canal and cruised out into the South Pacific. In February 1935, it promptly sailed into a typhoon off the coast of American Sāmoa. The *Seth Parker* took on water, leaving her wallowing and unmanageable in high seas. Following a radioed SOS by Captain Frank Eckmann, the HMAS *Australia* steamed toward the schooner. The *Seth Parker* survived but was trapped in another storm three days later. The governor of American Sāmoa, Otto Dowling, informed the floundering schooner that a navy tug would be sent out should it be found necessary to abandon ship. While the *Australia* stood by, having picked up nine passengers, the tug *Ontario* took the *Seth* safely in tow to Pago Pago.

The aging ship's hull apparently could no longer withstand the strain of strong winds upon the sails, even with its diesel engine. The masts would strain and spread the seams of the hull, allowing seawater to rush in. The damage to the ship during the typhoons was so great that the radio crew ended any thoughts of further broadcasts aboard the wounded ship and went home.[135]

In April 1935, Hawaiian Tuna Packers took an option on the schooner, then moored at Tutuila. Holmes had tanks fitted in the ship, with the idea of filling them with sardines to use as bait for tuna. The ship was sold to Holmes's company for $10,000, a tenth of what it cost Phillips Lord to buy and outfit for his exotic radio junket. The vessel sailed for Honolulu on 3 July and arrived on 16 September. The crew had complained that water was constantly awash on its decks from the bilge pumps. The ship's food supply was "down to one case of beans and a barrel of wormy flour." The beautiful beamed ceiling and homey paneled walls, the Frigidaires holding "great supplies of fruit and vegetables that are kept always plump and fresh," the rifle racks, broadcasting room,

and other fine appointments were all gone. The jib boom was full of dry rot, according to schooner captain Eckmann. Its hull was green with moss and algae—but eventually the reincarnated HMS *Bounty* limped into Honolulu.

Holmes had the *Seth Parker* towed from Honolulu Harbor to Kāneʻohe Bay and Coconut Island. Remarkably, the bait survived the voyage: Andy Anderson remembers that Holmes filled four of his Coconut Island fishponds with the sardines brought in from Sāmoa. But because of the general unseaworthiness of the schooner, Hawaiian Tuna Packers abandoned further ideas to use the ship as a bait hauler. The retired *Seth Parker* was towed to an artificial lagoon constructed adjacent to Coconut Island, where it was scuttled in a few feet of water.

Holmes modified the *Seth's* interior to use as a motion picture theater, laboratory, and bar. Guests could sunbathe on the deck, but generally they loved playing pirate. A few staterooms were equipped for overnight stay. Reflecting his avid interest in marine biology, Holmes installed laboratories in the stern of the schooner to serve Hawaiian Tuna Packers fisheries research. The movie theater on board was a major attraction in those pre-DVD days. Holmes's partner Alan Davis also ran Consolidated Amusement, so he could easily obtain all the first-run movies for Coconut Island gatherings.

The stately silhouette of the *Seth Parker* remained intact well into the 1940s. It was used as a prop in the John Wayne movie, *The Wake of the Red Witch*.

| *In the 1940s John Wayne filmed* Wake of the Red Witch *on Coconut Island. Note the man-eating octopus. Author's Collection*

| (above) An novel movie theatre and lounge transformed the Seth Parker. *Ann Holmes Terrell Collection*

| (far left) *The schooner was scuttled at Coconut Island, 1938. Ray Jerome Baker, Bishop Museum*

| (left) Seth Parker *always made a great photo op for Holmes's guests. Ann Holmes Terrell Collection*

| *A Seth party. Tai Sing Loo, Ann Holmes Terrell Collection*

Unsalvageable from the start, the ship slowly rotted away. The masts were removed around 1945. Robert Miranda dislodged the 400-pound anchor and dumped it into Kāneʻohe Bay, according to his son Steve. A fire in the 1960s accelerated the ship's demise. As the paint on the hull wore off, the ghostly name *Georgette* and homeport of San Francisco became visible. In the mid-1990s, all that remained was a mound of green vegetation where the proud *Seth Parker* once was berthed. For many years the wheel of the ship was on display in the main house on Coconut Island, but just before the sale of the private section of the island by Hachidai Corporation in the mid-90s, the wheel was donated to the Hawaiʻi Maritime Center at Honolulu Harbor, now a part of Bishop Museum.

END OF AN ERA

Dark clouds drifted over the island by the 1940s. In June 1940, one of Holmes's property supervisors, Gregario Benlaoro, was crushed on Coconut Island when a truck lost its brakes and rolled downhill upon him. He was rushed by speedboat to the hospital, but died from his injuries.[136] In August 1940, Holmes's beloved Linden Lodge in Santa Barbara was destroyed by wildfire. Mona and Christian were having marital difficulties, exacerbated by the latter's heavy drinking. Holmes's health began to give out, and he became an insomniac, roaming throughout his little island at all hours of the night. On 29 September 1941, his mother died at Sands Point.[137] The idyll at Coconut Island had come to an end; on 7 December 1941, Oʻahu itself was attacked.

The aggression on Pearl Harbor and other military sites on Oʻahu on 7 December 1941 is well remembered by Holmes's staff at Coconut Island. Located only a few hundred meters from the threshold of the main runway at Kaneohe Marine Corps Air Station at Mōkapu, Coconut Island was overflown and strafed by Japanese pilots on that eventful day. Christian Holmes and Mona were not at home, though. They were

Contemporary footprint of the main house, Linden Lodge, which burned down in 1940. P. Christiaan Klieger, Author's Collection

| (left) Aircraft landing and taking off at Mōkapu flew right over Coconut Island. Col. Ray Brashear
| (below) A PBY on fire at Kaneohe Base, Mōkapu. NH 97432

crossing the Pacific at the time on their way to attend to his late mother's affairs in New York.

During the attack on Mōkapu, nearly the entire fleet of PBY military flying boats was destroyed. Antonio Pagliotti, son of Holmes's cook and caretaker at Coconut Island, vividly recalled the event:

We heard all this commotion going on, early in the morning...we ran up to the [observatory] tower up there to see what was going on. We saw a few planes going over and they were strafing the [PBY] planes. Pretty soon we noticed the insignia on the planes, and we realized they were Japanese planes. And the help, the women help that we had here on the island, for some reason or another, all went up to that tower. And they all had red bandanas on.... Pretty soon my father ran up there and said, You'd better get out of here, this is a real attack. And we ran off that hill, we could hear the bullets going

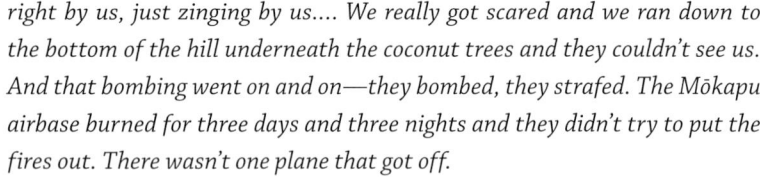

| *Burial of men killed at Kaneohe NAS raid at Mōkapu. NAS 80-G-32854*

| *Mōkapu after the raid. NAS 80-G-32943*

right by us, just zinging by us…. We really got scared and we ran down to the bottom of the hill underneath the coconut trees and they couldn't see us. And that bombing went on and on—they bombed, they strafed. The Mōkapu airbase burned for three days and three nights and they didn't try to put the fires out. There wasn't one plane that got off.

Coconut Island was cleared of inhabitants immediately after the raid. Ethel Uyehara recalls the evacuation:

We were quickly told to pack only necessities into a pillow case and gather at Mr. and Mrs. Mike Pagliotti's down at the guest house by the swimming pool. No lights were allowed—we whispered and were scared. Yes, it was a long night. The next day a food supply inventory was taken. There were two walk-in freezers and several refrigerators well stocked. Not knowing how long we would be isolated, the older employees started temporary plans. Bishop Trust [Alan Davis] in Honolulu notified us to pack all the valuable ivory carvings, etc. There were beautiful pieces of art from all over the world.

(I have never seen anything like them since). We were kept busy packing many trunks [that were] taken to Honolulu. A couple of days later military personnel came and took some of our permit cards away.

With the declaration of martial law in the Islands, the Japanese Americans that lived and worked in Kāneʻohe had to relocate to Honolulu. For about six months some members of the Holmes household maintained themselves at the Waikīkī property. Almost none of the employees on Coconut Island were allowed to return to their jobs for the duration of the war. Upon returning to Coconut Island the summer of 1942, Holmes gave his old Queen's Surf estate over to the U.S. military for use as a recreation center, just as his parents had given up their Cincinnati residence during World War I.

Christian Holmes was very concerned that the war would damage his collection of exotic tropical fish. He sent them to the Steinhart Aquarium at California Academy of Sciences in San Francisco.[138] By this time, an Englishman named Mr. Blackman had taken over the pet duties of Junior Lee, who had taken over the job of boatman transporting the few remaining guests to and from Coconut Island.

Life on Coconut Island during the war years was not full of the gaiety and jubilation so characteristic of Holmes's paradise. The dogs and exotic birds were gone. Holmes's drinking became more of a problem—his marriage with Mona Hind fell apart. His insomnia kept his staff on call at all hours in order to dash around Kāneʻohe Bay in one of his speedboats. Reminiscent of Howard Hughes and Bavarian king Ludwig II, Holmes became paranoid of many around him. Antonio Pagliotti recalls that his mother, the cook, would often have to taste Holmes's food in his presence. He would "just walk around with that fencing sword and his two chimpanzees," recalls Pagliotti. He was often clad only in a sarong and slippers or a Hawaiian *malo.*

As Holmes's alcohol consumption increased, only a few visitors were allowed to call. Among them was his loyal friend Duke Kahana-

moku, who liked to fish from the island. By 1943, Christian Holmes's health declined steeply. Efforts were made to transport him from the Islands to better medical facilities. Since it was wartime, however, securing transportation for private individuals was difficult. With the help of his friend Alan Davis of the Hawaiian Tuna Packers and Hawaiian Trust, a special request was made to Admiral Calhoun of the U.S. Navy. The application was granted, and Holmes left the Islands in December 1943, bound for New York.

Mona Hind, magic eye and all, divorced Christian Holmes in absentia on 19 January 1944. After nine years of marriage, she agreed to a relatively small out-of-court cash settlement of $233,175.45. Holmes adored Mona, so the divorce no doubt contributed to a further decline. While undergoing treatment for severe depression under the supervision of Dr. I. H. MacKinnon, Holmes was found dead on 5 February 1944, at the Hotel Savoy-Plaza in New York City. He was only 47 years old. His passing was announced the same day that Kwajalein Atoll in the South Pacific fell to U.S. military forces.[139]

THE LEGACY

Holmes's ashes were brought to Hawaiʻi and scattered in Kāneʻohe Bay by Alan Davis and the skippers of Hawaiian Tuna Packers. It is a sad irony that this scion of the Fleischmann family, pioneers in fermentation research and the distillery business, son of a renowned physician and anti-Prohibitionist, was dead from chronic alcoholism.

In his will, which was written prior to his divorce from Mona Hind, Holmes left $10,000 to Julia and Mike Pagliotti, the caretakers of Coconut Island. He left $5,000 to his private secretary, Marian Franks. Alan Davis was given the stock in Hawaiian Tuna Packers, worth over $1 million, and was a named executor at Davis's own Hawaiian Trust Company. The remainder of the estate was to be divided between his two sons, Christian III (at that time in the U.S. armed forces), William

Albertine Peck Launder, Holmes's first wife, in later years. Carole Holmes McCarthy

Dayton of New York, and daughter Ann in Santa Barbara. The bequests had provided nothing for then-wife Mona except the legally required dower right of one-third of the husband's estate. The children were allowed to choose a few mementos of their father, but most of the furniture and artworks were sold. An auction was held on the island for 129 lots of liquor, including "bonded bourbons, Napoleon brandy, and eighteen bottles of 112-year old rum."[140] The four Chris Craft motor boats were liquidated.

Christian's first wife Albertine Peck Holmes had remarried—first to Thomas Ward and then to Barry Lauder. The Lauders moved from New York to Reno around 1950, where they managed the Crescent L Ranch. She remained friends with former in-laws Max and Sarah Fleischmann who maintained a residence at Lake Tahoe. Albertine's son Dayton eventually purchased one of Max's giant ranches. Albertine died ca. 1972.

Katherine MacDonald, Holmes's second wife, and daughter Ann, stayed in Santa Barbara after the divorce, establishing a home on Hot Springs Road. The great silent film star, the American Beauty, died at a hospital in Santa Barbara on 4 June 1956. Ann became Mrs. E. R. Spaulding. In the late 1940s, the Spauldings lived with Christian III in the guest cottage at Linden Lodge. Later Ann married Donald Terrell— she still resides in Santa Barbara, enjoying tennis, her children, and her many grandchildren.

Christian Holmes III lived in Hawai'i from 1946–1947 and was a Marine captain in the Korean War. By his first wife, Elizabeth Lott, he had sons Christian IV and Michael. Christian III subsequently was married to actress Arlene Dahl from 15 October 1960 to 1964 (thus becoming step-father of actor Lorenzo Lamas). The couple had a daughter, Carole (Holmes McCarthy), on 3 August 1961. She lives in New York and is the mother of Patrick and Christine McCarthy. Christian III became an independent oil producer in Texas and bought a huge ranch in Paraguay. He died in 1999.

His son, Christian IV (author of a foreword to this book and a decorated military officer), became the CFO of the U.S. Environmental Protection Agency and directed the U.S. Trade and Development Agency. He is married to Noel Holmes who was for many years staff member of the House Foreign Affairs and House Appropriations committees. Christian IV's brother Michael is also a decorated officer. He married Ambassador Genta H. Holmes, head of the U.S. State Department's Foreign Service during the Clinton administration and ambassador to Namibia and Australia. Christian IV's son, Christian V, seems to be following his great-great grandfather into medicine, as has daughter Elizabeth who has founded a medical technology company in Palo Alto, California.

Christian Holmes II had nine employees on the payroll at his death. He left an orchid collection worth $7,650 and anthuriums worth $1,200. Household furnishings, personal effects, and machinery and tools totaled $76,889.10. When his entire personal estate was calculated in May 1945, a figure of $2,844,396.66 was realized. This was exclusive of his one-third interest in the remaining net assets of his late mother Bettie, whose estate had been in litigation with the federal government over tax matters since her death in 1941 (in 1951, the Christian R. Holmes Foundation in New York sold the Chimneys to a Jewish community center). Most of Holmes's personal assets were in stocks, including the local Hawaiian companies of Hawaiian Tuna Packers, Consolidated Amusement Company, and Hawaiian Trust Company. Holmes left a significant sum in cash and bonds as well.[141]

Holmes and his mother had been avid collectors of Japanese and Chinese art. In April 1946, a public auction was held to dispose of the antiques and other valuable furnishings from the old Queen's Surf estate at Waikīkī. Among the remaining items offered at the subsequent auction were a Spanish carved walnut chest, valuable tapestries, Persian and Chinese rugs, old teakwood and mother-of-pearl screens, and antique silver and iron. Fifty sets of book volumes from the library were auctioned, and rare wooden furniture were brought from Holmes's various bedroom suites. Most linen, draperies, kitchen supplies and equipment, plate, china, and washing machines were sold. A newspaper announcement understated that the collection "represents the finest collection of furnishings, painting, art objects, and antiques ever to be put on the auction block in Honolulu."[142] The legendary "Napoleon's sword" remains in family hands, as does the special Coconut Island china.

Mona Hind Holmes moved to her family's lands in Wailupe, ʻĀina Haina, Oʻahu. Returning to business life, she became an activist for several social causes. Mona adopted a boy, Robert K. Holmes. She became

| *Arlene Dahl married Christian Holmes III in 1961. Oakland Museum of California*

manager of the well-remembered Ranch House restaurant at 5202 Kalaniana'ole Highway. In 1946 she organized "We, the Women" during a threatened public utilities strike, and she fought for women's causes throughout the years. Later she moved to Kona and resumed her ranch management activities. She was associated with the giant King Ranch in Texas and became manager of her Semloh Ranch in Hōlualoa, Kona on the Big Island of Hawai'i. She was a member of the Daughters of Hawaii, the Cattlemen's Association, the Hawai'i Civic Club, the Kona Historical Society, and the Kona Outdoor Circle.[143] Mrs. Holmes never remarried. Having lived an amazing life, she died at the age of 90 in May 1987.

Beckel the elephant, two of the chimpanzees, a camel, and other animals were shipped to Locey's Wai'alae Avenue dairy ranch, where some were allowed to roam all over the property. Sadly, the apes Butch and Maryann were kept in a wooden barn with a sawdust floor. Windows and doors were covered with iron bars, and the whole enclosed by a chain-link fence. The chimps were given to the City and County of Honolulu in 1947, but since zoo facilities were not yet available, the primates remained at the ranch for an additional two years. Visitors often gave the chimps cigars and cigarettes to smoke, causing the sawdust to catch fire and endanger the apes. According to Paul Breese, first director of the Honolulu Zoo, arrangements were eventually made to house the animals on land previously set aside at Kapi'olani Park for Holmes's aviary collection from Santa Barbara. A cage similar to that used at San Diego Zoo's primate house was constructed for Maryann and Butch. In this manner Holmes's private menagerie of birds and mammals became the nucleus of the City and County zoo. The chimpanzees were moved to the Honolulu Zoo in 1949, but in 1950 they were transferred to a zoo in Sacramento. No one seems to recall what happened to Whoopee, who

| *Beckel, renamed "Empress" at Honolulu Zoo. Honolulu Zoo*

may have previously died on Coconut Island. At Honolulu Zoo, Beckel was renamed Empress. After a persistent foot infection, she was put to sleep at a ripe old age of 54 at Honolulu Zoo in 1986.[144]

According to Lester Zukeran, Holmes' great malacology collection in the net house was pilfered shortly after the Pearl Harbor attack, and the model planes in the bowling alley also disappeared.

Christian Holmes II passed his control of Hawaiian Tuna Packers to Alan Davis in his will. Davis, who had been an executive vice president with Castle and Cooke, took over operations of the tuna cannery in 1944. In 1948, Castle and Cooke purchased 41 percent of the stock of the cannery, knowing that Alan Davis needed capital for expansion. A few years later they had 97 percent of the company.[145] In 1956, Castle and Cooke exchanged their ownership of Hawaiian Tuna Packers for 12 percent of Columbia River Packers Association of Astoria, Oregon, which marketed its products under the "Bumble Bee" label.[146] Although Hawaiian Tuna Packers cannery closed in 1984, both Bumble Bee and Coral Hawaiian brands of tuna (not to mention "Figaro" cat food[147]) are enduring symbols of the legacy of Bettie Fleischmann Holmes, Paul Beyer, Charles Lucas, Jr., and Christian Holmes in the production and marketing of canned tuna.

Holmes was a man of great complexity who tended to engender polarities in the people he associated with. Many people loved Holmes; some people who didn't know him personally were scandalized by his lifestyle. It was difficult to be ambivalent. He could be polite, considerate, and generous to a fault, yet also irrational, unrestrained, and demanding. These memories continue to the present day. He created a beautiful tropical retreat for his friends, family, and pets, yet he disturbed the natural ecology of Kāneʻohe Bay and the surrounding Oʻahu shoreline in the process. He was an extroverted war hero and a recluse, a cross between Errol Flynn and Howard Hughes. According to his grandson, Christian IV:

My grandfather['s]...art was that of dramatic contrasts—the contrasts of an eccentric and flawed lifestyle offset by creation of the beauty of Coconut Island and the collection of beauty in such forms as Japanese and Chinese art and rare flora and fauna. He was a warrior who created and collected beauty. He came from a tightly knit family, having a strong and accomplished father, mother, grandfather, and grandmother. Yet, he left behind not only the legacy of the beauty of Coconut Island, but also the transgenerational legacy of three broken marriages and three children of these marriages. He was a man who found and created great beauty in Hawaiʻi but ultimately seemed incapable of finding lasting happiness.

On 15 January 1945, Alan Davis of the Hawaiian Trust Company, executor for Holmes' estate, leased Coconut Island to the U.S. government.[148] Coconut Island would see many more reincarnations before the twentieth century was finished.

On the way to Coconut Island. Across the road is the barbed wire fence for the little-known Italian prisioners of war camp. Kāneʻohe Library

Away from War

...too isolated to suit the tastes of the fliers...

Maj. Gordon Roberts

For a period of about a year near the end of World War II, the Holmes's properties on Oʻahu were given over for utilization by the U.S. military as recreation and retreat centers. Even before the death of Christian Holmes in 1944, the beautifully furnished house at Queen's Surf was used as a recreation center by naval aviators. There was a strong ethic of public service in the Fleischmann/Holmes family: Charles Fleischmann's mansion at Avondale was granted to the City of Cincinnati for use as a public park, as was the estate in the Catskills; Julius Fleischmann II's Coral Gardens estate was transformed into the Naples Zoo in Florida; the Chimneys on Long Island was converted into a recreation club for merchant marines; Queen's Surf and Coconut Island followed suit for the U.S. military.

| (above) *Roosevelt, MacArthur, Nimitz, and Halsey meet at Queen's Surf. Author's Collection*
| (opposite) *President Franklin D. Roosevelt arrives at Kaneohe NAS in 1944. Hamilton Library, UH-Mānoa*

At Queen's Surf, bunk beds were installed upstairs to provide sleeping arrangements for about 30 men. Most of the home's furnishings remained from the Holmes days. A "charming Honolulu matron" and her husband were installed in one of the guest cottages to look after the naval pilots and their friends.

President Franklin D. Roosevelt, just after his unprecedented fourth-term nomination, stayed at the Queen's Surf estate in Waikīkī in the summer of 1944 for a mid-war meeting with his general staff. On 27 July, Roosevelt dined with General Douglas MacArthur and admirals Nimitz, Leahy, and Halsey at the Holmes mansion. The next day the President threw a lawn party, which included a Hawaiian orchestra, a vocalist, and a hula dancer. (Newspaper articles at the time painted the scene of an ebullient, effusive Roosevelt suavely rebuking his vain Pacific commander. In truth, Roosevelt was dying).

Soon after the war ended, the military gave up its interest in the Queen's Surf property. The estate was sold, then transformed into a nightclub by Spencer Weaver, who officially named it "Queen's Surf" in 1949. Sterling Mossman was hired as the lead entertainer at the club. The buildings and grounds of the old estate were demolished in 1971 for an expansion of Kapiʻolani Park and beach. Where Roosevelt had dined with MacArthur, a snack bar now served teriyaki plate lunches. In 1997, new public restrooms were erected at the site of the famous mansion at a cost of $900,000, approximately twelve times the cost of the original Deering structure.

The U.S. military, in particular the Army Air Force, became more interested in Coconut Island by 1944. Although Christian and Mona were gone, it was being maintained for the Holmes's children on a shoestring by the Pagliotti family, who stayed there until 1948.[149] The war left the Pagliotti family mostly alone on the island—with the exception of some friendly assistance: as incongruous as it may have seemed in the middle of the Pacific Ocean, an Italian prisoner of war detention camp was established in Kāneʻohe. It was a fairly low-security affair, with a

simple chain-link fence border and no guards. Prisoners were given food, and they could prepare it to their liking. Mr. and Mrs. Pagliotti, Holmes's caretaker and cook who were brought to Coconut Island in 1940 from Santa Barbara when Linden Lodge burned down, visited the prisoners from time to time. During the establishment of the camp, six to eight men were taken to Coconut Island daily to do yard work and other chores for Holmes. Although they did not get paid, Mrs. Pagliotti would prepare fine Italian lunches for them.

The military leased Coconut Island for $2,424 per month from real estate agent E. A. Bolles, who represented Alan Davis, trustee of the Christian Holmes Estate. The lease was brought before probate judge Matthewman who approved it only up to the close of administration of the estate of Christian Holmes or for the duration of WWII plus six months, whichever was shorter. The leased property consisted of the furnished island, 61,360 square feet of land fronting Kāne'ohe Bay at Punalu'u Makai (the pier), a barge, and the boat *Coconut*. It was hoped that the island could accommodate 300 personnel at a time.

One B-29 pilot, Colonel A. R. Brashear, spent two weeks on Coconut Island and took many rolls of black-and-white film. It had been very difficult for any individual to obtain film during the war, and amateur photographer Brashear had to take great pains to obtain and process the film. This record, however, provides a fleeting glimpse at one of the briefest episodes of life on Coconut Island. Brashear, as he recorded in an oral history, spent a very relaxing time on Coconut Island with his comrades.

| (above) *Hearty meals made fly boys smile. Col. Ray Brashear*
| (top right) *Pilots relax in the Main House living room. Col. Ray Brashear*
| (bottom right) *Guests arrive at the Net House pier. Col. Ray Brashear*
opposite:
| (left) *Ray Brashear on deck, Seth Parker, 1944. Col. Ray Brashear*
| (right) *Ray Brashear. Col. Ray Brashear*

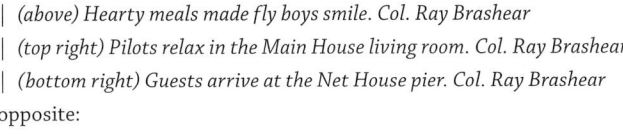

| *Holmes's shooting gallery was popular with the officers and their guests. Col. Ray Brashear*

The island was to be used primarily for Army Air Force personnel, but members of other branches of the Armed Forces were welcomed. Like in the heyday of Christian Holmes, parties with up to 200 individuals were held on the island. In its latest guise, Navy boats brought the guests over from mainland Oʻahu. Live bands were a prominent feature of life on the military's edition of Coconut Island, and great food and fine liquor flowed as before in an informal setting.

The U.S. military spent about $150,000 in improvements during its year's occupation of the islet. First, they staffed the observatory on the top of the hill with a full-time bartender.[150] Over a section of the east lagoon, the Army built a dance pavilion. Holmes's shooting gallery, shipped board by board from San Francisco, was a popular attraction for the young men and their guests. Bowling was also sought after. Rumors have it that a dozen slot machines were kept at Coconut Island, providing a substantial income for the Air Force. The machines were later found in Kāneʻohe Bay, according to the island commander, Major Gordon Roberts. One of Holmes's flower gardens on the top of the hill was converted to a tennis court.

A post exchange was established on the eastern shoreline of Coconut Island, roughly situated at the site of Holmes's storage sheds and the future site of the Hawaiʻi Institute of Marine Biology laboratories. One of the more intriguing projects was an experimental hydroponic garden where tomatoes and other vegetables grew in profusion.

The military soon realized the limitations of the island. The first reason the military rest and relaxation center on Coconut Island was not developed further was due to its infrastructural limitations. Sewage facilities on the island were not capable of supporting large numbers of personnel. Holmes had constructed a sewage collection system with a concrete treatment plant in the northeast corner of the island. From this point he extended a discharge pipe out across the reef to handle the primary treated sewage. Around 1960, a forced main sewage system was installed to pump all water through a pipe on Lilipuna Road.[151]

The second reason the island was not attractive to the military was that it seemed too isolated from the rest of Oʻahu and Honolulu and Waikīkī in particular. Frankly it must have been just a bit boring for the young aces of World War II.

With the end of the conflict in August 1945, the recreational camp at Coconut Island was decommissioned per the terms of the lease. The last of the military left January 1946.

For a brief interlude afterwards, Coconut Island was accessible to the general public, who could gawk at the decaying *Seth Parker* and other fixtures. The schooner was a fitting symbol of an age of gaiety now passed: a young Rick Rainalter, walking the main deck of the *Seth*, fell completely through the rotten deck boards, landing on a broken bottle on the deck below. Soon the entire island would be sold.

| *Experimental hydroponic farm on Coconut Island. Col. Ray Brashear*

Investors arrive in
Honolulu via United
Stratocruiser amid a
mountain of floral lei.
Ed Pauley is on the
left with the hat.
Pauley Collection

CHAPTER FOUR

More Dreams

God is going to have a hard time showing me
heaven after seeing Coconut Island...

Marge Woolman

The death of Christian Holmes in 1944 and subsequent abandonment of Coconut Island by the U.S. Army Air Corps in 1945 brought forward a sterling paradox—the tiny islet was both a paradise on earth as well as one of the most awkward of white elephants. Over the next 40 years, innumerable schemes, some of them reasonable, others harebrained, were planned for the little island. Collectively, they represent a full repertoire of the dreams and ambitions of some of the world's famous and not-so-famous. Thoughts ranged from an exclusive country club to a cemetery, from a religious cult compound to a nuclear power plant. The island always seemed to defy classification.

COCONUT ISLAND CLUB INTERNATIONAL

A certain reality took hold in 1946, however, when Allen Chase, a founder of Flying Tigers Airlines, approached Alan Davis, executor of the Holmes Estate, offering to buy the island for $250,000. While Christian Holmes III and his wife Elizabeth spent some time on Coconut Island in 1946, it was their wish, with the other children, to have the Holmes Estate liquidate the property. Chase represented a corporation of five businessmen: himself; Samuel Mosher, president of Signal Oil and Gas Company of California and chairman of the newly established Flying Tigers Airlines; Poncet Davis of Robbins Tube Company; Harold Pauley, a California financier; and his brother Edwin, also an independent California oilman. The latter would have a profound effect on the course of the little island.

Edwin W. Pauley had first visited Hawai'i when he placed first in Class A and second overall in the 1939 Transpacific Yacht Race from San Francisco to Honolulu aboard his schooner *Fandango*. Mrs. Pauley (née Barbara "Bobbe" Jean McHenry) met his boat and they both took the new Pan Am Clipper home to California.[152] Like many visitors, the Pauleys were fascinated with the beauty and setting of Hawai'i.

The Holmes Estate sold Coconut Island to the Moku-o-Loe Corporation, accepting the offer led by Allen Chase, who announced the intention to convert the island into an exclusive country club. Pauley was then special reparations emissary to the Far East under President Harry S. Truman. He recalled that his special interest in Coconut Island originated at that time when he "saw Coconut Island from the air. I said to myself at that time that if it wasn't so expensive I might buy it. And now...well."[153] Pauley asked his realtor, Earl Thacker, to look into the matter and promptly left for Korea. In the middle of an important war reparations meeting regarding Japan, a courier with a high-security dispatch arrived. Opening the letter, Pauley read the words relating to

Samuel Mosher, pioneer California oil independent. *Flying Tigers Retirement Club*

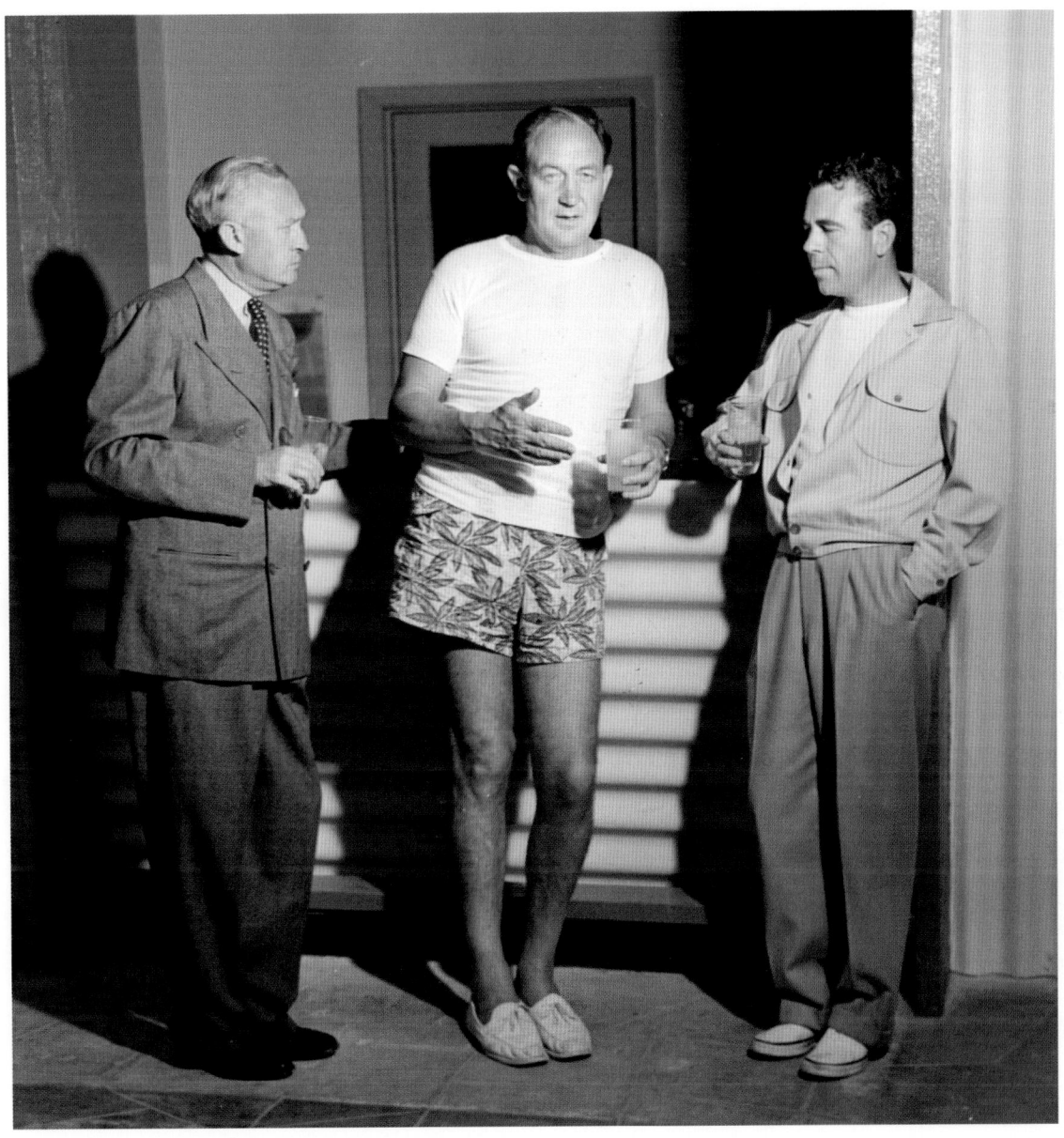

(left to right) Poncet Davis, Edwin Pauley, and Allen Chase on Coconut Island. Pauley Collection

COCONUT · ISLAND · CLUB, INTERNATIONAL ·
HONOLULU   T·H
PAUL R. WILLIAMS · A. QUINCY JONES · ASSOCIATE · ARCHITECTS
C. W. LEMMON   ·····   SUPERVISING · ARCHITECT

the sale by the Holmes Estate: "Congratulations! You have just purchased an island in Hawai'i."

Filled with enthusiasm, partners Chase, Mosher, and Harold Pauley soon hopped off a Constellation at John Rodgers Airport in Honolulu to unfold their plans for their proposed club.[154] Chase announced a three-stage plan: The first phase would accommodate 52 club members at any time from a membership of 250. Phase two called for accommodations for 80 guests, and phase three would accommodate all 250.[155] The corporation promptly leased the island for 25 years to the Coconut Island Club International, a corporation registered in California. Staff were to include F. M. Sandusky, managing director; Joseph P. Grey, resident manager; A. Quincy Jones, associate architect; and Robert O. Thompson, landscape architect. The designs were the height of modernity, with the fixtures and furniture reflecting the "jungle deco" style all the rage during the era. The first accommodations were to be ready by January 1947. Chase also announced that the *Seth Parker* would be open to the general public. Admiral John Heath, who had just retired as the respected commander of the Kaneohe Naval Air Station, was asked to be manager of the island.

The membership bylaws of Coconut Island Club International were organized around a strict quota:

The club, which will be organized on an international basis, has been given a regional membership quota. Of the 500 members, the owners would like to pledge 75 Hawaii residents, 75 Californians, 50 New Yorkers, 50 Chicagoans, 50 Texans, and about 25 each from England and Australia and the remainder from other regions of the United States....they expect to accommodate 250, their intended capacity. [156]

The club was dedicated to "furthering the interests of the Pacific area as well as offering unrivaled facilities for recreation, relaxation, and exchange of views in an ideal setting."[157] Membership was selected

·TYPICAL·LANAI·SUITE·
COCONUT·ISLAND·CLUB·INTERNATIONAL·HONOLULU·T·H·

| *(above) A Lanai Suite done up in subtle shades of pastel lime green, bamboo, and gray. Pauley Collection*
| *(opposite) Cabanas and club houses adorn this artist sketch of Coconut Island Club International. Pauley Collection*

on the basis of serious international accomplishment. It was hoped that oceanographers, ichthyologists, national park directors, and other scientists would join and share their knowledge with the world's business leaders at the Coconut Island Club.

In many ways, the proposed design reflected the reality of the island in Holmes's day when world-renowned explorers, celebrities, and business people retreated to the hermit isle.

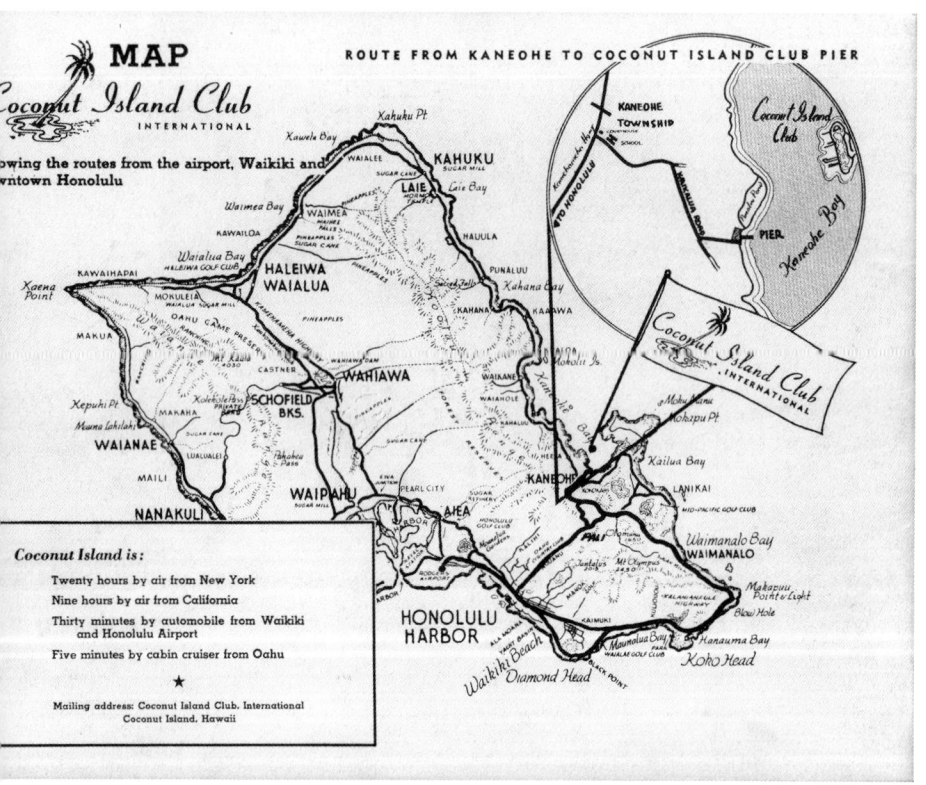

Only 20 hours by air from New York. Author's Collection

Major interior and exterior design changes were considered for the facilities at Coconut Island under internationally noted architect Paul Williams of Los Angeles. Up at the main house, the big glass picture windows overlooking the center patio and dining and lounge facilities were to be moved to the lanai. The shooting gallery of Holmes's day was to be remodeled as guest facilities, as were the additional housing structures built by the military during its year of occupation. The tennis court and dancing pavilion built by the Air Force were noted attractions in press reports.[158]

So eagerly anticipated was the success of the membership subscription that a U.S. post office was established on the island on 1 December 1947. A promotional brochure was produced that boasted of the verdant haven of the Coconut Island Club International:

...surrounded by numerous swimming pools and palm fringed lagoons. The trade winds, sweeping across the broad Pacific, caress the island and perform the miracle of cooling it to the most comfortable and pleasant climate in the Hawaiian Islands...The large, beautifully landscaped ponds of still water and the surrounding ocean abound with every description of ocean life and provide much interest and recreation to guests.

The flyer continues:

Governors, ambassadors and other members of international diplomatic circles, political figures, high-ranking army and navy officers and industrialists of international repute have been guests of the owners.[159]

A social kick-off was held in January 1947, the lei-bedecked investors and their wives arriving in the new-fangled Boeing Stratocruiser. An elaborate gala was convened to reintroduce the little island to Honolulu society:

One of the many terraces
where refreshments are served.

Patio Lounge.

Lily pond outside Dining Room.

| From Coconut Island Club International, "probably the most exclusive resort in the world." Author's Collection

Entertained in a lavish background of Hawaiian torches, music and tropical greenery were many of Honolulu's kamaaina couples and high ranking army and navy officers and wives last night when Mr. and Mrs. Edwin W. Pauley, Mr. and Mrs. Poncet Davis and Mr. and Mrs. Allen Chase were co-hosts at Coconut Island, the future home of the International Paradise.[160]

At first, club guests were transported the 1.25 miles across Kāneʻohe Bay either on the 36-foot diesel launch, SS *Coconut*,[161] or on the *Moku o Loe*. Kurt Johnson was hired during the summer of 1947 to convey guests from the Waikalua Road pier in Kāneʻohe to Coconut Island. He recalled that for smaller operations, one of the surviving Chris Craft vessels was used. Johnson also shopped for groceries for the island guests. Another boat operator was Randy Galt, nephew of Samuel Mosher, and husband of actress Ann Baxter.

By May 1947, however, it had already become clear to Allen Chase and the other investors in the not-for-profit Moku-o-Loe Corporation that the Coconut Island Club International would not be able to sell sufficient memberships to maintain the island. Memberships had been $25,000 each. Chase then proposed that the island facilities be converted into a modern, luxurious 117-room hotel. Part of this decision was based on a shortage of hotel rooms in post-war Honolulu.[162] At the time, though, Coconut Island had only seventeen bedrooms. Significant capital would need to be raised to build the hotel. By July 1947 the five owners had decided against the conversion for the time being.

When the club idea was abandoned, facility alterations had already begun under the direction of architect Cyril Lemmon. Commander Clyde Leo had been managing the property and over $500,000 worth of improvements had already been made for the club. About this time in 1947, Edwin Pauley offered Dr. Robert Hiatt of the University of Hawaiʻi the use of a portion of Coconut Island for a marine biology laboratory, a change that would greatly alter the future of the island (see Chapter 6).

Despite a lack of clear direction in its development, the island was hardly abandoned. In 1948 the Los Angeles Rams professional football team practiced at the Kaneohe NAS base and stayed on Coconut Island. Logically, Edwin Pauley was one of the owners of the team. The sports reporter covering the team was effusive in his description of the island, the "Pauley Paradise":

Whoever coined the phrase "Out of this world" obviously was stymied until he had succumbed to the lure of Coconut Island. Noah Webster's dictionbook just doesn't contain enough adequate adjectives to describe the place. It must be seen to be appreciated and one look merely whets the appetite.... To say the boys [Rams] live like kings is a masterpiece of understatement. No modern king has accommodations like this.[163]

When it was realized that the Coconut Island Club would not be as successful as hoped, rumors flew that the island might be sold again. In July, Edwin Pauley teased reporters from the *Honolulu Star-Bulletin* that the island could be purchased for $1 million. "The island is not up for sale, but that doesn't mean we wouldn't sell it," he intimated.[164] Pauley was responding to public rumors, but he nevertheless confirmed that two real estate brokers had approached him. Pauley and possibly other members of Moku-o-Loe Corporation were resisting the commercialization of Coconut Island. In December 1948, Don "the Beachcomber" Beach was rumored to be considering leasing the island.[165]

In 1949, Robert Miranda was hired by Allen Chase to be principal caretaker of Coconut Island under Admiral Heath. Miranda would remain in this position until the late 1970s and would raise his family of five children there, three of whom were named Edwin, Steve, and Robert after the Pauleys.

President Harry Truman had been scheduled to be a guest of his good friend Ed Pauley in 1949, but had to cancel due to a longshoremen's strike.[166]

Father of the tiki bar, Don the Beachcomber was the quintessential haole wanabee *Hawaiian. Author's Collection*

COCONUT ISLAND HOTEL

The hotel idea resurfaced when Allen Chase announced in December 1949 that Coconut Island had been leased to a group of local and mainland businessmen. Principal among the group was Walter D. Child, co-owner and manager of the Blaisdell Hotel in downtown Honolulu and president of the Naniloa Hotel in Hilo. Child had previously been a sugar chemist. Also investing was a group of Utah businessmen, among whom was Oscar W. Moyle, Jr., an attorney. A 10-year lease was signed between Child's group and the Moku-o-Loe Corporation. Clyde Leo was to be retained by the company as manager of the hotel.

In addition to supporting a public hostelry on the island, Coconut Island would retain its identity as a club with special privileges for its members. Child would manage the new club with a target of 400 members. The five owners of Coconut Island would be given honorary memberships in the new association.

In February 1950, the Coconut Island Hotel opened. Accommodations for 32 guests had been built on the island at a cost of $20,000. Amenities included transport on the launches from Oʻahu, skeet shooting, swimming, waterskiing, tennis, deep-sea fishing, dining, and dancing.[167] Most notable, however, were the honeymoon accommodations.

In actuality, only ten rooms were available at the opening of Coconut Island Hotel. While the bowling alley was still used occasionally, Holmes's shooting gallery had been demolished. The Pauleys thought it was too dangerous for the guests and their children. Andy Anderson tore it down.

The restaurant at the main house was the biggest attraction at the Coconut Island Hotel. Heʻeia *kamaʻāina* Anita Gouveia worked the summers of 1950 and 1951 at the hotel under Walter Child as the ticket cashier and operator of the launch: "He [Child] was so wonderful because he hired all the people from Heʻeia and Kāneʻohe." There were about

A TROPICAL HAVEN OF SPORTS AND FUN FOR ALL

Bowling . . .

. . . swimming

. . . skeet shooting

. . . tennis

. . . water skiing

| *Tennis, shooting, waterskiing, and sailing were touted. Most day visitors came for lunch. Author's Collection*

twelve employees of the hotel, including cooks, waiters, bartenders, gardeners, a maid, and boat handlers.

As hoped, the first honeymooners to visit Coconut Island continued the tradition of the Holmes era. Clark Gable spent part of his honeymoon on the beautiful isle with his new bride. Gable had married the former Mrs. Douglas Fairbanks Sr., Lady Sylvia Ashley, on 20 December 1949 and had sailed to Hawai'i aboard the *Lurline*.[168] But being

a public facility, the hotel also attracted everyday folks. Charles Gilbert Clark married Mary Alice Burns at St. Augustine's-by-the-Sea in Honolulu on 11 February 1950, and spent their honeymoon on the island.[169] The Gables and the Clarks were among the first, and last, guests of the Coconut Island Hotel. Mrs. Clark recalled the live Hawaiian music at dinnertime, the tiki torches, the open lanai. But she also remembers the solitude, "we seemed to be the only guests." Indeed, they were.

| (above) *One of the most romantic hide-aways conceivable. Pauley Collection*
| (right) *Eye-popping rates from the C.I. Hotel fare card. Author's Collection*

Coconut Island Hotel

COCONUT ISLAND, HAWAII

•

TARIFF CARD

RATES ON SLEEPING ACCOMODATIONS:
AMERICAN PLAN BASIS

Lanai Suites, Single Occupancy	$28.00
Lanai Suite, Double Occupancy	35.00
Bedroom, Main Unit, Single Occupancy	20.00
Bedroom, Main Unit, Double Occupancy	30.00
Deluxe Grass Shacks, Single	18.00
(Available April 1)	
Deluxe Grass Shack, Double	25.00
(Available April 1)	
Retreat (Private Pool) Single or Double	60.00

•

PRICES OF MEALS

Breakfast	$1.50
Lucheon	2.50
Dinner	3.00 to 4.50
Dinner-Dance—*cover charge plus tax*	1.00

•

RATES FOR RECREATION

Swimming	No Charge
Tennis	No Charge
Bowling	No Charge for alleys
Skeet Shooting, per hour, per person	$2.00
Water Skiing, per hour	3.00
Sailing, per hour	3.00
Torch Fishing, per hour	2.00
Cruising in Bay, 8 people, per hour	5.00

•

Glass Bottom Boat Trip to Coral Gardens	$1.00
Cycling, per hour	1.00

•

Minimum Check for Daily Visitors (per person)
$3.00

It was hoped by other investors that Allen Chase and Sam Mosher would establish a system of charter tours funneling guests to the hotel via their Flying Tigers Airlines—it did not happen. Other than the Honolulu overnighters on Friday and Saturday nights, most of the visitors to Coconut Island during the hotel era were day tourists. The essential problem of the Hawaiian resort hotel concept in the early 1950s was that the city of Honolulu offered an unparalleled nightlife.[170] Guests would come for lunch at the main house, or possibly dinner, then return to Waikīkī for the evening. Rooms remained empty night after night. Although lunches could be quite busy, "it was always a slow time at Moku o Loʻe. ...we would just sit and wait," exclaimed Anita Gouveia. "It was such an unhurried time and people were lovely."

The hotel was not well known on the national or international tourist circuit; there was little money to advertise. Letters from investors to Ed Pauley expressed their exasperation at the run-down condition of the island and Child's management. As if looking for a way out, when assistant manager Bob Herkes was drafted for the Korean War in late 1951, manager Dudley Child quit and went back to Cornell. The hotel closed a few months later.

After three very marginal years and average revenues of only about $27 per month, the tiny U.S. post office on Coconut Island also closed.[171] After 31 December 1950, the prestigious Coconut Island postmark became a souvenir of the past.

| Saints, Nudists, and the Dead

With the failure of the Coconut Island Club International and the Coconut Island Hotel, increasingly bizarre ideas for the practical use of Coconut Island appeared throughout the 1950s, none of which were ever taken seriously. Although the five Moku-o-Loe investors, Edwin Pauley, Mrs. Harold Pauley,[172] Poncet Davis, Allen Chase, and Samuel Mosher, held on to their investment, thoughts of finding a way

of making Coconut Island provide a good return were still entertained. It was one thing to keep the island as a playhouse for a fun-loving eccentric with unlimited funds, and another thing to make the 28-plus acres of rock and sand set in a beautiful paradise pay for itself. But despite their hard working business ethic, the owners thoroughly enjoyed their investment by spending as much leisure time as possible on the island. In 1952, Mosher also became a UC Regent, serving until 1972.

| *Father Divine sought out Coconut Island as a haven for his mission. Peace Mission International*

An outside idea for using Coconut Island came from perhaps a too literal visualization of the tiny offshore island as heaven on earth. In 1952 the rather infamous minister, Father Divine (George Baker), indicated interest in buying the island and converting it into a retreat for his cult followers.[173] Before his divine inspiration, Baker mowed lawns in Baltimore. Nothing came of the Coconut Island plan, however, except to cause a flutter in the Honolulu newspapers.

A more substantial design to utilize Coconut Island actively surfaced in 1955. Allen Chase approached Lt. Gen. Bruce C. Clarke, commander of the U.S. Army in the Pacific, with a blueprint to exchange Coconut Island for 72-acre Fort DeRussy in Waikīkī.[174] Clearly seeing the future, Chase hoped to develop the prime real estate in the heart of Waikīkī into a complex of ultra-modern hotels and apartment units. Developers had derided the Army's underutilization of Fort DeRussy for years—it would be a logical exchange.

Chase and his associates, Chase Syndicate, were willing to pay the cash difference between the two properties. At the time, Coconut Island was valued at $1–$2 million and Fort DeRussy was appraised at $20–$30 million. As part of the agreement, Chase would be willing to invest $6 million to develop Coconut Island into a luxurious military recreation center. The most important proposed change to the island, according to Chase's disclosure of 1957, was to fill the area between the island and the edge of the fringing reef, creating a parcel of 78 acres. A bridge would be constructed between the island and Kāneʻohe. On the island itself, clubhouses, living quarters, an amphitheater, and swimming and boating facilities would be constructed.

Military officials were reluctant to entertain the offer seriously, having learned a lesson with the Coconut Island R&R facility during the war. It was felt that Waikīkī was more centrally located and could offer better facilities for servicemen and women as well as tourists. Chase had said, "there has been considerable civilian agitation to have the area [Fort DeRussy] declared surplus and released for civilian needs.

Surveys show that the area, composing about 20 per cent of the total land in the Waikīkī district, is not now being put to its best and most valuable use."[175] He felt that the land was critically needed by the burgeoning hotel building boom in Waikīkī.

The Army's need for a military hotel facility was eventually satisfied years later, with the development of the Hale Koa Hotel on the Fort DeRussey property. This facility was remodeled and expanded in the 1990s. The Hale Koa Hotel concept owes much to the ideals of the 1945 military recreation camp on Coconut Island, coupled with the centrality and fame of Waikīkī Beach.

When Chase was talking with Army officials about a possible land swap in 1955, cemetery owner Edward L. Williams of Kansas City, Missouri, envisioned transforming Coconut Island from a paradise for the living to one for the dead. Certainly the infrastructural problems of sewage, electricity, and water supply that had contributed to limit the development of Coconut Island would not have been important issues under Williams's plan. However, nothing became of the cemetery concept.

In December 1955, the Territorial Tax Office raised the issue of the filled lands of Coconut Island. Although Holmes had clear title to Moku o Loʻe, the 16.3 acres of land created by his dredging and filling was apparently never assessed and taxed. The reclaimed land did not appear on tax maps. Federal law required that any accretion of land to an ocean shoreline become federal property unless overridden by an act of Congress. Clearly Holmes had no plans to create property for the United States. The attorney general stated that the territory would be interested in collecting back taxes should the man-made section of the property be deemed to belong to Moku-o-Loʻe Corporation.[176] Clearly a catch-22 for the investors—the matter would be held in abeyance for several more years.[177]

Still the old hotel idea didn't die—Coconut Island had a magnetic effect upon all who visited. To mainland investors and local businessmen, it seemed more Hawaiian than Hawai'i itself, a "hyper-real" Hawai'i where the myth of paradise could be commodified and sold to tourists. Around 1956, local innkeeper Harry Myers and a group of investors planned to turn the island into a resort, complete with aerial tram to connect it with Kāne'ohe. They were dissuaded by the territorial claim to Holmes's filled area and back taxes, and yet again another project fizzled.

In 1957, Admiral Heath, manager of Coconut Island for Moku-o-Loe Corporation, announced to the press that the owners of the property still had great plans for the island and hoped that the Honolulu City Planning Commission's proposed harbor and park development design for Windward O'ahu would take their facility into consideration. The plan, which conceived of a deep draft harbor and an industrial park, fell upon deaf ears.[178] Coconut Island was becoming a white elephant.

In March 1958, Samuel H. Price, Jr.[179] of Kailua, originated a scheme to convert Coconut Island into a residential home for children with cerebral palsy. Price had been the local director of a charitable group interested in helping children with the disease. The group eventually came under the control of United Cerebral Palsy. The persistent paradisiacal theme of the deserted tropical island was co-opted at Coconut Island, transforming its categories of escapism and luxury to those of healing and medical therapy. According to Price, the islet "could be a showcase of what can be done for cerebral palsy children under ideal therapeutic and climatic conditions.... Cerebral palsy doctors could spend their vacations there and make their reports to all parts of the world on observations made."[180]

Beautiful but isolated and set apart as if under quarantine, Coconut Island hadn't shaken its ancient reputation as a place of exile. Price's idea caught the attention of Samuel J. McConnell, executive director of United Cerebral Palsy. Together with Dorothy Ritter, regional director of the organization Rex Ravelle, Anita Diamond, a Mr. Borthwick, Reverend Bob Wallace, and an unidentified "fitness expert," Price and McConnell were appointed trustees. Price approached Ed Pauley and associates to ask them to make a tax-exempt charitable contribution of the island for the plan.

Price envisioned that the children might benefit from associating exclusively with others similarly afflicted. Although the relative isolation of Coconut Island was viewed as an asset, the difficulties of transporting disabled children over open water weighed heavily against the plan. Thus, this idea too fell by the wayside.

Allen Chase's interest in Coconut Island began to evaporate with the growing disinterest of the U.S. Army over the Fort DeRussy land swap. By August 1957, even Edwin Pauley was suggesting that the island be subdivided into house lots.

But new dreamers entered the story: Texas billionaire Troy Post invested in Coconut Island when his American Life Insurance Company of Birmingham, Alabama, bought Allen Chase's one-fifth interest in the property for $175,000 in early 1958.[181] This price reduced the value of the island from $1,000,000 to $875,000. One by one Post and Ed Pauley bought out Samuel Mosher,[182] Poncet Davis, and Mrs. Harold Pauley, the other partners in Coconut Island, for a total of $600,000.[183]

By early 1964, only Post and Edwin Pauley remained of the original Moku-o-Loe Corporation.[184] Post brimmed with enthusiasm over the potential of the island: "Hardly a month passes on the island that someone doesn't approach us on a project."[185]

But the problem of the areas of Coconut Island dredged and filled by Holmes kept coming up. Undoubtedly some potential investors had been discouraged by the ambiguity of the title to the filled land. When Pauley and University of Hawai'i officials wished to have the

| *(opposite) Troy Post (in suit) joins the group as the Pauleys and their guests christen a floating cocktail bar. (left to right) Mrs. Health, Ed Pauley, Ed Carter, Hannah Carter, Bobbe Pauley, Marie McHenry, Admiral Heath, Troy Post. Pauley Collection*

state rebuild the Hawaii Marine Laboratory after a disastrous fire in 1961, the legislature was hesitant to erect a state building on land of dubious title. The need for the new lab finally settled the matter.

In 1962, at the request of James Dunn, the state[186] surveyor, state attorney general Shiro Kashima rendered his decision that the filled land of Coconut Island belonged to the state. Citing English common law and other precedent, Kashima pronounced:

Thus, prior to the filling in of the submerged lands in question, the title to such lands was vested in the United States, holding such title in trust for the then Territory of Hawaii. Being that the United States Government did not grant these areas to Mr. Holmes, the question presented is whether the title to these areas was divested from the United States by the conduct of Mr. Holmes in filling in such area. We think not. The authorities are generally agreed that the riparian owner will not be permitted to increase his estate by himself creating an artificial condition for the purpose of effecting such an increase, and that the doctrine of accretion does not apply to land reclaimed by man through filling in land once under water and making it dry. The title to land thus filled in remains where it was before, unless the filling in was done wrongfully by another, in which case it will pass to the riparian proprietor.[187]

Ironically, such an accretion under traditional Native Hawaiian tenure would pass to the keeper of the land under which the fishery was attached. If Holmes held the fishing rights around the island, he would be able to claim the filled land made upon the fishery. With the U.S. law quite clear, Coconut Island was parceled into two legal entities. The man-made section of the island became part of the State of Hawai'i and was assessed under Tax Map Key (TMK) (1) 4-6-01, parcel 51. The original core of the island, Pāki's original Land Court Application 1134, remained private property as TMK (1) 4-6-01, parcel 1.

Despite the ruling, Ed Pauley and Troy Post consulted their attorneys in the 1960s on the possibility of disputing the findings of the

State Land Court. In 1967 a geologist, W. H. Easton, was commissioned by Post and Pauley to examine the island and write a report on its geology. There were a few surprises. Easton discovered remnants of the former rocky northern shore of Coconut Island along portions of the northern side of the lagoon swimming pool. The deep section of the pool seemed to have been excavated from volcanic bedrock rather than coral. The central groyne of the pool lay over this volcanic rock, and an igneous outlier cropped out "well above low water northeast (and seaward) of the east channel leading into the swimming pool."[188] Thus the lagoon swimming pool and some of the land to the north of it could be considered parts of the original Moku o Lo'e. Furthermore, the jetty connecting the island to the fishponds and net house was "manifestly... tied to Coconut Island by shore deposits which are normally exposed on far more days than they remain totally submerged."[189] Still, despite the fact that Pauley and Post probably had good legal grounds for reclaiming some of the adjudicated state lands fringing Coconut Island, they did not pursue the matter further.

In 1963 one of the more far-fetched rumors surfaced for the possible use of Coconut Island as a nudist camp. The compound was to capitalize itself on the sale of private memberships. Investigative reporters Bob Jones and George Marshall looked into the rumor but found only sketchy details.[190] Apparently a local promoter by the name of Jerome J. Campbell assured two *Honolulu Advertiser* employees posing as investors that there was indeed a plan to convert the island into a $1.25 million nudist camp. In February of that year, an ad appeared in a local newspaper that promoted a "Sunshine & Health Club." Interested investors were led to Asian Pacific, Ltd., Campbell's company. When interviewed again, Campbell, a "naturalist" himself, said he hoped to solicit 250 primary investors at $1,000 each and 750 secondary members at $250 apiece. The initial $250,000 would provide the down payment, a balance of $1 million to be paid within ten years. Investors were told that a mainland group was backing the plan with a potential advance of $382,000. When confronted directly by the exposed facts of *The Honolulu Advertiser* reports, both Campbell and the president of Asian Pacific, John W. Driver, refused to comment. Again the rumor came to a grinding halt with one short sentence from Ed Pauley: "The island is not for sale."

In 1964 it was announced that Post and Pauley would try again to transform Coconut Island into an exclusive membership club resort under their control. Post wished to include no more that 100 of America's top corporate executives: "What I have been thinking about is making Coconut Island over into something like the El Dorado Country Club in Palm Springs. It would become a resort for top executives, their families, and their friends with membership strictly invitational."[191] Post suggested that members build their own cottages on the island, and the club would arrange for a small, single building for members' guests—no high rises. The think-tank as envisioned would be sort of a Pacific Bilderberg Conference, held for the world's most influential people. Other amenities considered included turning the existing three-hole pitch and putt green into a nine-hole golf course.

One measure completed in 1964 that helped Post and Pauley along with thoughts of renewing the club concept was the construction of a new $150,000 pier and access road directly off Lilipuna Road, immediately across from Coconut Island. The pier was 315 feet long and 20 to 30 feet wide. Its completion made the island only 200 yards away from a mainland landing and effectively rendered the old Kāneʻohe Pier obsolete. The Coconut Island pier was built amid controversy, however. First, Bishop Estate, which still owned large sections of Heʻeia and Kāneʻohe, did not relish the plan. Local opponents claimed that the wharf would create a traffic nuisance and destroy the natural beauty of the landscape. Quelling dissent, Pauley simply bought the two adjacent waterfront lots from Aaron Jong, and the pier was built.

Atoms were friendly in the 1960s. One of the more grandiose plans for the region of Heʻeia was the construction of a nuclear power plant, perhaps on Coconut Island. Fortunately, environmental concerns and the economics of the resulting over-capacity of electricity discouraged the idea.

| Troy Post

Unlike J. R. Ewing of television's *Dallas* and many of the fabulous and flamboyant real oilmen of Texas, Troy Post's fortune was solidly based in banking, insurance, airlines, and finance. His fundamental business philosophy was his "theory of irreplaceability," which is that banking and insurance have existed for hundreds of years and nothing can foreseeably replace them. The same could be said for flight as a basic type of transportation. These services are irreplaceable, thus subject to perpetual demand and continual growth. This hypothesis worked for him, as he began to amass a great fortune by 1960. Post's first major move was to help bankroll the merger of James Ling with the Chance Vought Corporation to form the technology firm Ling-Temco-Vought (L-T-V). In 1962 he bought and merged various insurance companies to form GreatAmerica Corporation. In 1964, GreatAmerica was able to buy 55.5 percent of the outstanding stock of Braniff International Airways.[192] Post, with the help of CEO Harding Lawrence and Mary Wells's marketing firm on Madison Avenue, turned the staid regional carrier in to a sexy, psychedelic styled international player with Easter egg-colored planes and flight attendants clad in Emilio Pucci's swinging jet-age couture.[193]

Though he owned a huge mansion in Dallas, Troy Post spent about two months every summer on Coconut Island throughout the 1950s and 1960s.[194]

In addition to his interest in Coconut Island, he made local investments in Oʻahu's Sea Life Park and Bay View Golf Course, the latter managed by James L. Ukauka, who was interim manager of Coconut Island in 1964.[195]

By the 1970s, Post's major financial interests were solidly with other resorts, but he still maintained an interest in life insurance. He was largely responsible for the creation of Acapulco as a major vacation destination, frequented of course by his Braniff International airplanes. Post got his wish in establishing a very exclusive international country club in Acapulco, the Tres Vidas en la Playa. This $35 million private resort sold memberships for $8,000 each and still charged a rate of $45 per day in 1973. As he recalled, "Every man has some deep-rooted ambition if he ever gets rich. Maybe it's vanity, too. In my case I think it was a mixture of both. I had an ambition to build a beautiful resort."[196]

Post bought properties in Aspen, Colorado, and had plans to develop a ski resort in Flagstaff, Arizona. But he did not abandon Hawai'i. During the 1970s he made arrangements with Bishop Estate to develop three hotels on a 489-acre plot in Keauhou, Kona, Hawai'i. Post was a philanthropist who believed that an individual amassing a great fortune should put something back into the community, or "else pretty soon you don't have anything else."[197]

In 1973, Post sold his 50 percent share of the private section of Coconut Island to local businessman Sheridan Ing, through his successor companies, Apco Oil and Gulf Interstate.[198] Troy Post died on 26 May 1998 at the grand old age of 92.

GILLIGAN'S ISLAND

In 1964, while the dreams of both the solidly successful and wildly ambitious multiplied on the tiny island in Kāne'ohe Bay, the twice-told tale of castaways making a paradise of a deserted tropical isle made its debut on television. This series was a direct descendent

| *Encased in a bubble helmet, a pouting Pucci-clad flight attendent stands in front of a Braniff jet engine. Author's Collection*

of the Hollywood film, *Bird of Paradise*. The popular sitcom *Gilligan's Island*, starring the late Bob Denver and Jim Baccus, was the story of a ship's mate (Gilligan), his skipper, a brainy professor, a movie star, a simple farm girl, and a millionaire and his wife shipwrecking on a small island in the tropics. It was to have been only a "three-hour tour."

The pilot for *Gilligan's Island* was filmed in Hawai'i. The lead trailer shows the tour boat leaving Kewalo Basin in Honolulu and getting caught in a storm. The next scene is of the real Coconut Island in Kāne'ohe Bay. It was a fate reminiscent of the last *Seth Parker* voyage. Although no other episodes were filmed on the island, it would nevertheless be identified forevermore as "Gilligan's Island." Despite the obvious coincidences, the show's creator, Sherwood Schwartz, was completely unaware of the social history of the real Coconut Island, with its millionaires, movie stars, sailors, and professors. When asked about the similarities Schwartz said, "The studio just gave me a photograph of an island...I didn't know where it was or who might be associated with it." Coconut Island will remain, at least for those who were weaned on television, the real Gilligan's Island.

The Pauleys never lost interest in their island. Pauley Collection

CHAPTER FIVE

Edwin Pauley's Island

Ev'ry body has an Island fair

Tucked away in his heart somewhere

On a Coconut Island by Cherry Zeller

As extraordinary in philanthropy as he was in business, Edwin Wendell Pauley was a man of exceptional intelligence and fortitude, a kingmaker, and a successful diplomat, educator, and industrialist. He was the sustaining genius behind the Hawai'i Institute of Marine Biology on Coconut Island. From 1946 to 1981, Ed Pauley personally stewarded the unique treasure called Coconut Island, keeping the myriad of loopy schemes and would-be developers and subdividers at bay. This responsibility was passed on to his wife Bobbe, and on to the next generations of Pauleys. As with Christian Holmes, Ed Pauley shared a vision of the island as a natural laboratory for the study of aquatic biology. The Edwin W. Pauley Foundation continues to sustain his legacy and maintain the integrity and beauty of Coconut Island.

Among his many accomplishments, Ed Pauley is fondly remembered for working tirelessly to help make the University of California one of the greatest institutions of higher education in the world, through his leadership on the board and his generous donations. In the era framed by the Pauley years, the University of California went from a relatively sleepy state school on the banks of Strawberry Creek to a world leader in engineering, business, and liberal arts. And he turned his magic touch to the University of Hawai'i as well, ushering in perhaps the world's best situated school of marine biology. Those who knew Ed Pauley were well familiar with his extraordinary humanitarian interest in the promotion of science, education, and the arts. Like the innovative Christian Holmes, Edwin Pauley would eventually dominate life on Coconut Island, making it into his own version of paradise on earth. Together with his wife Bobbe, an extraordinarily talented and gracious woman, Pauley would relish its special beauty. For the Pauley kids in particular, Coconut Island would become their very own Robinson Crusoe summertime adventure.

Edwin Wendell Pauley was born on 7 January 1903, just six years after Christian Holmes, to Elbert L. Pauley and Ellen Eliza Van Petten

Pauley. Unlike the Holmes and Fleischmann families, the Pauleys had for many generations resided in the United States. In 1700, Adrinne Pauley of Liege, France, a landowner on the Isle of Man and the Isle of Wight, left for America. The first Van Petten to settle in America was born in Holland in 1641; he established himself in Schenectady, New York. Ed Pauley's paternal grandfather was Calvery Pauley, a merchant and farmer in West Virginia. He married Amanda Vickers (of the British armament family), and Elbert L. was born to the couple on 3 December 1877 in the town of Lewiston.[199]

| *(above) Ellen and Elbert Pauley. Pauley Collection*
| *(opposite) Toddler Edwin Pauley. Pauley Collection*

Elbert was born and raised in West Virginia. Growing up tall, blond, and powerfully built, Pauley became a construction foreman by age 16. Elbert married Ellen Van Petten of Peoria, Illinois, around 1902 at Elmwood. Her father had been a professor of theology. At 18 Elbert quickly earned a reputation as a fine salesman for new employer, Standard Oil, selling lubricating products throughout Indiana. It was at Indianapolis where Edwin was born.

Rising star Elbert was sent to New York to be groomed as a petroleum engineer and was introduced to founder John D. Rockefeller. He then left for Standard Oil of Kentucky, rising to vice president and eventually settling with his family in Birmingham, Alabama. A second son, Harold R., was born here in 1910.

Growing up in Birmingham, Ed Pauley developed a soft Southern accent that remained with him always. The family lived in a stone house near Glen Iris Park in the city, and as a youth Ed worked part-time for Curtis Publishing Co. as a magazine salesman. His youthful enthusiasm was difficult for his father at times, and Ed was eventually sent to a special school, White and Dixon, to help instill more discipline in his life. He spent 6th grade in California with his maiden aunts, where his classmates teased him mercilessly for his accent and being towheaded. His third year in high school was spent at Gulf Coast Military Academy in Mississippi. His senior year was spent at Georgia Military Academy in Atlanta.[200] Here, under the careful instruction of Colonel and Mrs. West, he developed a passion for learning and a life-long respect for education, which continues through the Edwin W. Pauley Foundation.

While Ed finished up his studies, his family left Alabama in 1918 to move to Pasadena, in southern California. After more than 20 years, Elbert had resigned from Standard Oil. The following year Ed joined them and enrolled at the new University of California branch at Los Angeles. Due to difficulties in commuting, Ed transferred to Occidental College. Ed took up a part-time job to make the increased expenses of this private college—he sold sandwiches, and took photographs for the Tournament of Roses. During the summers he worked hard labor, once working with the Edison crew on the Kern River Dam project. The next summer he switched to roustabouting on an oil platform, learning all the jobs in no time.

Ed Pauley took acting lessons at Pasadena Playhouse in addition to his regular business administration courses at Occidental. He played football and swam. After two years he expressed a wish to enroll at UC-

Berkeley, which he did in 1921. Here he was on the football team and rowed with the crew. He acted at the Greek Theatre, was a member of Phi Kappa Psi fraternity, and sold *Encyclopedia Britannica* in his spare time. Pauley received his bachelor of science degree from the UC-Berkeley College of Commerce in 1923, and returned the following fall to commence graduate work.

The senior Pauley, upon settling in Pasadena, initially took employment as a car dealer, selling Packard, REO, and Dort automobiles. The business thrived and he was soon able to open a branch dealership in Alhambra. Civically minded, Elbert became a Mason, president of the local Merchants Association, and served as the director of the Tournament of Roses Association. These public service values he instilled in young Ed. Ellen Pauley was devoted to her family and church.[201]

Elbert Pauley, however, quickly returned to his first professional passion, the oil business. In 1923 he formed the Pauley Oil Company, initially designed to distribute gasoline to retailers in the infancy of the California automobile boom. He soon realized that by integrating production, refining, and distribution, more efficiency and profit might be realized. He leased a refinery at Whittier until he could build his own refinery, in 1924, on Bandini Boulevard in south Los Angeles near the booming Signal Hill oilfields.

Pauley quickly became the largest independent gasoline distributor in Los Angeles, with his "Eureka" brand selling at gas stations throughout Los Angeles.[202] Ed was pulled from graduate school at UC-Berkeley to help with the family business. The refinery had some design difficulties, and it was Ed, with his great hands-on experience from roustabouting and evaluating crude oil, who came to the rescue. In addition to his technical expertise, Ed also helped raise capital by selling stock in the new company. Pauley went about securing supply guarantees from other producers to insure that the valuable distribution networks were safeguarded while the Bandini refinery was reassessed. With gasoline supply assured, Pauley converted Bandini

| *A notable woman of Pasadena, Mrs. Elbert Pauley in the 1920s. Pauley Collection*

| *(above left) Pauley's Bandini Boulevard refinery next to the Los Angeles River. UCLA Dept. of Geography*
| *(above right) Tanker, driver, and the early refinery on Bandini. Pauley Collection*
| *(bottom right) Eureka was a well-known brand during Los Angeles' early motoring days. Pauley Collection*

to the primary production of asphalt under the name Eureka Refining Company.

On 24 June 1924 Edwin married Norma Barrett, still in her teens, who he had met at the Pasadena Playhouse. They moved to Altadena just north of Pasadena, where Ed joined the Athletic Club and became a Mason. Sailing became Ed's main recreational activity, a factor no doubt in his later interest in acquiring Coconut Island. On 26 October 1925 Edwin W. Pauley, Jr. was born, but the marriage would not last.

On 16 September 1926 Ed Pauley was involved in an incident that would change his life. He and Helmar Duncan, area representative of Pauley Oil Company, and pilot Roman Warren, flew off to the Imperial Valley off in the desert on a sales trip in a new bi-plane. Landing at El Centro, they consummated several deals in the valley and across the border in Mexicali. Spending the night in El Centro, they took off early the next morning. The airplane barely cleared 150 feet when it lost power, clipped a high-tension wire, and plummeted to the ground and flipped over in a tangled mass. All three passengers were taken to El Centro hospital, where Duncan died and Warren was treated for minor injuries. Ed Pauley suffered multiple fractures to the neck vertebrae, right arm, pelvis, and both legs—32 fractures in all, it was later learned.

Ed was placed in traction and put in a body cast. Pauley had to remain at the El Centro hospital for a month, and was fitted with a Thompson collar to relieve pressure on his cervical nerves. During this time, Pauley reflected upon his short (23 years) and athletic life, and his possible future physical limitations. Ed had also recently separated from Norma. Recalling the accident, Pauley commented, "It changed my whole pattern of life, which had been neither inspirational nor profitable. You decided you had to think about doing good for your fellow man, as well as creating a living for yourself. You realized the value of charities and public service and started thinking in terms of that. I had mostly ignored that before."[203]

Ed Pauley was prepared to resume a more sedate life in Berkeley graduate school and go on to teach. However, he was cognizant that his competitive strength came from a great knowledge of crude evaluation. He knew better than most how to gauge the yield and profitability of a barrel of oil. All this just as Henry Ford perfected the Model T for the average American consumer, launching the voracious, insatiable demand for gasoline and other petroleum products.

Paramount for Pauley, however, was to pay the hospital bill, now over $11,000. The insurance company denied liability for injuries from the airplane crash. He was getting stronger day by day, but the oil business was by then in a costly price war and the prospects of returning immediately to employment were dim. Elbert Pauley struggled to secure enough producers to keep his once-strong distribution networks active. He began to run into serious debt.

To help recuperate, Ed and his brother Harold rented a small house on Balboa Island at Newport Beach. Ed took to swimming to help build up his shattered body, and began a small boat repair business. These were all youthful occupations that would reappear much later in a continuation of Pauley's leisure time activities on Coconut Island. But Ed, still facing the pressing need to pay his medical bills, crafted a deal to buy and sell oil that independently of Eureka Petroleum garnered him exactly $11,000 in commissions. This impressed his father, who encouraged him to return to work at Eureka.

Gas prices began to stabilize, but the demand for petroleum products went unabated in booming southern California. By now the Pauleys had 60 retail gas stations. Unfortunately, however, Senior Pauley had invested in old wells at Huntington Beach that were long past profitability. Ed realized that the only way to remove the cash crisis was to merge or sell the company outright. Fortunately, a suitor arrived in L.A. looking to purchase a refinery. On 14 August 1928, the Italo Petroleum Corporation assumed the assets and liabilities of Eureka Petroleum Corporation for guarantees that the refinery would be remodeled and various credits would be made available. The new operation retained the Eureka brand name and Elbert Pauley as a director. Ed remained as sales manager.

As deeper wells were sunk at Signal Hill, new fields up at Bakersfield came on line. The resulting surplus exceeded demand, dropping prices again. Nevertheless, Pauley promised to supply retailers for up to six cents per gallon less than Standard Oil's price. Italo defaulted on many of the promises to rebuild Eureka, however, and the Pauleys subsequently sued them for $400,000. Then in November of 1928 the banks foreclosed. Elbert Pauley's business headed into receivership.

Ed Pauley worked tirelessly and skillfully through the receivership, ultimately repurchasing Eureka's assets at the subsequent foreclosure sale and creating a new entry, the Petrol Corporation. He saved the family business—a few weeks later Edwin Pauley turned 25.

Pauley had to reestablish confidence in his name, establish new credit lines, and finally fix the nagging refinery issue. Instead of straining to distill gasoline, he switched to producing 80 percent asphalt at the Bandini refinery, a formula that was well-suited to the heavy crudes he was receiving from the wells at Huntington Beach. It seemed obvious, considering how natural asphalt, once the bane of mastodons in places like La Brea, was clearly abundant in the region. Ed resold others' gasoline to retailers, keeping his lucrative distribution networks happy. Profits soared and Pauley never looked back. New installations were finally constructed at the Bandini refinery. Crude processing at Petrol jumped from 8,000 barrels the first quarter of 1929 to 84,000 for the month of October of that year.

Prosperity, and a little free time, allowed young Edwin the freedom to pursue outdoor hobbies such as sailing and football. Physically he was able to rebuild his large frame and resume most normal activities. Petrol made it through the Wall Street Crash of October 1929, and during the next year, the Pauleys won their suit against Italo Petroleum and prevailed over the insurance company regarding the old medical bills.

Ed Pauley, having tasted great success as an independent, was faced with a new challenge—government control over oil production. Politicians had been responding to the public concern over fluctuating prices and supply, and there was a movement afloat to regulate the industry under federal and state control. Under the guise of oil reserve conservation, state Senator Will Sharkey introduced a bill that would place allotment authority over every producer. This measure would essentially remove market forces from the oil business and would potentially favor the major producers, such as Standard Oil, over the independents. Pauley jumped into the lobbying effort on behalf of the independents at Sacramento. The state bill passed, however, and was signed into law by the governor. But by that uniquely California procedure known as referendum, Pauley raised significant funds to collect the needed signatures to place the issue directly before the public. Due to Pauley's determination, the Sharkey Bill was soundly defeated at the polls in 1932. This success brought Pauley the attention of both state and national policymakers.

Elbert Pauley still remained an influence in Petrol, and second son Harold was placed in charge of general operations while Ed was up in Sacramento. Nancy and Ed had reconciled to some extent, and moved to a fine house on La Vereda Road more suitable for entertaining clients and friends. Ed Pauley, flushed with his success in defeating Sharkey, became more astute in his political abilities. He aligned with Democrats against the old Republican big business and the oligarchy of the major oil producers.

In 1932, Pauley was introduced to a fellow Democrat who had clearly inspired Pauley in overcoming his physical disabilities, Franklin Delano Roosevelt, now Democratic candidate to the presidency. Pauley would become an important member of Roosevelt's administration in the 1940s.

Petrol continued to expand, as Ed drilled wells in new sites in Ventura and Kern (Bakersfield) counties. The country was now suffering from overproduction of oil, and slackening demand due to the Great Depression. Pauley remained steadfast in his opposition to federal or state regulation of the oil industry, anything that would provide an advantage to the major producers. It was in this context that he met his nemesis, Interior Secretary Harold Ickes, who let it be known that he was inclined to nationalize the oil industry. Ickes set up a system whereby representatives of Standard and Shell, the big producers and Pauley's competitors, oversaw the production and regulation of the small independents. Needless to say, Ed Pauley was outraged at the injustice of having his competitors control his business. For the next decade and a half Pauley would be vilified by Ickes and a sympathetic press as the epitome of the laissez-faire capitalist.

Ed Pauley continued his lobbying efforts on behalf of the independent oil producers. Under the National Recovery Act, part of Roosevelt's grand plans for emerging from the Depression, Pauley represented independent oil producers on a federal planning committee. Fittingly, he became president of the Independent Petroleum Association in 1934 and served until 1938. This position gave him visibility as a national public figure and provided a platform for his role as a leading lobbyist for the oil industry.

With both Edwin and Harold running Petrol Corporation, Elbert finally retired. Having borrowed or rented yachts for years, Ed finally purchased a splendid vessel named *Fandango*. He would eventually sail to Hawai'i in the Trans-Pacific race on this yacht. By now, Ed and Nancy were divorced.

In 1936, Edwin Pauley met Barbara "Bobbe" Jean McHenry, a charitable UC-Berkeley student from an old California pioneer family from Modesto.[204]

Bobbe's family settled in California during the first wave of "Yankee" immigration to the old Mexican province just after the discovery of gold along the American River. It was around 1849 when Bobbe's great grandfather Robert McHenry arrived from Ohio and purchased

2,640 acres of land along Stanislaus River in California. He married Matilde Hewitt, also a pioneer from Ohio, in 1859. They had one son, Oramil, born 14 November 1861. Most likely the McHenrys raised wheat on the vast Bald Eagle Ranch. Unlike the irrigated salad bowl that the Central Valley is today, the arid region then was most suitable for dryland agriculture and pasturage. In the 1870s, Robert McHenry became involved in banking, establishing the first such institution in the new town of Modesto, six miles from the ranch. The town itself was established by Charles Crocker in conjunction with his Central Pacific Railroad, the western portion of the first transcontinental railroad.

| (above) The Bald Eagle Ranch house near Modesto. *McHenry Mansion Museum*
| (opposite) *Marie McHenry with her two children, Ora Louise (left) and Bobbe Jean. McHenry Mansion Museum*

| *Teenager Bobbe Jean (right) with other Red Cross volunteers, Berkeley. Pauley Collection*

In the 1880s McHenry built a fabulous mansion in the town, which is still standing today. Robert did not have long to enjoy it however, dying in 1890. His son Oramil, who had married Louise Bilicke, continued the family businesses and ranch. Three sons and a daughter were born, Robert, Albert, Russell, and Ora Louise. Oramil built a two-story Queen Anne Victorian at Bald Eagle Ranch, which had now grown to 4,000 acres. Robert Jr. and Albert inherited the ranch (the other two children died young), growing prize chickens and Kadota figs. Robert Jr. married Marie Jane Rogers and had two daughters, Ora Louise and Bobbe Jean.

Early on Bobbe exhibited strong community spirit, a characteristic that persevered throughout her long life. At Berkeley she became president of the freshman class, vice president of the student body, and in her senior year a member of many clubs and committees. Bobbe McHenry graduated in 1930 from Berkeley with a bachelor of arts in public speaking.

The athletic director of the University of California, Bill Monahan, and his wife Betty are credited as introducing Ed Pauley to Bobbe Jean. Ed was of course a big sports fan and was frequently at Berkeley. In October 1937 Ed and Bobbe were married, "just before the big game," according to the bride. They had three children by that union: Susan (born 1938), Stephen (born 1940), and Robert "Buzz" (born 1945).

Pauley, due no doubt to his somewhat populist battle with big business, became one of the few businessmen of his time to support FDR's New Deal. This program of wide-reaching governmental economic assistance (e.g. Social Security, the FDIC, and SEC agencies) was in opposition to the old oligarchy of Republican capitalists. FDR was generally unpopular with most conservative American industrialists. The attractiveness of the New Deal to the public, however, was its goal to bring America out of the Great Depression and help create a stable, confidence-building atmosphere in banking, finance, and the stock market.

Roosevelt and his liberal social policies of course gained wide acceptance, and Pauley emerged in the 1930s as a power broker within the Democratic Party. It was Pauley's refined social consciousness, however, that was his most engaging feature. He was not just concerned with making money; as he realized after his airplane accident, he would utilize his fortune and influence for the long-range benefit of society, especially in educational endeavors. Like Chris Holmes's mother and uncles, Pauley would give a substantial portion of his wealth for the public good.

Ed Pauley was twice appointed to the University of California's Board of Regents: first by Governor Culbert Olson in 1939 (serving 1940–1954), and second by Governor Goodwin Knight in 1955 (serving until 1970). Pauley would remain at this post for 30 years, sitting twice as board chairman (1956–1958; 1960–1962). He never missed a meeting of the regents. Working closely with, and sometimes against, the great chancellor Clark Kerr, the University of California system became one of the foremost in the world.

Pauley's abilities as a fundraiser for the formerly debt-ridden Democratic Party led to his being appointed as secretary of the organization. In 1942 Roosevelt named him party treasurer. Later during World War II, Roosevelt appointed Pauley to a position that helped shape the administration's petroleum policy. As head of the Petroleum Administration for Defense, Pauley built the first transcontinental oil pipeline, which extended from Texas to the East Coast. Ironically Pauley became the oil czar whose position he had so strongly opposed ten years earlier. He was also appointed to supervise the lend-lease program that supplied fuel to Great Britain and the Soviet Union during the war.

One of the more interesting and internationally significant of Pauley's actions was his promotion and support of Missouri senator Harry S. Truman to become Franklin Roosevelt's vice president and ultimate successor as president of the United States. Essentially, Pauley was Truman's kingmaker. Many on the inside knew that Roosevelt was

dying by 1944, and the likelihood that an unpopular Vice President Wallace would succeed during the upcoming term was great. Pauley choose the right moment to place Truman on the ticket, and all of course succeeded.

When World War II ended in Europe during the spring of 1945 and in the Pacific in the summer, Truman appointed Ed Pauley to be his personal ambassador extraordinary and U.S. representative to the Allied War Reparations Commission, which was responsible for dismantling the German and Japanese capacities for war.[205] Ambassador Pauley

stated that he was not a "soft peace man." After all, Pearl Harbor would not easily be forgotten.

Pauley attended the Potsdam Conference with Truman, Churchill, and Molotov. The president's objective was to renegotiate the terms set at the earlier Yalta Conference attended by Churchill, Roosevelt, and Stalin. Pauley succeeded in getting the other allies to settle on a percentage settlement of war damages from Germany, rather than a dollar amount. Pauley was tough. In a letter to Truman he wrote:

I do not mean to imply, Mr. President, that we should "coddle" the Germans. The Russians are not coddling them. Quite the contrary, they are making them get down to business cleaning up their own mess. Berlin wrecked as it is almost beyond recognition, is nevertheless being cleaned up. And the Germans, under German supervision, are doing the cleaning up…. They are told in no uncertain terms, in posters on the buildings, that if they try to engage in plunder, they will be shot.[206]

| *(above left) Pauley (center) leaves the Dai Ichi building with MacArthur (left) and aide. Pauley Collection*
| *(above right) As reparations chief, Pauley found these bars of gold and platinum at Toyko's central bank. Pauley Collection*
opposite:
| *(top left) To the victors…Pauley attends Potsdam Conference (third man to the left of Truman). Other notables around the table include Winston Churchill, Clement Attlee, and Joseph Stalin. Pauley Collection*
| *(top right) Pauley with General Eisenhower and the Allied Forces. Pauley Collection*

| (top) Pauley with Chiang Kai-shek and Madame Chiang. Pauley Collection
| (bottom) '50s chic at Pauley's headquarters in Los Angeles. Pauley Collection

After Hitler's defeat and Japan's capitulation, Pauley was sent to Japan in November 1945. Among his duties was to examine the gold and the looted treasures collected by the Japanese government during its imperial aggression throughout Manchuria and Southeast Asia. A mission to Korea was launched in May of 1946. It was in this capacity as special ambassador that Pauley saw Coconut Island for the first time—from his airplane while landing at Kaneohe Marine Corps Base. He had been on a brief stopover en route to Korea—the island was directly under the final approach.

Pauley's reparations duties in Asia included examining the Japanese assets in Korea and Manchuria. He studied the ability of those two regions to produce raw materials for East Asia. He also decided how much machinery and assets could be taken from the region to help reconstruct the Philippines and China. Despite difficulties, Pauley and his group moved above the 38th parallel in Korea, the region then occupied by the Soviet Union. They were the first of the non-Soviet allies to do so. From this experience, Ed Pauley was in a position to warn the U.S. of the Soviet and communist threat to the Far East and Korea. Manchuria, ruled since the 1930s by the Manchu emperor Pu Yi, returned to China under communist rule, while Korea resumed its sovereignty as a divided country. His work took him to China, where he advised the Nationalist president Chiang Kai-shek.

Back in Los Angeles, Ed Pauley continued his active interest in the petroleum business, and was involved in numerous enterprises. As previously noted, in 1945 he had become a minority owner of the Los Angeles Rams football team. Pauley obtained controlling interest in Pacific Tire and Rubber Company. In 1948 he sold Petrol Corporation (which had retailed gasoline under the "P.D.Q." brand), and created Pan-American Oil. His father Elbert passed away in San Marino, California, in 1950. Ed restored the Pauley name to the oil empire in 1958, incorporating Pauley Petroleum. He built stylish offices at 10000 Santa Monica Boulevard and moved to Sunset Boulevard in Beverly Hills.[207]

Pauley did not seek high political office, but he did enjoy being in service to his country behind the scenes. He was considered for the post of Secretary of the Navy, but he was blocked by the opposition of Ickes and others, and quietly withdrew his name. He cultivated friendships with rulers of the Middle East, including King Hussein of Jordan and Shah Mohammed Reza Pahlavi of Iran. Ed Pauley was a strong supporter of Edmund "Pat" Brown, Sr., who became governor of California, and a friend of Eleanor Roosevelt. Pauley met Soviet premier Nikita Khruschev during his famous visit to California in 1959, as well as Marshall Tito of Yugoslavia. Years later he advised Democratic presidents John F. Kennedy and Lyndon B. Johnson on petroleum matters.

| (above) Pauley entertained King Hussein at his home. Pauley Collection
| (left) Bob Hope was introduced to the Shah of Iran. Pauley Collection

| *Empress Farah, Shah Mohammed Reza, and the Pauleys. Pauley Collection*

| Edwin Pauley, with Governor Pat Brown (white jacket), host Eleanor Roosevelt. Pauley Collection

(left) Pauley talks with Marshall and Madame Tito. Pauley Collection

(opposite) Cold warriors: Nikita Khruschev meets Ed Pauley in Los Angeles in 1959. Pauley Collection

| *President Kennedy is given an honorary doctorate at Berkeley. Pauley Collection*

Pauley was instrumental in guiding the University of California system through a period of substantial physical and intellectual growth, as well as student discontent. Pauley literally helped build the campuses. After the sale of the Rams to Carroll Rosenbloom, Pauley made a donation of $1 million to UCLA to build Pauley Pavilion, one of the most famous sports arenas in the West. Another gift was made to fund a building in honor of Elbert and Ellen Pauley at Occidental College. A $25,000 gift also aided development of the Jules Stein Eye Institute at that campus. Other grants over the years resulted in the Pauley Nuclear Science Pavilion and the Barbara McHenry Pauley Ballroom at UC-Berkeley. He led the fundraising drive to establish Dr. Ernest O. Lawrence's first cyclotron and the Chester W. Nimitz Room at Berkeley. Pauley donated funds for scholarships, medical and scientific research, alumni and student facilities, athletics, development of musical talent, and other purposes. His support helped the famed Berkeley band perform in concert tours abroad. Use of instructional television got its start at UC-Santa Barbara with Pauley's gift of cameras and other equipment for televised lecture-demonstrations to supplement classroom and laboratory sessions.

Pauley's political clout no doubt helped in bringing in the seemingly limitless amount of federal grant monies being poured into UC-Berkeley and Lawrence's cyclotrons during the Cold War. Pauley helped develop a powerful board of industrialists and philanthropists. While the funds no doubt helped make the university one of the best anywhere, its links to the feared "military-industrial complex" was a major issue of contention in the student protests of the 1960s. Both Pauley and the first Berkeley chancellor Clark Kerr had serious issues

Pauley founded the People's Bank of California and was a partner in the real estate firm that developed such communities as Lakewood and Hastings Ranch in California. He became a director of a rapidly growing Western Airlines, of First Western Bank and Trust Company, and of Surety Life Insurance Company. With Dr. Lee DuBridge of Cal Tech, he founded the PBS station KCET in Los Angeles. Pauley also became a director of KTVU, a television station in the San Francisco Bay Area.

| (above left) Lyndon Johnson is also given an honorary doctorate. Pauley Collection
| (above right) Pauley joins Brown and Kennedy in the presidential motorcade.
  Pauley Collection
| (bottom right) UC Chair Pauley sits at the head of the regents. To his left is Sam
  Mosher (standing) and Clark Kerr (sitting). To his right are Edward Carter and
  Mrs. Randolph (Catherine) Hearst. Pauley Collection
| (opposite inset) Lawrence and an early cyclotron. UC labs went on to synthesize
  plutonium. Author's Collection

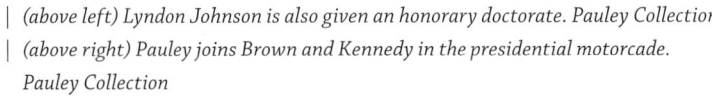

to contend with during their tenure at Berkeley. The problem began early on with the Oath of Loyalty forced upon the faculty in the early 1950s. It divided the regents, and the regents from the administration. Kerr was known in some circles as the "Red Chancellor" for opposing the oath. Kerr became president of the University system in 1958, despite the pro-oath regents, including Chairman Pauley. The Free Speech Movement was fought between Berkeley students and the administration beginning in 1964 over the ban on campus political activities and the ideals of academic freedom, and Kerr did not seem to be able to control matters successfully. Finally in 1967, under pressure from the new, conservative Republican governor Ronald Reagan, Kerr was dismissed by the regents.[208]

While devoting his attentions to his businesses and minding his duties as a University of California regent, Ed still found enough time to play tennis, bird hunt, and sail. The Pauley family also began their summer residence on Coconut Island. Being an educator at heart, Ed had adjusted his life to flow with the academic year, which always included an idyllic summer away from business.

| The Long Summer Vacation

From the onset of Ed Pauley's purchase of a share of the Moku-o-Loe Corporation in 1946,[209] he and his family began to spend their summers on the island. Bobbe, Ed, the children, and grandmother Marie McHenry would leave Beverly Hills just as soon as the school term was over. Because Marie McHenry didn't savor flying, the Pauleys would usually take Southern Pacific's overnight *Lark* to San Francisco, then sail to Hawai'i on the *Matsonia*, the *Lurline*, or the *President Cleveland*.

One of the most memorable visitations to Coconut Island in the early 1950s occurred when Ed Pauley's long outstanding invitation to his friend, Harry S. Truman, was finally fulfilled. The president would spend a month with the Pauleys.

(left) Kingmaker and king. Pauley Collection
(opposite) The Pauleys arrive in Honolulu. Pauley Collection

The Trumans returned home to Missouri in January 1953, soon after Dwight Eisenhower had become the new president. In March, Truman and his family left Independence for a much welcomed holiday in Hawai'i as guests of the Pauleys. The trip to Hawai'i was a dream for the Trumans, much like those nurtured by hundreds of thousands of other elderly winter-weary couples from the Mid-West. Since he was recently the president of the United States, however, there was a difference.

Harry, Bess, and daughter Margaret crossed the continent in the elegant private car of Union Pacific's scion Averell Harriman. At San Francisco, they boarded the P & O liner *President Cleveland*. A few days later Harry Truman awoke to see Diamond Head and Honolulu, with the Nu'uanu Pali in the background, rainbows, clouds, sunshine and the beautiful city "all in one scene."[210] Like Pauley, Truman had first glimpsed Coconut Island from the air—in Truman's case, as president en route on the historic trip in 1951 to dismiss General Douglas MacArthur during the Korean War.

Truman's ship arrived in Honolulu amid wild celebration and greetings. Truman had been the first presidential advocate of statehood for Hawai'i. The former president and his family were swarmed by the press and a dozen reception committees. Swaddled in lei, he was given honorary degrees and flown and driven around the territory before finally settling in on Coconut Island.

Ed and Bobbe Pauley made available the Retreat house for Harry and Bess, while Margaret stayed in the main house. The local newspapers reported with anticipation: "To people who want to get away from it all, this feeling of being cast adrift on a Pacific island might be refreshing."[211] This time, the reporters managed to faithfully describe the spirit that had always been Moku o Lo'e's.

The Retreat house on the island was rejuvenated, and the bowling alleys, swimming pools, pianos, and other amenities of the island were spruced up. Upon arrival, the former president could even ascend to the Lookout Bar on the top of the hill and survey one of his former charges

as commander-in-chief of the Marine Corps Air Station on Mōkapu. The newspapers gushed, "[Truman] is writing another chapter in the fabulous story of Coconut Island which probably will become known as 'the place where Truman stayed'."[212] Time has shown us that this label did not stick, but Truman's big Hawaiian vacation was nevertheless frontpage news in post-war Hawai'i.

Presidential biographer David McCullough stressed that the one-month stay on Coconut Island was one of the Trumans' most enchanting experiences.[213] But McCullough missed seeing the lighter side of the former president, first lady, and daughter Margaret. The normally staid and shy Missouri family really relaxed as guests of the Pauleys on Coconut Island, in ways that no biographer has ever captured. In many ways Ed Pauley was similar to Harry Truman: heartland bred, down-to-earth, earnest, and straight shooting.

No doubt one of the reasons Coconut Island made such a fine presidential sanctuary was the degree of security it afforded. Isolated from the mainland of O'ahu, yet only a few hundred yards from the protection offered by the Marine Corps Air Station, Truman could truly loaf after his ordeal of the past eight years, which, among other matters, included the task of ending World War II. This Easter time visit to Coconut Island was anything but routine for the Pauley children, however. Buzz, who was nine years old at the time, remembers the days just before the Trumans visited. As he was playing on the beach, Navy frogmen in black wetsuits suddenly rose up from the lagoon and stormed the island. A startled boy was quickly reassured by the men that they were only on a training maneuver, not creatures from the Black Lagoon.

The Trumans soon developed a routine of leisure on Coconut Island. The ex-president came in contact with many employees during his stay. Bess and Margaret often took the launch to go shopping in town, but Harry preferred to stay put. He enjoyed rising early and walking around the island. Sometimes he would pick up island caretaker Robert Miranda's toddler son, David "Kawika", on his sunrise jaunts.

| (above) Presidential commission on Easter eggs: (left to right) Dean Gayaro, President Truman, Buzz, Ed. Pauley Collection
| (opposite) The Pauleys relax with Harry S. Truman at the Beach House. Pauley Collection

The avuncular former president had a special effect on the children of the island. Truman organized swimming races with the Pauley kids. He and Ed gave away prizes such as Outrigger Canoe Club patches for the children's shorts and bottle caps for their shirts. They also helped the kids dye Easter eggs.

The Trumans became the butt of several April Fool's jokes devised by the mischievous Pauley children. Among other pranks, Margaret

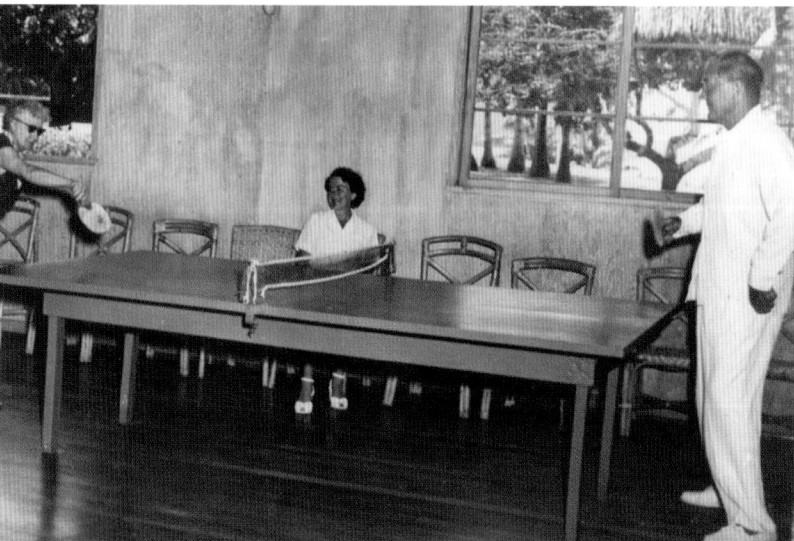

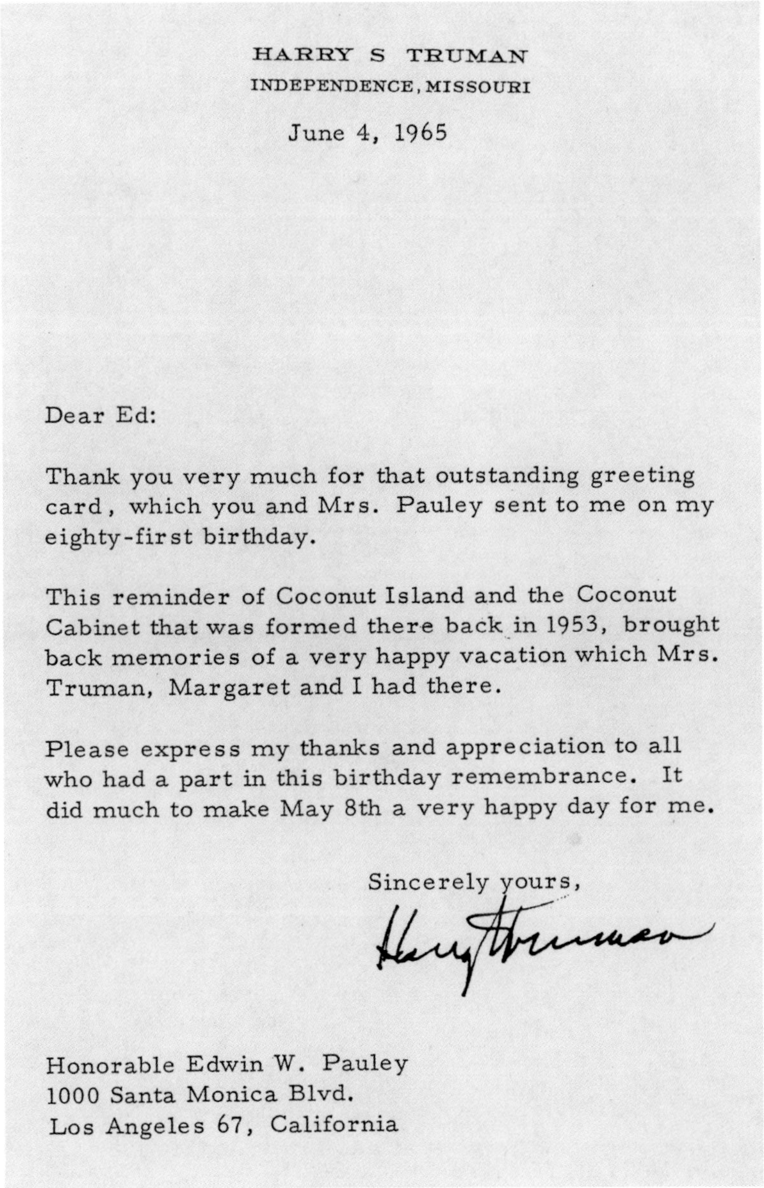

HARRY S TRUMAN
INDEPENDENCE, MISSOURI

June 4, 1965

Dear Ed:

Thank you very much for that outstanding greeting
card, which you and Mrs. Pauley sent to me on my
eighty-first birthday.

This reminder of Coconut Island and the Coconut
Cabinet that was formed there back in 1953, brought
back memories of a very happy vacation which Mrs.
Truman, Margaret and I had there.

Please express my thanks and appreciation to all
who had a part in this birthday remembrance. It
did much to make May 8th a very happy day for me.

Sincerely yours,

Harry Truman

Honorable Edwin W. Pauley
1000 Santa Monica Blvd.
Los Angeles 67, California

Truman awoke on that day to find a frog statue, normally located at the fishpond on the front lawn, in her room. Then there was the shaving cream on the toilet seat. When the president complained that his daughter was getting special treatment, the kids shortsheeted the presidential bed and put corn flakes in his pillow slip that night, and did the same or worse to everyone else. Susan Pauley French, chief architect to the short-sheeting, recalls the experience vividly: With two other teenage girls, the Pauley's daughter went up to the Retreat cottage after the president had left. They rang the bell and Bess Truman answered. Summoning her courage, Susie asked the former First Lady if they could play a joke on Mr. Truman. Suddenly they were escorted back into the bedroom, and with Mrs. Truman supervising every detail of the bed making, the deed was quickly done. At the family breakfast table the next day, Susie cautiously asked the president how he had slept. "Fine!" he chirped. A long pause followed. The president eventually resumed, "I did have one problem. I had to walk to breakfast on my knees."

Truman took the matter in hand and appointed a "Coconut Cabinet"[214] with each child becoming Secretary of Nuisance, Trouble, Laughter, or Mischief. In this capacity, Truman gained control over his tiny principality while teaching the kids a few lessons in government. On the island, Bess took to ping-pong, while the president enjoyed exploring the little island, lounging around in Bermuda shorts, and bowling a few games.

| (left) Truman remembered his vacation for the rest of his life. Pauley Collection
opposite:
| (far left) Truman and his "Coconut Cabinet." Truman Library, National Archives
| (top right) A very rare photo of Bess Truman (left) at play. Pauley Collection
| (bottom right) Harry and Margaret Truman bowling in the Recreation Center, Coconut Island. Pauley Collection

| *Susie and her friends learn hula. Pauley Collection*

| *Bobbe and Robert (Buzz) row in the lagoon swimming pool. Pauley Collection*

| *Volleyball on the lawn. Pauley Collection*

After about a month in Hawai'i, though, it was time for the Trumans to leave. It was back to Independence, where Truman, feeling refreshed but "very lazy," began to write his memoirs. For Christmas 1957, Truman printed official certificates, complete with the presidential seal, accrediting his cabinet with their special accomplishments in the realm of hijinks.[215] Truman would fondly remember the magical Pauley hospitality and the "Coconut Cabinet" for the rest of his life.

The summers on Coconut Island were an idyll of swimming,

waterskiing, sailing, and enjoying the good life in paradise. Bobbe Pauley recalls:

Everyone used to ask, "What do you do on Coconut Island?" There were more than enough activities besides relaxing in the sun with a good book and doing nothing. In the golden days, before we found out that too much exposure to the sun was harmful, we used to bake ourselves black. Ed's secretary, Gaye Bjornsen, won an award for being the darkest. The award was probably a sea cucumber. The "awards" were anything we could find on Coconut Island, including a 1920 typewriter for a scrabble winner. There was one promise that we had from our guests and that was to do nothing but what one wanted to do. In other words, relax!

A mother with three small children in the 1940s, Bobbe distinctively remembered the earthquake that rolled through the Pacific in 1947 (and described by her son in the Foreword):

It was a severe one and we were worried about a tidal wave coming in. So we took the children from the beach house along with the nurse and my mother up to the lookout and the highest point of Coconut Island. The earthquake didn't do any damage to the beach house but it did knock all of the big glass windows out of the dining room and cracked the wall over the fireplace in the Retreat.

Before the eight lanai suites were built on the west side of the island as guest facilities, the Pauley children, Edwin Jr., Stephen, Susan, and Buzz, the nurse, and Bobbe's mother Marie McHenry stayed next to the saltwater swimming pool in the beach house formerly occupied by Holmes's caretakers from the Holmes days, the Pagliottis.

Rose Wailehua was hired as "the best cook that ever was," according to Stephen Pauley—her mahimahi was legendary. Mrs. Pauley Pagen recollected Rose's special banana pancakes with coconut honey.

Caretakers Robert and Rosita Miranda, Charles "Naka" and Shizuko Nakamoto, Lorrain Chinen, Lorraine Lopez, and Eleanor Santana also worked for the Pauleys at Coconut Island. Grace Oyama was the children's 17-year-old caretaker/nurse. Andy Anderson, the master storyteller of octopus lore but known by everyone as "Andy Fix," had a reputation for being able to build and repair anything. Ms. Oyama recalls:

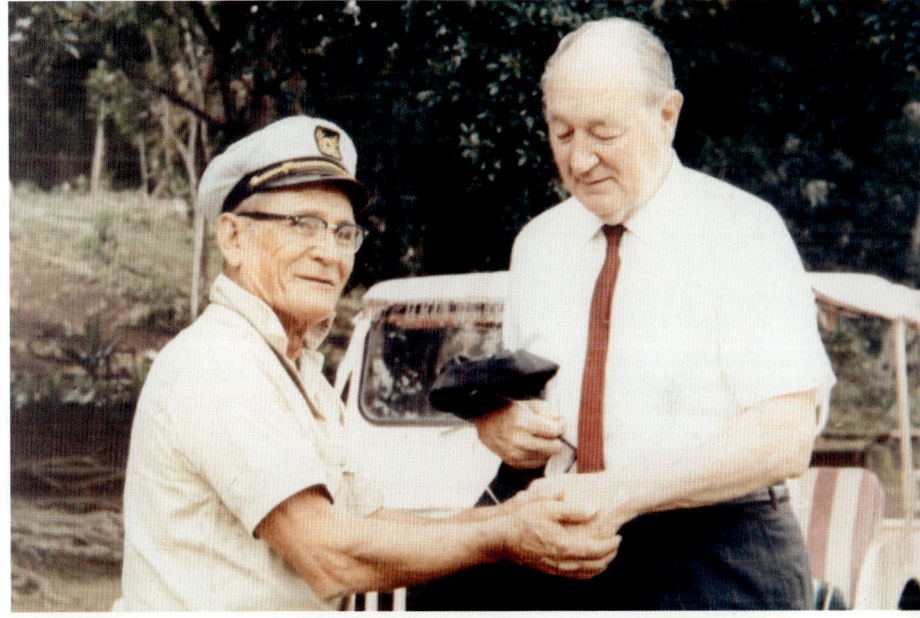

| *Ed and Captain Andy Anderson (left), who helped build Coconut Island under Christian Holmes. Pauley Collection*

In the early days when one of the seaplanes, a PBY from the marine base, got stuck on the coral around our island, Andy Fix removed the leaking oil from the swimming hole by using burlap sacks. As usual he did a good job.

Bobbe Pauley Pagen maintained lifelong contacts with many of her former employees; Steve Miranda recalls that Ed Pauley, although clearly a powerful, commanding individual, was very soft spoken and always showed compassion and care towards people. He had a good heart, and education was always his main concern. The Mirandas were particularly fond of the Pauleys and named their children after them. The first Miranda granddaughter was named Bobbe.

| *(above) The Suzie Q built by Andy Anderson. Pauley Collection*
| *(above right) Buzz sails off Andy's ski jump. Pauley Collection*
| *(bottom right) Ed waterskiing. Pauley Collection*

Like in the days of Holmes, boating and sailing was a popular past time around Coconut Island. Ed Pauley commanded the 30-foot Columbia sloop *Ku'uipo* (H. "my sweetheart"). Andy Anderson built the catamaran *Susie* for the Pauleys' daughter. Waterskiing also was an important recreational activity, with Andy Fix building a waterski jump. Bobbe Pauley Pagen recalled the pastime:

I was opposed to the children jumping at such an early age, although they were all good swimmers. Ed asked me if I would allow the children to jump if he "got the best ski instructor in the world, Bono Batani," whom Marcella Courtright had recommended. The Hernando Courtrights were visitors to Coconut Island many times. Marcella convinced me that it could be safe with Bono Batani. Bono agreed and was on his way from Mexico. I couldn't look at their jumping during those days, but fortunately they all learned without any injuries and became excellent jumpers and skiers.

Mrs. Pauley Pagen recalled her frequent trips to the lanai suites to attend to the first aid of the children and their guests. Unusual for most landlocked mothers, every night Bobbe would take a bottle of peroxide with her to treat the wounds that the kids received from scraping their feet and legs on the coral heads of the surrounding reef. On one occasion, Buzz attempted to hit a croquet ball with his mallet, missed, and broke Steve's nose instead.

The Pauleys continued the Holmes's tradition of entertaining a variety of guests on Coconut Island. And like the Fleischmann heir,

| *(top right) Comedian Red Skelton (front row, center) and the swim team at the Beach House. Bill Smith, two-time Olympic gold medalist, sits to the right of Ed Pauley. Pauley Collection*
| *(bottom right) John Wayne, surrounded by tritons, returns to Coconut Island as guest of the Pauleys. Pauley Collection*

Hollywood was no stranger to the social world of Ed and Bobbe Pauley. We are fortunate that the Pauleys usually had a photographer on hand. Long-time friend Red Skelton and his wife, and John Wayne were visitors. Greer Garson, Dinah Shore, George Montgomery, Ann Miller, and Eddie Albert also stayed. The Pauleys hosted opera diva Dorothy Kirsten French and her husband Jack French, director of the Brain Research Institute at UCLA. The Pauleys welcomed actress Jane Meadows.

Mr. and Mrs. Henry Walker had been frequent visitors to Coconut Island since the times of Christian Holmes. Henry Walker's mother, Una, was among Bobbe Pauley's greatest friends. One day she suggested that Bobbe invite the famous dancer ʻIolani Luahini to the island to teach them hula:

| *The great* kumu hula *ʻIolani Luahini performs in the Main House, Coconut Island.* Pauley Collection

When ‘Iolani thought we were ready to perform, which most of us were not, we'd show our husbands at dinner what we had learned, which again brought forth much laughter.

Una taught Bobbe songs on the ukulele and they sang them together. Mrs. Walker was a great help to Bobbe during the early days on the island when the children were still young. It was Una that brought over Grace Oyama as the first and only children's nurse through the years.

The family dog at the time was a little dachshund named Brandy. The pup was "on loan" from manager Admiral Health to the Pauley children during their summers on the island. Bobbe recalled:

One evening when the children were very little there was a fire incident in one of the lanai suites where all the guests and children were sleeping.... The children used to take turns having Brandy sleep with them. Brandy's barking awakened everyone to the flames started by the mosquito punk which had ignited some hanging clothes. Thanks to Brandy's barking and Susie's presence of mind to carry out the chair on which the clothes were starting to burn, a possible tragedy was prevented. Susie turned on the water hose, which we always kept in front of the lanai's in case of an emergency. We had a dinner honoring Brandy, who sat at the head of the table and enjoyed his steak with the rest of us. My mother gave Brandy a silver metal, with "hero" engraved on it and a "hero" or "heroine" medal to all those who took part in the action.

| *Departing guests toss their lei into the seas in the hope of returning. Pauley Collection*

Like a ship, the danger of fire on the isolated islet remained a major cause of concern for the inhabitants of Coconut Island. Early during the Pauley years, fire drills were held regularly.

The Pauleys always specially welcomed guests to Coconut Island. Andy Anderson painted guests' names on coconuts and they would be used as place cards at Aloha parties. The family had a parsimonious system of recycling lei. Since the island had a limited supply of flowers, the family would keep all the lei presented to arriving guests and returned them upon their leaving. When the guest departed, they tossed their lei into the water, an old Hawaiian custom reflecting the hope of returning. Lei floating in the water, the Pauley boys and Susie would swim out and retrieve them after the guests had departed. Mrs. Pauley Pagen recalled that the oldtimers who had been to Coconut Island many times felt honored when they received a tired looking lei.

Pan Am Stratocruiser flies swim team to Los Angeles with coach Sakamoto (1st row, far right). Pauley Collection

In later years the Pauley boys were given various island chores. They worked diligently to keep the grounds clean, and hammered rust off iron grids separating the laboratory fishponds. The Pauley children became so familiar with the work at the lab that they eventually gave tours of the facilities for Pauley guests. Working with the marine biologists at the lab sparked Stephen Pauley's interest in science and biology, and led to an outstanding career in medicine.

Every summer the family would hold a luncheon for the students and staff of the Hawaii Marine Lab. Everyone looked forward to the event and the food cooked by Mrs. Miranda, Rose Wailehua, and Eleanor Santana. Among the favorite treats for the group was homemade banana cake with coconut honey (instead of pancakes, this time). Ed Pauley used to say that he enjoyed serving the island-grown bananas and papayas as a way of "making the place pay for itself."

The endless summer for the Pauleys continued on Coconut Island throughout the 1950s and 1960s. Swimming, like waterskiing, was an important activity. Celebrated coach Soichi Sakamoto taught the Pauley kids how to swim. One of Sakamoto's swimmers, Keo Nakama, became the first person to swim the treacherous Moloka'i Channel between that island and O'ahu. An ambitious Stephen Pauley joined the Hawaii Swim Team during the summer of 1955:

I was the youngest swimmer. My hero at the time was George Onokea, an excellent distance swimmer, who was pushing for a world record in the 1500-meter freestyle. He was a fun guy and we became good friends.

In August I traveled with the team to Los Angeles for the AAU Nationals at the pool next to the Los Angeles Coliseum. Coach Sakamoto entered me in the 1500 meters (30 laps). I had never swum a 1500-meter race before. I not only came in last in my heat, but was lapped by several swimmers. I had learned how to lose and didn't particularly like the feeling. But the training helped me go on to do well in the 200-yard freestyle in high school.

| *Steve Pauley (left), George Onokea (2nd from left), Buzz Pauley (2nd from right) with swim team. Pauley Collection*

Other swimmers included Jon Hendrix, Al Wiggins, and Bill Smith. Some members of the swim team, like Dick Cleveland, had been friends of the Pauley kids for years. Swimming was also a popular past time for the guests of the Pauley family, as Bobbe recalled:

Down at the swimming lagoon there were a lot of sea cucumbers, which were a type of sea slug, and we would pay the kids 10¢ a piece to get these out of the shallow waters. The children got very, very proficient at this and the price dropped down to 5¢ and then later down to a penny.

It was a custom that any of the children's guests leaving the Island receive a "surprise" plate at dinnertime. Sometimes a covered plate was presented to the departing guest and when the cover was removed there would be a plate full of live sea cucumbers.

One year a venomous puffer fish also took up residence in the pool. Inflated when alarmed, the puffer was removed by the Pauley boys and taken to the lab. Ed Pauley, like Christian Holmes before, took an avid interest in marine biology.

During the Kennedy administration (1960–1963), the well-known composer of *The Music Man* Meredith Willson and his wife visited several times. Inspired by the natural beauty of Coconut Island, Willson composed the theme song for President Kennedy's physical fitness initiative. Bobbe remembers that the jingle had something to do with chicken fat, and that her son Buzz and his friend ended up doing push-ups to the music, thus feeling they had contributed to the presidential effort. The Willsons returned several times to the island over the years.

Also during the Kennedy administration, the Pauleys and the Hawai'i Institute of Marine Biology were hosts to a vice-presidential visitor, Lyndon Johnson and his wife Ladybird. The vice president was in

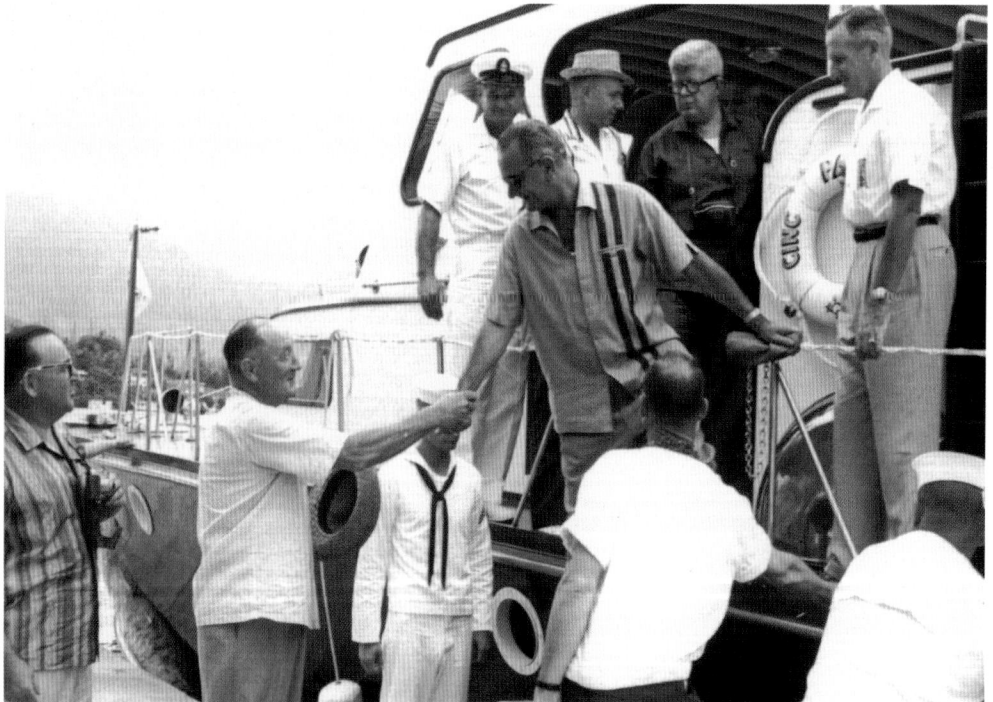

| *(left) Huge sharks continued to lurk in the waters off Coconut Island. Pauley and tiger shark. P. Helfrich, Pauley Collection*
| *(right) Pat Brown and Ed Pauley welcome LBJ to Coconut Island. Pauley Collection*

| (left) Della Ried and Sydney Townsley chat with the Johnsons at the labs on Coconut Island. Pauley Collection
| (right) Bobbe Pauley became friends with Ladybird Johnson from the start. Pauley Collection

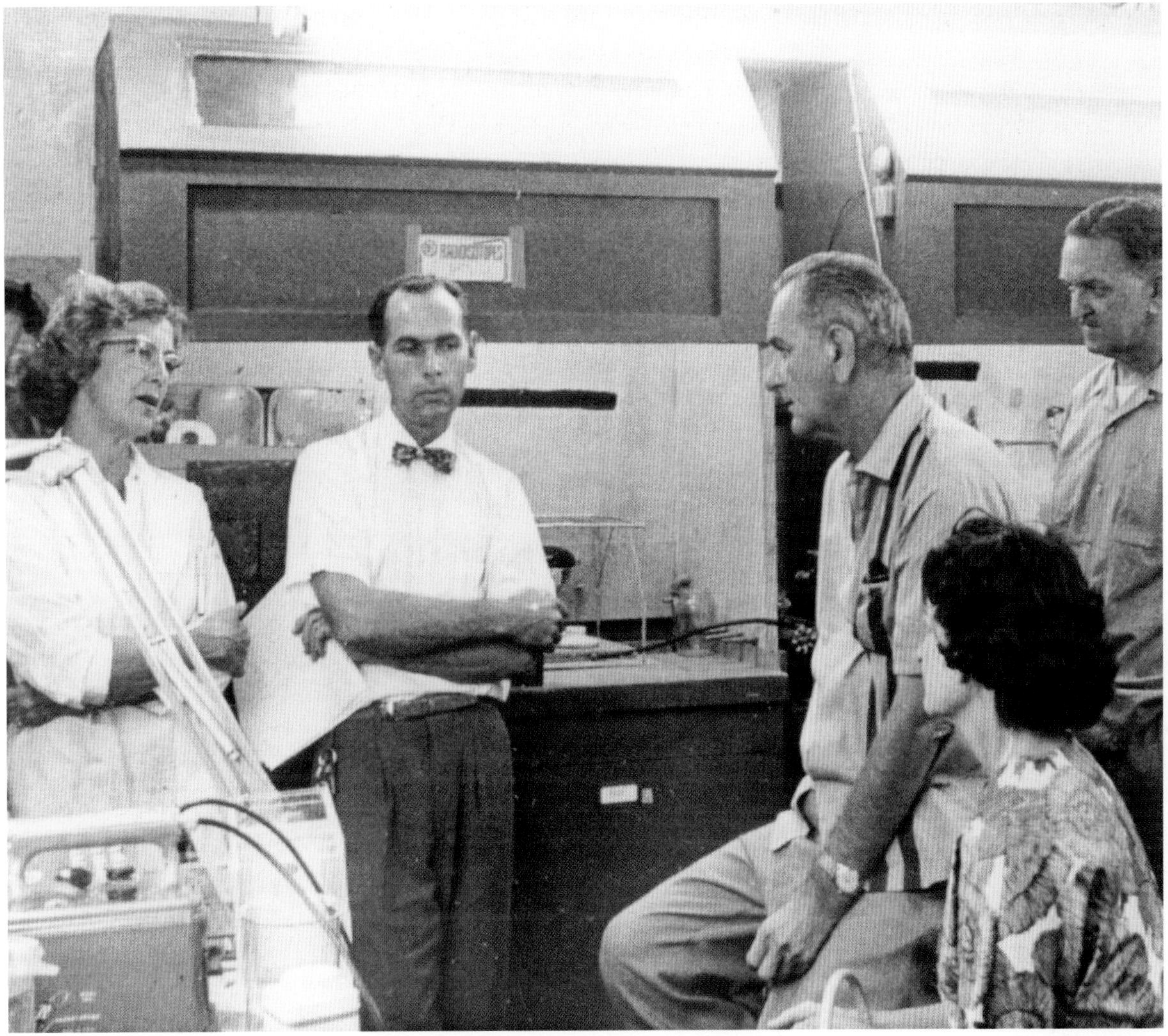

| *(above) Cal power. Regent Edward Carter, Regent Chair Ed Pauley, Governor Pat
  Brown at Coconut Island. Pauley Collection*
left column:
| *(top)* Gilligan's Island *cast. Author's Collection*
| *(middle) Nature imitating art. The professors, millionaires, and movie stars of
  Coconut Island. Note author's former boss, Oakland mayor Jerry Brown (standing)
  Pauley Collection*
| *(bottom) Marge Woolman, UC Regents secretary, tosses her lei. Pauley Collection*

the Islands to attend the governors' conference being hosted in Hawai'i in May 1961. Arriving by naval launch, the Johnsons were given a tour of the laboratories as well as the residential portions of the island. Bobbe remembers showing Ladybird their designated picnic luncheon table upon arrival. After the tour of the facilities, the party was shocked to notice that the appointed table was missing—it had been moved by the Secret Service.[216]

During this era, General and Mrs. Mark Clark also enjoyed relaxing on the island. Long-time family friend and associate California governor Edmund "Pat" Brown and his family were entertained on the islet. Jacqueline Kennedy, Caroline, and John Jr. visited the island once, but the Pauleys were not in residence at the time. Frequent guests included Chancellor Vernon Cheadle and his wife Mary, from UC-Santa Barbara. A botanist, Chancellor Cheadle used to occupy himself discovering rare cacti in Christian Holmes's impressive cactus garden up at the retreat. Famed UC president Clark Kerr also enjoyed his visits, swimming at times with the dolphins. Fellow UC regent Edward Carter and his wife Hannah were good friends of the Pauleys.[217] Other frequent guests included the Maisons from Los Angeles, the MacBrides from Sacramento, and UC Regents' secretary Marge Woolman, who called Coconut Island "her" island. She often said "God is going to have a hard time showing me heaven after seeing Coconut Island." Marge came to Coconut Island every year for decades.

When summers were over, however, the family would pack up and return to California. The Pauleys' business and social life was even more active as the years went by. In the late 1960s and despite their political

| (top right) *Swimming with dolphins. Clark Kerr and Ed Pauley. Pauley Collection*
| (bottom right) *Harold (left) and Ed Pauley riding on a ranchero in California in 1955. Harold died of a heart attack soon afterward. Pauley Collection*

| *The Pauleys' 15th wedding anniversary with Ethyl Merman in Los Angeles, 1952. Pauley Collection*

*Dear Ed
Just a Reminder as well as
proof we were working —
Best Regards
Ron*

| *Conservative governor Reagan pressured the UC Regents to dismiss Clark Kerr. Pauley Collection*

In those days the Royal Hawaiian Hotel used to require formal attire and later coat and tie, so the children would dress up in their best at night and would wear their shoes without argument. The kids would go out all day on their surfboards and we would all take outrigger canoe rides. They generally were swimming and in the water all day long. We would come in and have dinner at the Royal Hawaiian and then we would go back to Coconut Island. The kids were always anxious as we all were to get back to Coconut Island, our home. And they couldn't wait to take off their shoes.

Bobbe's mother greatly enjoyed her visits to Coconut Island. Grandmother McHenry would stand watch over her grandchildren boating in the bay, passing the word on should she detect trouble. According to Stephen Pauley, she had a sixth sense about her grandchildren. Daughter-in-law and daughter of two great and venerable California families, Marie McHenry spent the last ten years of her life living with Bobbe and Edwin Pauley in Beverly Hills before she died in 1962.[218]

Maintaining Coconut Island and its infrastructure had always been a formidable task. Holmes had spent $1,000 Depression dollars a day on the island. Many of the problems were based in the exposure of the island to the elements—saltwater, head-on trade winds, moisture, and strong ultraviolet light. Oxidation, actinic deterioration, and dry rot were ever-present, and landscaping overgrowth was a nightmare. However, before the Pauley summer visits, manager Admiral Heath assured that all was in readiness. The areas where the family stayed were always well maintained, with lawns manicured and trees trimmed. Bowling was always a main recreation. Remarkably, the simply constructed building remained intact until winter storms in 1996 destroyed the roof. The children were growing up by the 1960s: Susan married Rick Hillyer and Stephen married Marylyn, and the next generation of Pauleys began to enjoy the island. Not all entertainments were formal, as much of the photographic documentation would indicate—in fact both Bobbe and Ed enjoyed silly parties and great amounts of laughter.

| *In San Francisco's exclusive Bohemian Grove, Pauley shared hot dogs with Reagan and Nixon. Pauley Collection*

differences, regent Ed Pauley worked with the new governor Ronald Reagan and other Republicans.

Summer life at the Coconut Island paradise was never allowed to become a routine for the Pauleys. Bobbe Pauley Pagen recalled that occasionally the family would go into Waikīkī and stay at the Royal Hawaiian:

| *(left to right, front row) Mrs. Roos, Marie McHenry, Katie Jurado. (left to right, back row) Bobbe Pauley, Mr. Roos, Allen Chase. Pauley Collection*

| (above) *Steve and Susie follow where Bettie Fleischmann and*
Harry Truman once bowled. Pauley Collection
| (right) *Mother and daughter at the lagoon pool. Pauley Collection*
| (opposite) *Bobbe as pin girl. Pauley Collection*

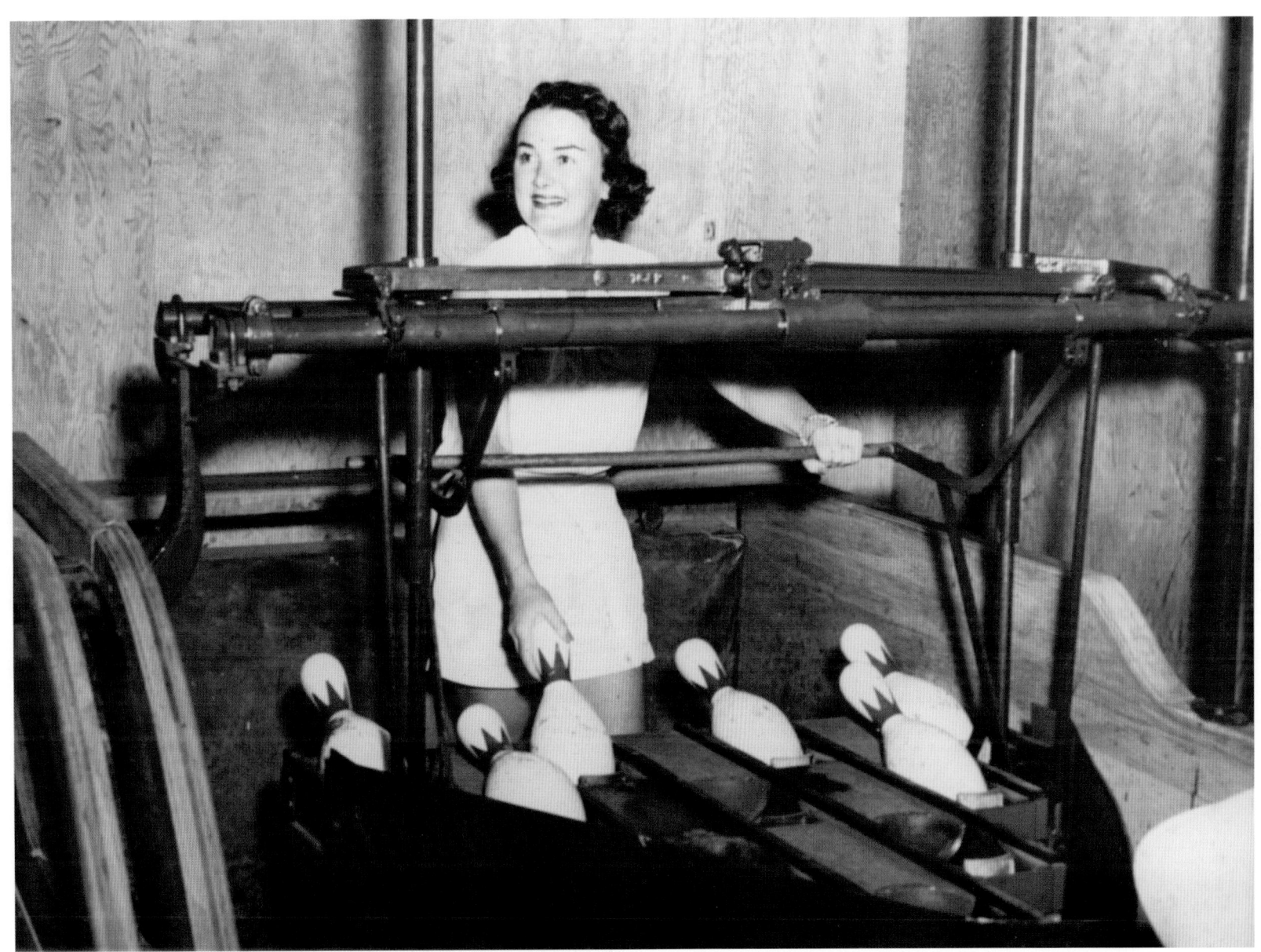

| *Marylyn (right), Steve's wife, joins the Pauley family in the 1960s. Pauley Collection*

| (above) Dress up ball at Coconut Island reveals the fun of Coconut Island. *Pauley Collection*

| (left) Bobbe and her two grown sons, Steve (left) and Buzz (right). *Pauley Collection*

Sheridan Ing, Ed Pauley's last Coconut Island partner. Julia Ing

The first and only rock concert held on Coconut Island took place in 1969, two years after San Francisco's pivotal "Summer of Love." The festival was sponsored by Honolulu Symphony's Junior Guild.[219]

On 10 October 1970, Dr. Philip Helfrich, acting director of the Hawai'i Institute of Marine Biology, declared the first Ecology Day on Coconut Island. It was an occasion to clear the island of plant debris and the encroaching mangroves, ironwoods, *koa haole*, and other vegetative pests.[220] Helfrich, together with the Pauleys, was to maintain an active interest in maintaining the special beauty of Coconut Island and the concept of the place as a natural or naturalized paradise.

In 1973 real estate developer Sheridan Ing became Pauley's sole partner in Coconut Island. His wife Julia recalled with delight the large *lū'au* held on Coconut Island during that time. According to Mrs. Ing, her husband and Ed Pauley had planned to put in a large housing development on the island, but Bobbe Pauley requested that they continue to leave the island relatively undeveloped. The Pauley family had become deeply attached to their summer home, and they certainly recognized its special beauty and unique nature—Bobbe's wish was ultimately fulfilled. Eventually, Sheridan Ing traded his interest in Coconut Island for a lot along Kāne'ohe Bay Drive. Except for the filled acres along the shoreline that were claimed by the state, the Pauleys now owned all of Coconut Island.

Ed Pauley, the sole surviving Moku-o-Loe partner, had finally given up the idea of developing Coconut Island as a semiprivate or public resort facility. In addition to the problems of access, parking, infrastructural limitations, and high maintenance costs, the U.S. Marines had brought over a wing of Navy jet fighters to the base on Mōkapu Peninsula. Throughout the Vietnam War and into the 1980s, the serenity of Kāne'ohe Bay was shattered by the roar of fighters practicing carrier landings over Coconut Island.[221] No one could seriously conceive of putting a hotel, club, or private homes essentially at the final approach of a major airport runway. But the noise was not new.

Stephen Pauley recalls a brief victory during a previous decade of island overflights:

One particular summer night I remember my grandmother, Marie McHenry, at her wit's end. [My father] called the base commander to ask if they could please stop the continued "creep" of the flight path toward the center of the island and return to the correct path north of the swimming pool.

Dr. Pauley reminisced that his father offered to take his mother-in-law to the Royal Hawaiian Hotel, but she wouldn't abandon her post. The marines complied with Grandmother McHenry's wish and corrected the flight plan.

In general, the relationship between the marines and the Pauleys was one of cordiality and cooperation that grew over the years. The marine commander often invited the family over to see the planes or helicopters at the base. And the Pauleys often had the marines over to the island for recreation and refreshment. In times of medical or any other emergency, the servicemen at Mōkapu were always at the assistance of the residents of Coconut Island.

By the 1970s, however, the Pauley visits changed in nature. Stephen, Susan, and Buzz had grown up and moved off with families of their own. Now it was a time of discovery for the grandchildren of Ed and Bobbe Pauley. For a new generation of residents, this place of eternal summers began to work its magic again. Ed and Bobbe never lost their love of Coconut Island.

| (top, left to right) Brian Hillyer, Scott Pauley, Kevin Hillyer, Clarke Pauley at the C. I. lanes, early 1970s. Kevin Hillyer

| (right) Puka shells and pageboy haircuts were the style for ca. 1979 Pauley grandchildren. (left to right) Brian Pauley Hillyer, Kevin Pauley Hillyer, 'Dallas', Rosita Miranda (red pants), 'Eleanor', Bobbe Pauley, Scott Pauley, Clarke Pauley. Seated, Christine Hilte. Pauley Collection

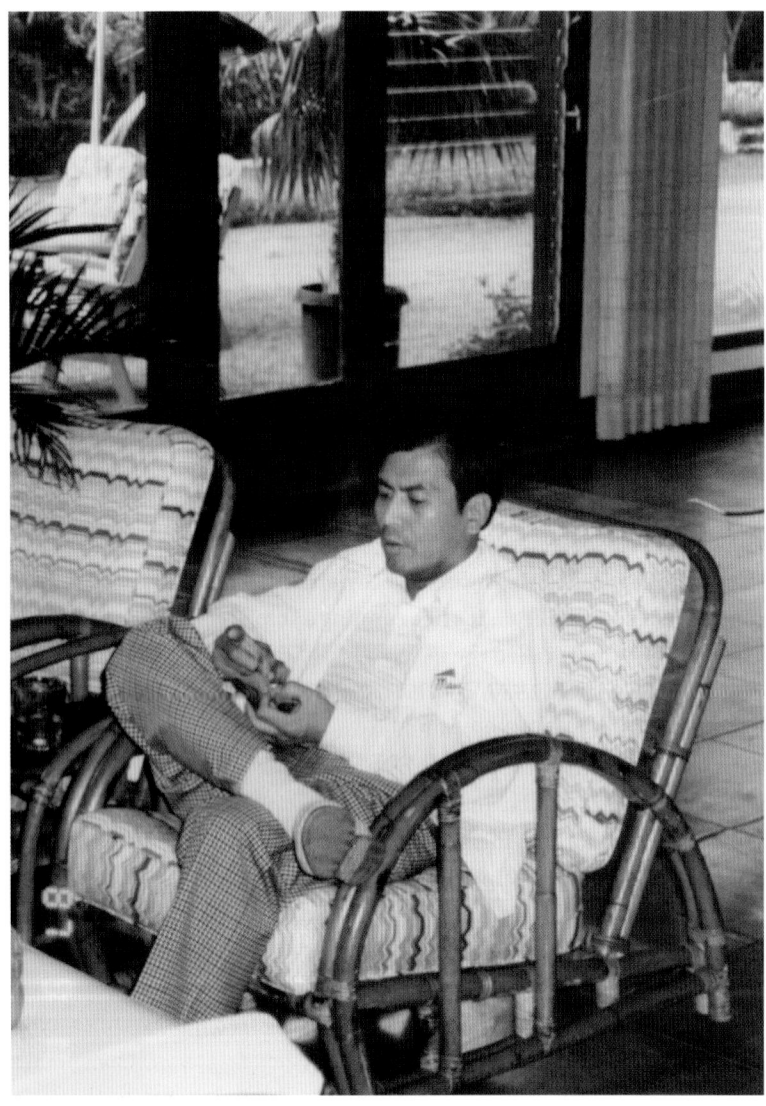

| *Rare portrait of Katsuhiro Kawaguchi in the Main House at Coconut Island.*
  P. Helfrich, HIMB Collection

| AN INVESTOR FROM JAPAN

The real estate market had exploded in Hawai'i in the 1980s, largely fueled by Japanese investment. Coconut Island itself would be brought into the speculation bubble, launching an era of intrigue and uneasiness.

Not too much was ever publicly known about Katsuhiro Kawaguchi in Hawai'i. According to reporter James Dooley,[223] he was known in Japan as a *jiageya*, a partisan of a business practice that obtained older properties, forced out tenants with the help of organized crime gangs known as *yakuza*, then demolished the buildings in order to develop new ones. Although he was not a member of the *yakuza*, Kawaguchi testified before the U.S. Congress in 1992 that he had used loans brokered by an organized crime group to finance his Hawaiian real estate deals.[224]

Philip Helfrich vividly recalls the investment climate that brought Kawaguchi to Hawai'i:

Japanese investors were discovering Hawai'i in the '80s. Hawai'i was warm and beautiful, easily accessible from Japan, the economy was stable and it seemed like a safe place to invest. Many Hawaiian residents were receiving lucrative offers for homes and property and there was a definite feeling in Hawai'i that longtime residents were being edged out by Japanese real estate investment. Kawaguchi did his best to alleviate some of the anger toward himself and other Japanese investors. He immediately revealed his plan to invest $10 million to assist in improving the marine lab as well as bringing the island back to some of its original grandeur. He did not seem to be a threat to HIMB and in fact seemed quite pleased to be associated with such an endeavor.

In fact, Kawaguchi gave HIMB a $50,000 grant.

In addition to his real estate development elsewhere, Kawaguchi had plans to develop Coconut Island into a luxurious corporate retreat and entertainment center. Thus, he added himself to the long list of would-be developers of the tiny island. Kawaguchi also envisioned turning Coconut Island into a grand "hospitality lounge" for morning-arriving Japanese tourists whose rooms in Waikīkī were not ready until the afternoon.

During the transition from the Pauleys to Hachidai, Capt. Charles Forquer stayed on as manager of the island for a few months. He was succeeded by Betty Ozaki as property manager. Red Miller, who was originally hired by Ed Pauley, remained the head caretaker until he retired. Akira Kato was vice president of Hachidai-USA and was in charge of Hachidai in Hawaiʻi. Kawaguchi, who was then in his late 40s, his wife, and children owned 100 percent of Hachidai, a multi-billion dollar corporation at the time he purchased Coconut Island.

The Hachidai Corporation was also concerned with establishing golf courses worldwide and selling golf club memberships and tours. Kawaguchi purchased Eaton Square in Waikīkī for $13 million in 1987 from John and Eaton Magoon and Rick Rainalter,[225] Kawaguchi envisioned purchasing all the individually owned condominiums in the complex to use as courtesy units for his golf club members. Hachidai owned a large hospital in Japan, a penthouse in Vancouver, golf courses, and other real estate.

Barely had Kawaguchi begun to operate in Hawaiʻi when he ran into major legal problems. On 9 May 1988, he was arrested at Honolulu International Airport upon arrival from Japan on a charge of visa fraud. He was held for a time at Kuakini Hospital in Honolulu in order to undergo necessary kidney dialysis. Subsequently, Kawaguchi was released from custody, after posting a $240,000 bond.

Kawaguchi was represented by Kevin Chang at the Immigration Court of federal judge John C. Williams in San Diego. The president of Hachidai Corporation was found guilty of fraudulently obtaining a visa to the United States by concealing his criminal record in Japan. He was fined $100,000 and was excluded from staying in the United States for

one year. Ironically, he could not be officially deported since, technically, he had not legally arrived in the United States. This particular exclusion of course placed a severe restriction on Kawaguchi's activities in the United States and made it increasingly difficult for him to do business in Hawaiʻi. It again relegated the private portion of Coconut Island into a white elephant.

At this point, Hachidai radically changed its plans for Coconut Island. Of particular interest was the establishment of a dolphin research center on the island. Sharon Core, owner of a large beverage firm, was interested in supporting the project. On the recommendation of Jacques Cousteau, Core was led to Louis Hermann, one of the world's leading dolphin specialists who was based at Honolulu's Kewalo Basin. About this time, Honolulu Waterfront Redevelopment Agency was looking to relocate the Kewalo dolphins, and Core and Hermann believed that Coconut Island would be an ideal place. Ed Pauley had had a particular interest in dolphin research as well, and they flourished there.

Plans for the porpoise facility at Coconut Island progressed to a great extent. A board of directors was put together, with Dr. Jacques Cousteau of the Oceanographic Institute of Monaco, Ed Eisner of Disney Corporation, and Steve Wynn of the Mirage Hotel in Las Vegas, among other members. Hermann had acquired permits from China and Peru for the export of freshwater dolphins. National Geographic Society wanted to film the entire project, and Warner Brothers was to provide musicians for the score. Proposals were made to the Bishop Estate to repurchase the island, but because of the prospects of state condemnation the Estate was not interested.

Development manager Grieg Porter was hired in November 1989 and became the immediate supervisor of the employees of Kawaguchi's Coconut Island. He was also the main planning manager until 1992, when Bill Drake was hired as manager. In addition to the dolphin center, Porter wished to construct a Hawaiian fishing village on the island.

Another idea was to hold Honolulu Symphony concerts on the property for fundraising. "Project Esteem" for homeless Hawaiian youths was another possible use of the island, as well as a nature center involving the Nature Conservancy. But none of these projects came to be.

The restrictions put on Kawaguchi's activity cost him dearly. By the beginning of the 1990s, Hawai'i's real estate boom had fizzled. Local residents, having watched their property taxes or rent skyrocket, were no longer as open to foreign investment in the state as they had been previously. Kawaguchi appeared to not have known the zoning restrictions placed on Coconut Island, which had been recorded as a conservation district.

Manager Porter did not recall seeing Kawaguchi ever at Coconut Island, but Drake remembered him staying overnight several times. Philip Helfrich visited the elusive developer in Japan:

I stayed at the Prince Hotel in Tokyo, and met with Kawaguchi there. Satoro Taguchi (a former colleague from Coconut Island) served as translator. Most of our initial discussions centered around how we had used the $50,000 gift he had given to HIMB. Kawaguchi's people had arranged to pick me up the next day to take me to another meeting. I was taken by limousine to a Tokyo heliport where a private helicopter awaited to take us to one of Kawaguchi's golf courses. We toured the facilities and had lunch there. I felt that Kawaguchi was managing a vast business enterprise, and that Coconut Island was but one of many activities in which he engaged. Through translators, I had a substantial conversation with Kawaguchi in his office on the following day, and I felt like he had a genuine interest in supporting the research at HIMB. In subsequent meetings before I left Tokyo, he conveyed a continued interest in Coconut Island but was frustrated by the bureaucracy that prevented his visits. He requested that I intervene on his behalf with Senator Inouye, but when approached the senator's staff did not feel that Kawaguchi's past actions warranted any special treatment, and they declined to intervene.

In Hawai'i, however, Kawaguchi and his persona were barely visible. Even Red Miller and his wife Mary, who were caretakers of the private portion of Coconut Island during the later Pauley years (1975–1987) and then under Hachidai until 1992, rarely saw him. Mrs. Miller recalls, however, that Kawaguchi was a generous man who showered his employees with gifts. Porter had met Kawaguchi in Japan, and thought of him as very personable and warm. And Bill Drake was convinced that Kawaguchi planned on the complete restoration of the island.

Estimates for the renovation of facilities that were in disrepair ran into the millions of dollars, perhaps $20 million. In 1992, faced with the possibility of state condemnation, Kawaguchi proposed a land swap with the state for the private section of Coconut Island, but officials at the Department of Land and Natural Resources (DLNR) indicated that they had no land suitable for Kawaguchi. William Paty, head of the DLNR, felt that it would have been easier for the state to buy the island outright.

COCONUT ISLAND RETURNS TO STATE CONTROL

Kawaguchi still wanted about $20 million for Coconut Island in 1993. By 1995, a recession and various other problems in Japan were resulting in severe financial difficulties. Kawaguchi owed $50 million to Muramoto Construction Company for the development of a golf course in Japan. The daily interest alone accounted for $4,800 per day. Kawaguchi took out mortgage loans on both Coconut Island and Eaton Square to keep up with the payments. In March 1995, Kawaguchi agreed to sell his acres of Coconut Island to the University of Hawai'i Foundation for $2 million.

The sale of the private section of the island was agreed upon after the Edwin W. Pauley Foundation pledged the necessary funds to the University of Hawai'i Foundation.[226] Hachidai-USA accepted ten times less than they originally wished because of the problems with the Muramoto golf course. Muramoto itself was having financial difficulties. In 1994, Muramoto filed for bankruptcy and attempted to foreclose on Kawaguchi's Hawaiian properties. This precipitated the sale to the University of Hawai'i Foundation.

The Foundation's $2 million was placed in escrow for several months while disputes raged between Hachidai and Muramoto over Muramoto's rights to the proceeds from the sale. According to Kawaguchi, the clubhouse roof at the golf course built by Muramoto was leaking, and its repair would cost several million dollars. This decrease in value would greatly reduce the amount owed by Kawaguchi to Muramoto.[227] Lex Smith, local attorney for Hachidai, attributed some of the delays to litigation in Japan.[228] In May 1995, Muramoto proceeded with the foreclosure action, and Coconut Island was sold through that foreclosure on 30 August 1995.

Once the sale was consummated, the UH Foundation leased Coconut Island to the University of Hawai'i for $1.00 per year for 99 years, with the university assuming all costs and expenses, including maintenance and repair. In addition to this sale, the 31-unit, 52,000 square foot Eaton Square complex was sold by Hachidai-USA for $8.2 million. Developer Bill Mills and investors Jay Shidler, James Reynolds, and ESQ Incorporated were purchasers.[229]

Kawaguchi lost $6.5 million on the Coconut Island purchase price alone. With Eaton Square, his losses amounted to an additional $5 million. Hachidai-USA subsequently filed for bankruptcy, and Kawaguchi released all his employees in Hawai'i. Finally, resident caretaker Steve Gates and his wife left the island toward the end of 1995.[230]

After the deaths of Ed Pauley and William Pagen (in 1993), Bobbe Pauley Pagen, through the Edwin W. Pauley Foundation, continued to support higher education, the arts, and research at Coconut Island until her own death in 2002. She was honored by the UCLA College of Letters and Science, was given an honorary degree, and served on several UCLA committees. The Barbara McHenry Pauley Ballroom is located at UC-Berkeley. The Barbara Pauley Gallery of Greco-Roman and Early European Art graces the Los Angeles County Museum of Art where she was a trustee. She was a generous supporter of the McHenry Mansion Foundation, which has restored her family's elegant Victorian home in Modesto, California, and the nearby Bald Eagle Ranch where she was raised. Her name is linked with Edwin Pauley on several other projects and institutions. Over the years, she graced many trusteeships and committees and was associated with numerous civic organizations. Bobbe Pauley Pagen was a director of Pauley Petroleum and received many additional awards.[231] One of her last public acts was the dedication of the new Pauley Pagen Laboratories on Coconut Island in 1998 (see p. 251).

To their enduring credit, Edwin W. Pauley and Barbara Pauley Pagen saw to it that the natural beauty of Moku o Lo'e, and the artificial splendors of Coconut Island, would remain largely intact for future generations. The Pauleys gave up much of their privacy on the island when they offered to share it with the scientists of the Hawaii Marine Lab and the Hawai'i Institute of Marine Biology. This unselfish act for educational purposes would again be underscored when the Edwin W. Pauley Foundation granted the University of Hawai'i Foundation the funds to acquire the private portion of Coconut Island.

Unlike the vast tracts of surrounding Kāne'ohe, which have been subject to unrelenting real estate subdivision and urbanization, Coconut Island has weathered the storm of progress exceedingly well. The careful stewardship of individuals such as Ed Pauley, Bobbe Pauley Pagen, Philip Helfrich, as well as Christian Holmes a generation before, has sustained this fragile image of paradise cast upon a coral sea. This has allowed the island to serve completely as one of the earth's most important and unusual platforms for the exploration of marine biology.

Shades of the old days at Moku o Lo'e. HIMB staff and students collecting specimens for the tuna baitfish study near Coconut Island. HIMB Collection

CHAPTER SIX

Hawai'i Institute of Marine Biology

by Philip Helfrich (Director Emeritus) and Jo-Ann C. Leong (Director)

Research conducted at Coconut Island has resulted in significant findings, and the education programs have enriched the lives of hundreds of students over the years.

Barbara Pauley Pagen

The story of the Hawai'i Institute of Marine Biology goes back more than 100 years. It involves the vision and determination of a small group of individuals who recognized the enormous potential for studies of marine biology in Hawai'i's superb mid-Pacific location. The evolution of this world-class present day institution was greatly enhanced by the interest and crucial involvement of many people, but particularly by Christian Holmes who created the ideal facilities for a marine laboratory on Coconut Island, and by Edwin W. Pauley, who supported and encouraged the University of Hawai'i's marine enterprise by providing the property upon which the laboratory is located, the resources, support, and encouragement for numerous programs. In 1995, the Pauley family, through an act of far-reaching vision and generosity, provided funds for the purchase of the privately held interior of the island for the University of Hawai'i Foundation and for the construction of a state-of-the-art marine biology laboratory for the Hawai'i Institute of Marine Biology.

Charles H. Edmondson and Robert W. Hiatt were two visionaries who played key roles in the early development of marine science and the facilities to support major educational and research programs in marine biology.

| ORIGIN AND EARLY YEARS

The Waikiki Aquarium, Hawai'i's first shore-side marine facility, was opened to the public in March 1904. It was built as a private project by the Honolulu Rapid Transit Authority (HRTA) to attract the public to Kapi'olani Park that was served by its electric trolley cars. In addition to the aquarium, the park included a horse track, polo fields, a bandstand, ponds, gardens, and a public bath house. Frederick Potter, a clerk for HRTA, was appointed the first director of the aquarium, a position he held from 1904 to 1940, when he was replaced by Spencer Tinker.[232]

In a prophetic statement made in November 1906 by William T.

Brigham, the first director of the Bernice Pauahi Bishop Museum, he described his vision of a teaching and research institution in Hawai'i, "a college to include a marine biological station."[233] What was to become the University of Hawai'i, was established as the College of Agriculture and Mechanic Arts in 1907. The first classes were held on 3 February 1908, "with five borrowed students, twelve valorous instructors, a token library, all gathered in a rented house on Young Street on the Waikīkī side of Thomas Square."[234]

While teaching courses in zoology and oceanography at the college in 1910, William A. Bryan made a plea for the establishment of a marine laboratory associated with Waikiki Aquarium. In 1913 Professor Allan Herbert articulated the need for a "Marine Biological Laboratory for Hawaii." His plan called for a seaside laboratory at Waikīkī, in the park adjacent to the aquarium. Such a laboratory "would give the college access to the fascinating world that lies hidden in the ocean."[235]

Bryan and Herbert's pleas apparently caught the attention of townspeople and after occupying a temporary laboratory on Pier 6 in 1916, another appeal was made in 1919 for a "thoroughly equipped marine biological laboratory."[236] Arthur L. Dean, then president of the College of Hawaii requested that the Territory turn over the property in Waikīkī, where the aquarium now stands, to establish a marine research laboratory in connection with the aquarium. This was accomplished by the Territorial Legislature in 1919, and in 1920 the Cooke Estate generously provided $10,000 to build the laboratory. The Charles M. Cooke Memorial Marine Laboratory, was ready for use in the summer of 1920.[237]

That same year, the legislature created the University of Hawai'i, and hired their first faculty member with training in tropical marine biology, Charles H. Edmondson. Dr. Edmondson received his Ph.D. from the University of Iowa in 1906, and the same year studied at the Carnegie Institution of Washington's Tortugas Laboratory in the Florida Keys. This first tropical marine laboratory in the U.S. provided Edmondson with an excellent background for his future work in Hawai'i. Edmondson arrived in Hawai'i in the summer of 1920 and was given a joint appointment as a researcher at the Bishop Museum, and as professor of zoology at the newly constituted University of Hawai'i. He also became the founding director of the Cooke Memorial Marine Laboratory, which at that time, was administratively separate from the Honolulu Aquarium.[238] In subsequent years it was referred to as the "Marine Lab" or more frequently the "Beach Lab."

According to Kay, "Edmondson reigned supreme at the Cooke Marine Biology Laboratory." The first Pacific Science Congress was held in Honolulu in August of 1920, and at that meeting Edmondson expressed the hope that it would stimulate interest in biology and encourage students to continue in research. He remained an active researcher until his retirement in 1943 and published many papers on corals, shipworms, starfish, and fouling organisms. He is best known for his classic, *Reef and Shore Fauna of Hawaii*, one of the first texts on tropical marine animals.[239]

Charles Edmondson and Christian Holmes might have met at some time. It would seem likely considering their common interest in marine biology, and the close proximity of the Cooke Laboratory and the Holmes mansion just a few yards away. However, they left no evidence of such a meeting. We do know that Frederick Potter, aquarium director from 1906–1940, did have an encounter with Holmes. The Potter family resided in a house on the aquarium property and in 1916 C. F. Case Deering constructed the fabulous three-story mansion that was sold to Christian Holmes in 1933. Holmes was well known for throwing lavish parties and *lū'au* at his Waikīkī mansion, and several all night revelries prompted a visit from the Potter family to express concerns about their ability to sleep. Despite their initial apprehensions, this visit resulted in a cordial relationship between the Potter and Holmes families, with invitations to visit Holmes's Coconut Island estate.[240] It is ironic, that the Holmes property was acquired by the City and County of Honolulu in 1957 and leased to the Spencecliff Corporation to become the Queen's Surf Restaurant. Its infamous Barefoot Bar also had a reputation for flamboyant entertainment and the parties continued until the building was razed in 1971.[241]

The Era of Pioneers, 1943–1963 (R. W. Hiatt, A. H. Banner, A. L. Tester, V. E. Brock)

Edmondson retired from the university in 1942, and was replaced by Christopher Hamre, and assistant professors Albert H. "Hank" Banner and Robert W. Hiatt were both hired in 1943. Banner was drafted into the army as soon as he was hired, and was not to return to Hawai'i until 1946. Due to war time civilian travel restrictions, Hiatt's arrival in Hawai'i was also delayed until the summer of 1944.

The Cooke Laboratory was a modest structure at the water's edge, approximately 40 meters east of the Waikiki Aquarium (and next door to Holmes's Queen's Surf estate). It was closely associated with the Department of Zoology and Entomology and from 1944 was directed by Hiatt. With his colleagues Albert Tester, George Chu, Pieter van Weel, Donald Matthews, Sydney Hsiao, and Banner, plus the assistance of several graduate students, the "Beach Lab" was used for teaching, research, and as a base for classes and field trips in marine biology.

| *The Charles M. Cooke Memorial Marine Laboratory, predecessor of the Hawaii Marine Laboratory on Coconut Island. P. Helfrich, Natatorium Collection*

This early version of the Hawaii Marine Laboratory (HML) was the precursor to the much larger Hawai'i Institute of Marine Biology that would be established on Coconut Island. The old "Beach Lab" was demolished around 1955, and the furniture and classes moved next door into the back section of the new Waikiki Aquarium building.

The University of Hawai'i in the post-World War II era was a small institution struggling to establish itself, focusing on a few areas of emphasis that the tropical environment and the geographic setting made obvious: Asian studies, tropical agriculture, and marine biology. At that time, academic marine science was evolving from an era of exploration with emphasis on taxonomic description and classification of animals and plants to an era of experimental science, particularly in ecology, animal and plant physiology, and animal behavior. Oceanography was emerging as a separate discipline, and molecular biology was on the horizon. The enrollment in 1946–1947 was only 2,960 students; the budget was $2.7 million.[242] Remember that the research conducted by faculty in the late 1940s was largely non-funded. The tradition of federally funded research in marine science was virtually non-existent. It was a labor of professional fulfillment and personal gratification rather than monetary compensation, and it required a high level of dedication and commitment. A young and resolute faculty had been recruited in response to the demands of a new generation of returning servicemen and women. The G.I. Bill provided them opportunities for higher education that were previously unavailable and, like elsewhere in the United States, college enrollments increased.

In the Department of Zoology and Entomology, marine biologist Robert W. Hiatt was aware of the potential that existed for marine studies in a territory surrounded by ocean, and whose mostly benign climate allowed year-round access to the marine environment. A doctoral program was offered in zoology for the first time; the journal *Pacific Science* was inaugurated. The wartime and postwar federal support of university research established a whole new mode of funding for scientific

Dr. Robert Worth Hiatt, the founding director of the Hawaii Marine Laboratory. An inspirational leader, he has been called the "Father of Marine Science" at the University of Hawai'i. Elizabeth Hiatt

enterprise that would nurture research in an unprecedented manner for decades to come.

Early in his career in Hawaiʻi, Hiatt recognized the need for a vessel for the marine biology program. Before the wide availability of SCUBA, the principle means of sampling the sub-surface marine environment was through the use of plankton nets, bottom grabs, and dredges, all operated from a surface vessel. Hiatt obtained the diesel-powered *Salpa*. It was a 46-foot converted naval vessel originally used to tow targets during World War II. Hiatt named it for a marine invertebrate animal and equipped it with a winch and other equipment for the collection of marine organisms.

In 1947, Hiatt was conducting research in Kāneʻohe Bay using the *Salpa*, which was operated by Lester Zukeran. Zukeran was a recently repatriated World War II veteran who had worked for Christian Holmes at Coconut Island in the 1930s. The vessel was berthed at Kewalo Basin in Honolulu, and whenever it was needed in Kāneʻohe Bay, it was sailed around Mōkapu Point and moored at the Waikalua pier near Coconut Island.

The 1947 research involved a plankton and *nehu* (baitfish) sampling program in Kāneʻohe Bay. Every Thursday, Lester Zukeran would bring the RV *Salpa* around from Honolulu for use during evening collections. One Thursday a storm came up, and the *Salpa* dragged anchor in Kāneʻohe Bay. The next morning, Zukeran found the vessel aground in the mud and, with help from an *aku* boat, pulled it into deep water. Zukeran then sailed the boat over to the old pier once owned by Holmes off Waikalua Road and asked permission to tie up during the bad weather. Permission was given, and when Hiatt came to inspect for damage, he met the new owner of Coconut Island, Edwin Pauley.[243]

From this first meeting grew an enduring friendship. Both Hiatt and Pauley attended the graduate program at UC-Berkeley (although not at the same time), and both had a strong commitment to higher education. Pauley's regency at the University of California lasted for 32 years,

| RV Salpa, *the first vessel dedicated to marine research at the University of Hawaiʻi. HIMB Collection*

and Hiatt had a distinguished career in higher education, progressing through major administrative positions at the University of Hawaiʻi. Understandably they shared a vision for what would become an important adjunct to the educational facilities of both Hawaiʻi and California. This historic meeting on Coconut Island was the beginning of an important institutional relationship between the University of Hawaiʻi and

the University of California that probably exceeded the initial expectations of either man, but has endured for more than half a century.

During the course of this and subsequent conversations between the marine scientist and the University of California regent and visionary, Pauley recognized the benefits that might be realized from the study of marine biology. Such endeavors would not only provide food from the sea for a world recovering from a devastating World War, but would also strengthen the ties between the University of California and an emerging university located in the center of the Pacific Ocean. Pauley also had a desire to make more productive, year-round use of his Hawaiian property while still having it available for summer recreation. Acting on behalf of himself and the co-owners of Coconut Island, Pauley extended an invitation to move the Hawaii Marine Laboratory to Coconut Island.[244] Pauley then invited University of Hawai'i president Gregg Sinclair to a luncheon on Coconut Island to extend the formal invitation to establish a university marine laboratory there. They agreed that the University of Hawai'i would occupy the existing structures Coconut Island as part of the Hawaii Marine Laboratory. Initially Pauley offered the net house and adjacent pier and ponds.

Pauley then asked Hiatt to look around to see what else he might be able to use. Hiatt chose several wooden structures adjacent to the east lagoon, built by the military during World War II for rest and recreational purposes. In addition, Pauley donated $10,000, a substantial sum of money in 1947, to convert the buildings for use by the university faculty and students.[245] University of Hawai'i maintenance staff and "volunteer" marine laboratory faculty and students put in many hours of work to bring about the relocated Hawaii Marine Laboratory.

Shortly thereafter, Hiatt invited the director of the Rockefeller

The original Hawaii Marine Laboratory building on the east lagoon on Coconut Island. This former military barracks was destroyed by fire in 1961. HIMB Collection

Foundation to visit Coconut Island. During the visit, Hiatt described his attempts to build a laboratory to conduct research on corals and other tropical marine organisms that might have pharmaceutical properties beneficial to human health. At the time there were no laboratories in the world engaged in the study of corals. The Rockefeller Foundation was favorably impressed and offered another $10,000. With $20,000 and a good supply of volunteer labor, a seawater system was constructed on the island and the selected buildings were remodeled into laboratories.[246] A new dock was built so that a research vessel could be docked nearby and Holmes's ponds and aquaria were renovated. Laboratory tables were constructed in the main building, and offices were built for Hiatt, Tester, and Banner. At the north end of the lab a small workshop was established, and at the south end of the building a lunchroom with adjacent kitchen and shower room were built. This also served as the social center of the new marine lab.

ROBERT W. HIATT, FOUNDING LABORATORY DIRECTOR AND RESEARCHER (1948–1955)

Robert Hiatt served as the founding director of the Hawaii Marine Laboratory on Coconut Island as an extension of his management duties of the "Beach Lab" and as chairman of the UH Department of Zoology. In 1949 Hiatt took legislative action to designate the 64 acres of coral reef around Coconut Island as the Hawaii Marine Laboratory Refuge.

In 1951, the Coconut Island laboratory officially became the Hawaii Marine Laboratory (HML) of the University of Hawai'i; it was the first designated research unit on the UH campus and the beginning of the "organized research units" as proposed to the UH administration by Hiatt.[247] It was in these early years that Hiatt aggressively pursued funds for research in marine biology from the Office of Naval Research, National Science Foundation, and the National Institutes of Health. He was away from Hawai'i, mostly in Washington D.C., about three months every year. His initial efforts were to obtain funds for HML, and at one point, he had obtained more than half of all of the research funds at the University of Hawai'i.[248] It was Hiatt's inspirational leadership, vision, energy, and dedication to higher education and research that propelled the Hawaii Marine Laboratory of the late 1940s toward the fine institution that exists today.

ROBERT HIATT'S RESEARCH ON THE EFFECTS OF RADIOACTIVITY ON MARINE ECOSYSTEMS

After tests of U.S. nuclear devices at Bikini Atoll in the Marshall Islands, in which Hiatt and Vernon Brock participated as observers, HML became involved in studies sponsored by the Atomic Energy Commission (AEC) on the fate of selected radioactive nucleotides in the marine environment. Hiatt hired Howard Boroughs as an associate professor in the Department of Zoology. Boroughs gave a course entitled "Isotopic Tracers in Biology" and all of the members of Hiatt's team participated. Boroughs had been a member of the Committee on Biological Effects of Atomic Radiation established by the National Academy of Sciences.[249] He presented a report, *Fission Production Metabolism in Marine Organisms*, to the committee in which he and his colleagues had conducted their pioneering feeding experiments of tuna kept in captivity on Coconut Island. The isotope used in this experiment was strontium-89. Sidney Townsley, who by then had obtained a Ph.D., was a member of this research team, which also included Della Ried and Winifred Ego. These were some of the first experiments that provided information on the effects of radioactivity on marine ecosystems.[250]

HAWAII MARINE LABORATORY IN THE 1950S

The original staff of the Hawaii Marine Lab circa 1950 included all the marine biologists on the faculty of the Departments of Zoology and

Lester Zukeran, first staff member of the Hawaii Marine Laboratory and formerly an employee of Christian Holmes on Coconut Island. Bridging the Holmes to HIMB era was unique. HIMB Collection

Botany, as well as three lecturers in fishery biology affiliated with federal and state programs in Honolulu (see Appendix, Table 2). The main theme of the applied research program was fisheries, aimed at assisting the local skipjack tuna fisheries that had been the focus of Christian Holmes and his Hawaiian Tuna Packers enterprise. The operation and maintenance of this initial, emerging marine lab was the responsibility of its only two full-time employees, Lester Zukeran, boat operator, and Charles "Naka" Nakamoto, the resident caretaker.

I (Helfrich) joined this small laboratory during this formative early period, along with other graduate and undergraduate students: Don Strasburg, Austin Prichard, Sidney Townsley, Jack Randall, Michio Takata, Susumo Kato, Alison Kay, Richard Nishioka, Jim Yount, and Shirley Trefz. The students moved into the lab on the east lagoon. It had bare concrete floors and 4-foot wood frame walls topped by screens reaching to an open-beamed ceiling. Laboratory benches, sinks, a fume hood, and other furniture were installed.

Resident caretaker Charles "Naka" Nakamoto and his family lived in one half of an old bachelor officer's quarters at the south end of the east lagoon. The other half provided living quarters for resident students and visitors. A second military building utilized on the east lagoon was affectionately dubbed "Hale[251] Dry Rot." During the military occupation, Hale Dry Rot had been a recreation pavilion where dances were held. It was initially converted into offices and laboratories in 1954.

A portion of the building became a lunch room and social gathering place in the 1970s and 1980s where students and faculty could sit down to lunch. I recall many lunch hours spent overlooking the east lagoon at tables fashioned from lumber salvaged from the deck of the *Seth Parker*. An adjacent building, formerly a small military latrine, was also converted into a staff lunchroom (later dubbed "Gilligan's Hut"). A barracks structure next door became living quarters.

The *Salpa* was the flagship of the little HML fleet. Two surplus launches for transportation from the Waikalua Road pier and two

| *The original marine laboratory building. HIMB Collection*

| (top) The original marine laboratory building and a second former military building, "Hale Dry Rot" (right) converted for laboratory use at Coconut Island in 1954. HIMB Collection

| (bottom) The main laboratory building on the east lagoon that replaced the original laboratory destroyed by fire in 1961, ca. 1985. P. Helfrich

wooden skiffs powered by 3- and 5-horsepower outboard motors made up the remainder of the fleet. The largest of these, a planked boat christened "Hiatt's Skiff," was salvaged by Zukeran from Kāne'ohe Bay in the early 1950s and was the mainstay of the small boat fleet for a decade until it was replaced by several Boston Whalers.

Edwin Pauley took a personal interest in the research on Coconut Island particularly those projects that addressed the world food problem. He often alluded to the vast resources of the sea, with its great potential to meet the nutritional needs of the developing world. He was regularly supplied with research reports, and tours of the HML research facilities when he visited the island. An annual event that was greatly anticipated by the HML faculty and staff was a luncheon hosted by the Pauleys. The faculty, students, and the entire staff were always invited and made to feel very welcome by the Pauley family. On these occasions, Ed and Bobbe Pauley demonstrated a remarkable ability to remember the names of staff and students at HML, and their research interests. Edwin would frequently ask probing questions, and would challenge his guests to pursue an area of research that he thought was important. I had fond recollections of attending these annual affairs, and meeting his many distinguished guests. Pauley frequently asked me to conduct tours of the Marine Laboratory for his guests, and he would refer to it as "my marine lab," a designation that the HML staff and students considered totally appropriate.

As the Hawaii Marine Laboratory was established to support the university's goals of teaching, research, and service, informally as an adjunct of the Zoology Department, it basically served as a field station in which faculty and students pursued their personal research interests. It also served as a base for field trips for classes such as ichthyology, invertebrate zoology, and marine ecology. An undergraduate introductory course in oceanography (Oc 201) has been given for many years. This is a lecture course, but it had a required Saturday field trip to Coconut Island for all enrolled students; an experience that changed the lives of hundreds of students over the years, and was often cited as the experience that directed many into a career in marine science.

| Albert Tester's Research on the Tuna, Baitfish, and Sharks

The Hawaiian Tuna Packers enterprise of Christian Holmes, evolved on Coconut Island, had moved its base of operations to Kewalo Basin in Honolulu. The fishery was based on pole and line capture, primarily of the abundant skipjack tuna (*aku*). The tuna were attracted to the vessels and stimulated into a feeding frenzy by tossing live bait, mostly the Hawaiian anchovy (*nehu*) into the water around the fishing boat, and then catching the frenzied tuna with hooks suspended from short poles. The two main sources of baitfish upon which the fishery depended were in the sheltered waters of Pearl Harbor and Kāneʻohe Bay. Because Pearl Harbor was a major military installation with restricted access, Kāneʻohe Bay became the primary source of baitfish. Early baitfish research at Coconut Island was done by Albert Tester on the population dynamics, capture, and holding of these delicate animals, and in the response of tuna to various chemical stimuli, as well as to artificial bait.[252] Tester's baitfish studies ran from 1948 until he joined the federal fishery service in 1955.

Baitfish research was continued by Garth Murphy, Wayne Baldwin, Tom Clarke, and others at HML. The tuna baitfish program was one of the longest-running research efforts at Coconut Island. It is a happy irony that the legacy of Christian Holmes's interest in tuna translated into the focus of research on the island that he developed and with the commercial enterprise he nurtured.

When Tester returned to the University of Hawaiʻi in 1958, he pursued a program on the ecology, behavior, and sensory physiology of sharks. A shark attack that killed a young surfer, Billy Weaver, at Lanikai Beach on Windward Oʻahu, did much to propel Tester and his graduate

| *Dr. Albert L. Tester, whose early research at Coconut Island was on tuna baitfish. His later research was on sharks. Masao Miyamoto*

| *A floating laboratory at Coconut Island that allowed 24-hour observations of baitfish upon which the local tuna fishery depended. HIMB Collection*

students in this line of research. In response to the Weaver incident, Tester directed the Cooperative Shark Research and Control Program for the State of Hawai'i from 1967–1969. It had as its goal to determine the distribution, abundance, and behavior of sharks in inshore waters mostly around the island of O'ahu, and to learn more about their habits. In addition, observations were made on a few captive sharks held in the ponds at Coconut Island. Tester and some of his graduate students also conducted this research at Enewetak, where sharks were abundant, and observations and experiments could be conducted on captive animals as well as those found in their natural environment.[253]

The Enewetak Marine Biological Laboratory (EMBL)

Robert Hiatt had established a close relationship with Sidney Galler, director of the Office of Naval Research. Galler asked the eminent marine biologist, H. Burr Steinbach of the University of Chicago to visit Enewetak to consider the feasibility of establishing a marine biological laboratory that would focus on studies of radiation exposure on marine organisms. Steinbach recommended that such a laboratory be established, and that it be operated by the University of Hawai'i. A contract was signed in June 1954 to establish the Enewetak Marine Biological Laboratory (EMBL) on the island of Medren on Enewetak Atoll, with Robert Hiatt appointed as the inaugural director.[254] Buildings were

| (top right) Charles "Naka" and Shizu Nakamoto by the caretaker's residence on the south side of Coconut Island. The current resident caretaker for HIMB is Naka's nephew, Wayne. Nakamoto Collection

| (bottom right) The Enewetak Marine Biological Laboratory (later named the Mid-Pacific Research Laboratory) on Medren island, Enewatok atoll, Marshall Islands. The laboratory was managed from Coconut Island, providing access to an extraordinary marine environment for more than thirty years. Ernst Reese

modified, a seawater system installed, and occupancy and research was encouraged between the scheduled test nuclear detonations, the last of which was conducted in 1958.

The operation of EMBL was managed by Hiatt with assistance from the maintenance and clerical support staff of HIMB. The laboratory operation was supported by a contract with the AEC and its successors, the Energy Research and Development Agency and the U.S. Department of Energy. For more than 30 years it provided extraordinary opportunities for HML and HIMB researchers and students. From 1954 to 1987, 1,028 persons—scientists, their assistants, graduate students—conducted research at the Enewetak Laboratory. The environment at EMBL was very conductive to research productivity. Food, lodging, transportation, and a variety of support services were provided to those scientists whose proposals were accepted by the EMBL directorate. Hiatt was director until 1969; myself, 1969–1975; Stephen V. Smith, 1975–1977; Ernst S. Reese, 1977–1979; and myself again, from 1979 to 1987 when the lab closed.[255]

The Enewetak Laboratory hosted several groups engaged in major research efforts relying on the EMBL facilities and support services. One such team research effort supported by the National Science Foundation was code named SYMBIOS, and organized by HIMB scientist Robert Johannes. Twenty-three scientists (including six from HIMB) and the Scripps Institution research vessel *Alpha Helix* spent nine weeks at Enewetak Atoll conducting what has been described as "one of the most comprehensive studies of a coral reef ever undertaken."[256]

| ALBERT BANNER, LABORATORY DIRECTOR (1955–1963)

Albert "Hank" Banner served as the second director of the Hawaii Marine Laboratory while a full-time professor of zoology, and actively researched the fish poison, ciguatera, as well as Alphaeid (snapping shrimp) taxonomy. While Banner was serving with the military on

Saipan in the Marianas Islands, he encountered this problem and devoted his research to it. Ciguatera is widespread in the tropical Pacific and Caribbean. The toxin appeared to originate in an alga, and was passed

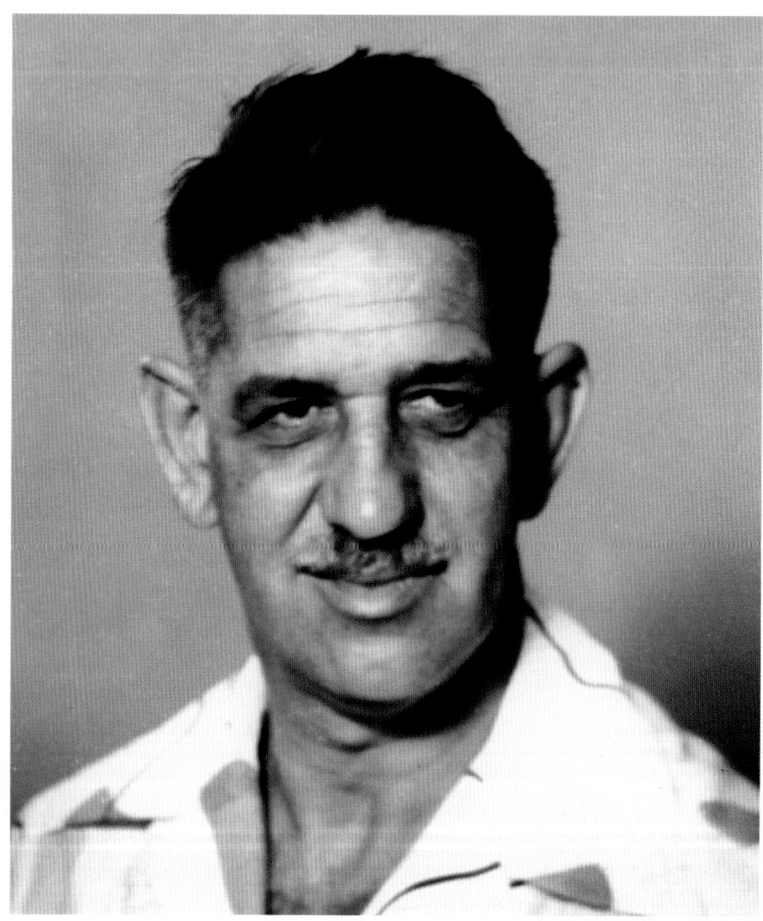

| *Dr. Albert H. "Hank" Banner, the second director of the Hawaii Marine Laboratory from 1955–1963. He was the principal investigator on the ciguatera fish poisoning study and also conducted research on snapping shrimp taxonomy. HIMB Collection*

through the food chain to top carnivores. Banner assembled a team of researchers in the mid-1950s to determine: 1) the molecular structure of ciguatoxin; 2) the origin of the toxin in the marine environment; 3) a diagnostic test to distinguish toxic from non-toxic fish; and 4) to find an effective human therapy. The team consisted of scientists and technicians with diverse backgrounds and interests. They included chemists Paul Scheuer, Tamao Yoshida, Takeshi Yasumoto, and Satoshi Sasaki; marine biologists Hank Banner, Jack Randall, Twesukdi Piyakarncha-na, and myself; physiologists Martin Rayner and Charles Alender; and the many other technical and support people that were needed to collect, process, and analyze large quantities of toxic fish from throughout the Pacific.[257, 258] Field stations and expeditions for the collection of epidemiological data and specimens were established at Palmyra and Christmas Islands in the Line Islands, New Caledonia, Fiji, Samoa, Tonga, Cook Islands, Kiribati (Gilbert Islands), Johnston Island, Marshall Islands, Tahiti, and in the Ryukyu Islands.

| THE FIRE OF 1961

On a quiet New Year's Eve afternoon in 1961, Bob Miranda, resident caretaker for the Pauley estate, was on a routine boat run to the Lilipuna pier. As he looked back toward the island he saw smoke rising from the main laboratory building and sounded the fire alarm. In those days that meant alerting the Nakamoto family on the island and calling

| *(top right) Phil Helfrich (right) and Hank Banner (center) of HML and biochemist Satoshi Sasaki of Tokyo University with a specimen of red snapper that was implicated in many cases of ciguatera fish poisoning in the Pacific. They were part of a research team that was attempting to discover the origin of the toxin in the marine environment and determine its molecular structure. HIMB Collection*
| *(bottom right) Hank Banner and his wife, Dee, collaborating on snapping shrimp taxonomy. HIMB Collection*

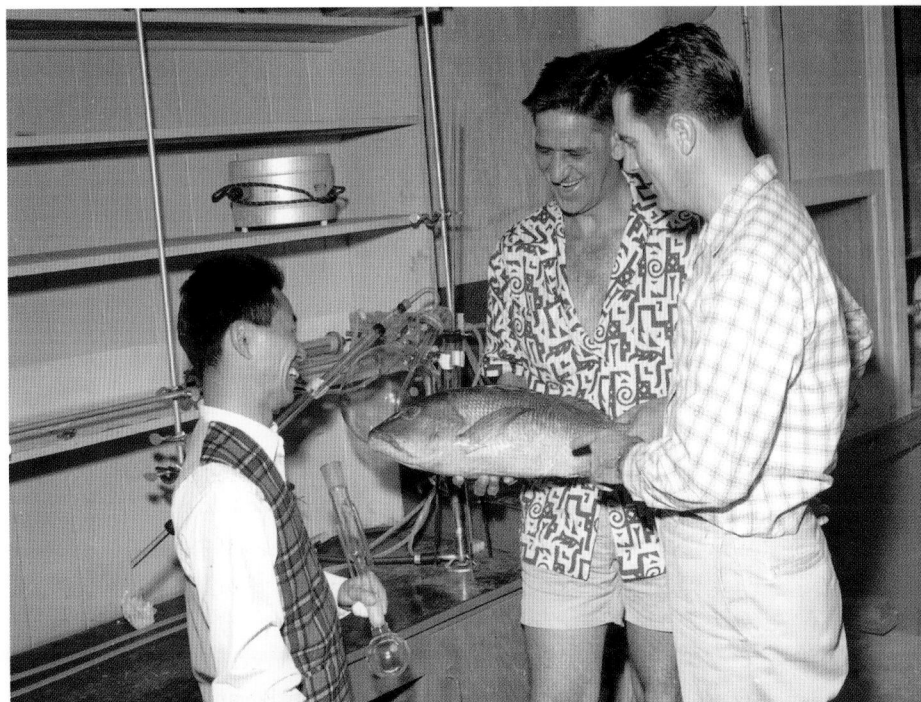

Lester Zukeran and the Kāne'ohe Fire Department for help. The marine base at Mōkapu sent a fire boat to help control the inferno, and the fire department dispatched firefighters to the island, but by the time they arrived the main laboratory building was completely engulfed in flame. As near as anyone could figure, the fire started in the center of the building, in a room that housed the laboratory's only fume hood and a storage area for highly flammable solvents such as ether and alcohol. It was assumed that since this was the area in which combustible solvents were stored, they were somehow the cause of the fire. As important in many ways as the loss of the building itself, researchers' notes and papers were destroyed, representing months and years of work. Dr. Banner and I lost four years of data on fish toxins, and Banner lost seven years of data and collections of snapping shrimp. Numerous manuscripts in preparation burned to ash, including one almost-completed doctoral dissertation. These were the days of manual typewriters and carbon paper—no back-up computer files! It was an enormous loss to UH marine science programs.[259]

After the 1961 fire, steps were taken to assure that research programs funded by the federal government could indeed be sustained. Banner took the initiative to maintain the momentum of the ciguatera research program. He arranged with the U.S. Air Force to transport a group of 25 volunteers from HIMB to the island of Palmyra for a week of intensive collecting of toxic fish over the New Year's holiday (1962–1963). Several thousand pounds of samples of the highly toxic red snapper *Lutjanus bohar* were returned to Hawai'i to sustain the program.

After the fire, Hiatt initiated an emergency request to the National Science Foundation, and they responded with a grant to construct a new 2,000 square-foot classroom-laboratory building. A basic single-story, concrete block classroom-laboratory was completed in 1964 on the east lagoon with a $350,000 grant. It was appropriately named the NSF laboratory and is still in use.

In addition to Hiatt's request to the National Science Foundation, an appeal was also made to the State of Hawai'i for funds for an additional building to replace the destroyed laboratory. The legislature was interested but had some concerns about establishing a public facility on privately held land. They asked the attorney general's office to investigate the land ownership on Coconut Island. Coconut Island developer Christian Holmes added around sixteen acres of coral reef and sand dredged from the subtidal zone for the expansion of his original island. As mentioned in Chapter 4, the attorney general's office judged that land accreted from the subtidal area properly belonged to the State of Hawai'i.

(top) Ceremony laying the cornerstone of the new laboratory on Coconut Island. Right to left: Robert Hiatt, Philip Helfrich, Vernon Brock, Rev. Charles Ke'ekumano, and an unidentified representative of E. Black Construction Co. Masao Miyamoto

(bottom) Dedication of the new Hawai'i Institute of Marine Biology on Coconut Island in August 1966. Right to left: Vernon Brock, Edwin Pauley, and Robert Hiatt. HIMB Collection

Once the land issue was settled, the services of an architect were obtained to design a building that would meet the growing needs of HIMB. Once again, Edwin Pauley showed his generosity and willingness to help in a time of need. The planning and construction of the new marine laboratory for Coconut Island was under the direction of the state Department of Accounting and General Services (DAGS). It went out to bid, and all bids came in substantially over the budget allowed by the State Legislature and Edwin Pauley. DAGS solution was to hire the low bidder to redesign the building to be accommodated within the existing budget. The result was a building with unfinished laboratories, exposed steel beams, and many features that were to become a challenge to future directors of HIMB. But the lab had a new laboratory, and students and scientists looked forward to occupying it after so many years in temporary, sub-standard quarters.

The many delays in the planning process and the urgency to get research projects into permanent quarters caused much pressure to get the project under way, and it was decided to forgo a groundbreaking ceremony. As the construction started, however, Hawaiian workers employed by the contractor pointed out that the site had not been properly blessed, and all work immediately ceased. Considering local customs, it was deemed advisable to hold a blessing ceremony. Since ground had already been broken, an observance was planned with the laying of a cornerstone. The ceremony took place on 2 August 1965, with the blessing conducted by UH Regent, Reverend Charles Keʻekumano. The building was completed on schedule, and the dedication of the laboratory was attended by Edwin and Barbara Pauley, Robert Hiatt, Vernon Brock, and myself, all of whom had been agents in the creation of the new structure.

With all its terrible losses, the fire was a turning point for HIMB. Two new laboratory buildings were constructed, and this modest field station started down the road toward becoming a world-class marine laboratory.

| (top) The newly dedicated Hawaiʻi Institute of Marine Biology main building on Coconut Island. HIMB Collection
| (bottom) An aerial view of the newly constructed laboratory building, Hawaiʻi Institute of Marine Biology on the east lagoon, Coconut Island. P. Helfrich

Under the sponsorship of the Office of Naval Research and the National Science Foundation, a U.S.-Japan Cooperative Research Program in Marine Toxins was funded in 1966–1969. This involved Hawai'i (HIMB/University of Hawai'i), Japan (Fisheries Biochemistry/Tokyo University), and France (L'Institut de Recherches Medical Louis Malardé, Tahiti) in a collaborative research program on ciguatera. A major milestone in this program was in a "Symposium on Ichtyosarcotoxisme" held in Tahiti in August of 1968 to report significant progress on all aspects of the research.[260] This was the first of several multinational collaborative research programs and was instrumental in establishing HIMB as an internationally recognized marine laboratory.

After 35 years of intensive research effort by Banner's team in Hawai'i, with collaborators in Japan and Tahiti, significant progress was made in accomplishing all of the original goals of the program.[261] The molecular structure of ciguatoxin was illucidated by Scheuer and collaborators; its origin in the marine environment was determined to be a dinoflagellate, *Gambierdiscus toxicus*.[262] A simple and rapid test for toxic fish was developed,[263] and a treatment for persons stricken with ciguatera was found.[264]

VERNON BROCK, LABORATORY DIRECTOR (1963–1969)

A native of California, Vernon Brock came to Hawai'i in 1944 to take a position as director of fish and game for the Territory of Hawaii. He later joined the National Marine Fisheries Service.

In 1963, Hiatt, then dean of research, was convinced of a major opportunity for marine research related to the expansion of the fishing industry of the central Pacific. He recruited Vernon E. Brock from the Federal Fisheries Service to become the new director of the Hawaii Marine Laboratory.

In February 1965, Brock published *A Proposed Program for Hawaiian Fisheries* in which he proposed a major initiative in fisheries development

based on research centered at HML.[265] The 1965 Hawai'i State Legislature passed a bill authorizing twelve new professional and technical positions to develop a fisheries program, and by doing so, transformed

| Vernon E. Brock, eminent fishery biologist, the third director of HML/HIMB from 1963–1969. Masao Miyamoto

the lab into the first organized research institute at the University of Hawai'i. It was renamed the Hawai'i Institute of Marine Biology (HIMB).

The events of Vernon Brock's directorship clearly follows Hiatt's strategy for HIMB. Brock was a fisheries biologist of international stature with a vision for the sustained rational management of the vast tropical Pacific oceanic fisheries. He demonstrated considerable insight and innovation in dealing with a large spectrum of research problems in development of pelagic fisheries in the tropical Pacific in order to insure a maximum sustained yield in the principal component pelagic fisheries.

| PAULEY–UNIVERSITY OF CALIFORNIA VISITING SCHOLARS PROGRAM

One of the most successful early programs at HML was the Pauley–University of California Visiting Scholars Program. At the time he invited Hiatt to establish the laboratory on Coconut Island, Edwin Pauley envisioned mutual involvement of faculty and students of the University of California and the University of Hawai'i. He hoped they could take advantage of the superb environment that Coconut Island offered. The program, administered for many years by professor Theodore Papenfuss of UC-Berkeley, and later by professor Leonard Muscatine of UCLA, brought faculty and students from the California campuses to Coconut Island for scholarly work. It is uncertain how this arrangement was formalized, however the University of Hawai'i catalogue for 1948 notes that the newly founded Hawaii Marine Laboratory on Coconut Island was jointly administered by the University of Hawai'i and the University of California. Pauley-sponsored researchers came for a few weeks during school holidays, for the summer, or for a sabbatical leave that extended up to a year. They were able to reside on the island, or in the nearby community, in close proximity to their work. Typical of field stations and marine labs of the day, housing accommodations on Coconut Island

were primarily communal, although single faculty apartments could be made available.

Among the University of California eminent visiting scholars who received Pauley Foundation sponsorship was Dr. Howard Bern, a distinguished scientist and member of the U.S. National Academy of Sciences. Bern has been a regular visitor to Coconut Island for more than fifty years, and has been a valuable influence on the faculty and students at Coconut Island. The Pauley Foundation also sponsored other outstanding visitors from UC campuses including Drs. Leonard Muscatine and Joseph DiStefano from UCLA, Donald Crosby from UC-Davis, and Robert Trench from UC-Santa Barbara. The program sponsored

| *Lyndon Johnson observing experiments in the shark pond on Coconut Island. HIMB Collection*

many faculty and students who had a positive impact on University of Hawai'i scientists and students. Examples of productive exchanges, collaborative relationships, cooperative research efforts, and lifelong friendships among academics and the Pauley family abound. Students received the added benefit of working with experienced researchers on a day-to-day basis, allowing them to get a real feel for their area of marine biology and inspiring them to continue in the field. Strong ties and working relationships were established with all the University of California campuses, and frequently a visiting student would benefit from the program and later return as a UC faculty member. Three early Pauley-supported beneficiaries of the program, Ernst Reese from UCLA, and George Losey and Richard Grigg from Scripps Institute of Oceanography, would go on to become distinguished members of the University of Hawai'i faculty at Coconut Island.

| John Bardach, Laboratory Director (1971–1977)

In 1969 Vernon Brock resigned from the position as director of HIMB due to failing health. I assumed the interim directorship of HIMB (1970–1971) while a decision was implemented to engage a new director via national recruitment. Dr. John Bardach was appointed HIMB director in 1971. A recognized scholar and researcher (he co-authored a definitive text on aquaculture[266]), Bardach had a broad range of interests.

As a recognized scholar-researcher, Bardach spent a great deal of time traveling to conferences and symposia around the world. The operation of a marine laboratory was not his principal interest, but as his associate director, I was able to assist in this area as well as gain valuable experience running a marine lab. This arrangement continued until 1 January 1975 when I accepted a position as the founding director of the International Center for Living Aquatic Resources Management (ICLARM), The WorldFish Center of the Rockefeller Foundation.

| Dr. John E. Bardach, Director, Hawai'i Institute of Marine Biology, 1971–1977.
Masao Miyamoto

The late 1970s were a period of concern for the future of HIMB. Several HIMB faculty moved their offices to the UH-Mānoa campus as there was a vocal element that felt Coconut Island was too isolated and inconvenient. An external committee was convened which called for a revitalization of HIMB. They noted that the institute lacked leadership and recommended that it be moved to the more convenient location at Kewalo Basin in Honolulu.[267] The plan for the Coconut Island facilities was to relegate them once again to the 1940s status of part-time field station. Fortunately for the future of HIMB, this recommendation was largely ignored.

Bardach directed HIMB until 1977 when he resigned to take a position as a senior advisor in the Resource Systems Institute of the East-West Center in Honolulu. Upon Bardach's resignation, William

Coops, executive director of the Research Corporation of the University of Hawai'i became interim director (1977–1978), and in 1978 the position was offered to an HIMB researcher, John Caperon. He resigned in 1980 to pursue personal interests in Australia.

AQUACULTURE RESEARCH AND DEVELOPMENT AT HIMB

Aquaculture research at HIMB began in the late 1960s and gained momentum through the '70s and '80s. During this early period the research was mostly applied, aimed at identifying species and determining the feasibility of developing commercially viable production systems. Attempts were made to develop plans for the culture and husbandry of a variety of organisms that showed promise for commercial or recreational use. This activity was in the context of education, and those involved were researchers, technicians, and primarily students. As the program progressed, with mentors like John Bardach, Ed Laws, Arlo Fast, and E. Gordon Grau, HIMB became a credible place to pursue this discipline.

Early aquaculture research was exploratory with little experience in the fish culture to draw on beyond the salmonids, carps, and some shellfish. Some of the first candidates for culture were tropical abalone, octopus, *ogo* (edible Hawaiian seaweed), penaeid shrimp, black- and gold-lipped oysters, rabbit fish, mahimahi, catfish, tilapia, and freshwater prawn (Macobrachium). Development of a program for the culture of a species usually involved the establishment of a brood stock or a reliable source of seed, suitable feed for the various life stages, strategies for stocking grow-out ponds/enclosures, disease/predator control, harvesting and post-harvest preservation, and marketing.

Aquaculture development at HIMB benefited from several federally funded programs. The one with the greatest impact was the Sea Grant College Program at the University of Hawai'i. It provided seed money and funds in competitive grants to investigators exploring new aquaculture systems, species, or culture techniques. Sea Grant developed an effective extension program that provided dissemination to private commercial ventures of new techniques and discoveries generated on Coconut Island. In the 1960s and '70s most of the students in aquaculture programs at HIMB were at least partially funded by Sea Grant.

The early 1980s presented a challenge to HIMB. There was a need to invigorate the organization with individuals who were first-class scientists with the potential for highly productive research careers and the capacity to integrate the efforts of many people and use them effectively as a team. E. Gordon Grau was hired on a joint appointment (HIMB-Zoology Department) in 1982 and proved to be such a person. He was a well-trained scientist and organizer, an excellent teacher, and a dedicated scholar-researcher in both the theoretical aspects of environmental physiology and endocrinology, and their application to aquaculture.

With the arrival of Grau in 1982, research on aquaculture took on a whole new dimension. His research on some of the basic life processes at the cellular and molecular level allowed those working to develop culture systems in fish to better understand and regulate nutrition, growth, reproduction, and saltwater balance, and interactions of fish with their environment as controlled by the release of hormones of the neuroendocrine system.

In 1983, HIMB was chosen to participate in a program of the U.S. Agency for International Development called the Pond Dynamics/Aquaculture Collaborative Research Support Program (PD/A CRSP). Its objective was to bring technology developed at U.S. universities to the developing world. HIMB and UH-Mānoa were coupled with the following universities: Oregon State, Michigan, Michigan State, California-Davis, Arkansas at Little Rock, and Auburn. Counterpart institutions were in Indonesia, Thailand, Philippines, Panama, Honduras, Rwanda, and Kenya.

In 1987, the U.S. Department of Agriculture established regional centers to support aquaculture research programs. HIMB, the UH Sea Grant Program, the Oceanic Institute, and the University of Guam participated in the Center for Tropical and Subtropical Aquaculture (CTSA). The programs allowed HIMB researchers to interact with colleagues across the world, and to exchange ideas, and hopefully work out common solutions to aquaculture problems in different settings.

ANIMAL BEHAVIOR RESEARCH

Drs. Ernst Reese and George Losey have been active and productive scholar-researchers on the behavior of marine animals at both the Coconut Island and Enewetak laboratories. Reese studied the social behavior of reef fishes, the relationship of food and feeding behavior, the co-evolution of corals and reef fish, and the use of certain groups of coral feeding fish as indicators of conditions of coral reefs. Losey's research interests include various aspects of ethology and behavioral ecology of reef fish. For several years he conducted research on the

| Distinguished animal behaviorist and Nobel laureate Konrad Lorenz (left), fish collector Lester Zukeran, and HIMB's well-known ethologist Ernst Reese. Lorenz spent several weeks at Coconut Island as a guest of Dr. Reese, interacting with students and staff on a daily basis. Ernst Reese

behavior of fish that pick parasites from the bodies of other fish. His current research is centered on ultraviolet vision and coloration in coral reef fishes, and the effects of UV light on tropical fishes.

Reese and Losey have participated in Pauley Summer Programs on reef animal behavior, sex change in fishes, and ultraviolet light on coral reefs. They pioneered research on the many relationships between behavior, feeding ecology, and the overall condition and health of coral reef communities. Notable in the many activities of this program was a six-week visit by Austrian Nobel laureate Konrad Lorenz in the 1970s. Lorenz interacted with the entire staff of HIMB, and all benefited from his insights into the behavior of Hawaiian reef fishes.

CORAL AND ENVIRONMENTAL STUDIES

Coconut Island, located in the inner waters of Kāne'ohe Bay and protected by an extensive barrier reef system (16 sq. km), supports a rich and diverse biota. Research on corals and coral reef ecosystems have always had a special significance at Coconut Island because of the access to a live coral reef immediately adjacent to the Point Laboratory on the island. Researchers have direct access to the fringing reef on the windward side of Coconut Island as well as to a facility in an ideal location for conducting replicate controlled studies of corals to monitor various physical and chemical parameters of the local environment.

Environmental concerns were of major importance to HIMB researchers long before the creation of the Environmental Protection Agency. The Hawaiian Electric Company proposed to build a power generating plant near He'eia Kea on Kāne'ohe Bay. Coconut Island scientists heard of the plan at the last minute. They immediately sought a two-year delay in the project while the impact of heated water from condensers associated with an electric plant could be explored. They set out to determine the thermal limit of Hawaiian corals, and set up the appropriate experiments at the Point Laboratory. They discovered that corals live very close to their upper thermal limits, and the installation proposed by Hawaiian Electric would have disastrous consequences to the Kāne'ohe Bay ecosystem, killing its many ancient coral reefs.[268] This early work provided essential information to interpret current concerns about global warming and the resultant coral bleaching.[269]

HIMB research in the 1960s on coral reef communities in Kāne'ohe Bay also influenced the management of sewage discharges on Windward O'ahu, with far-reaching implications for other tropical marine ecosystems. Studies were initiated on the effect of the onset of a major municipal sewage discharge into the south end of Kāne'ohe Bay. The discharge, in excess of one million gallons per day from two outfalls had a profound affect on the ecology of the bay. It decimated coral reefs, reduced water clarity, and caused a proliferation of a blue-green bubble alga that smothered the corals. An organization called "Kaneohe Bay in Crisis" was created with leadership from a Coconut Island scientist. The public outcry resulted in a decision to remove the outfall from Kāne'ohe Bay entirely, and divert the sewage to a deep-water discharge pipe off nearby Kailua Bay where currents could disperse it to the open

| *The Point Laboratory adjacent to the fringing coral reef on the eastern shore of Coconut Island. Much of the HIMB coral research was centered at this facility since it was established in the early 1960s. J. O'Reilly*

| *(above) Paul Jokiel conducting experiments on corals at the Point Laboratory, Coconut Island. Jokiel began as an assistant researcher in 1969 and has done much to establish HIMB as a world leader in coral research. Kuulei Rodgers*
| *(right) HIMB biologists conducting an underwater suvey of coral reefs in the vicinity of Coconut Island. Kuulei Rodgers*

ocean. Both laboratory and field studies of the process and dynamics of eutrophication (nutrient enrichment) were conducted by John Caperon, Allan Cattell, Edward Laws, Paul Jokiel, Marlin Atkinson, Steve Coles, and others.

Removal of sewage from Kāneʻohe Bay in 1979, to the alternate outfall in adjacent Kailua Bay provided a unique opportunity to study the effects of the removal of a major perturbation from a coral reef community. The project was called the "Sewage Relaxation Study." The research was funded for five years by the Environmental Protection Agency[270] and was directed by Stephen Smith in collaboration with Richard Brock, Keith Chave, Evan Evens, Paul Jokiel, Edward Laws, W. J. Kimmerer, and T. Walsh. It provided fundamental information about the dynamics of various contaminants in a perturbed estuarine ecosystem.[271] Later studies would address the role of zooxanthellae (symbiotic algae in corals) on the calcification process, the effect of ultraviolet light on corals, and the impact of global warming and the bleaching phenomenon. A major discovery was made at the Point Laboratory, when a visiting investigator from Germany, Ludwig Franzisket, demonstrated that corals could live autotrophically.[272] Recent conservation-oriented research has led to the development of coral transplantation, allowing the recolonization of reefs denuded by shipwrecks, dredging, or by natural disasters such as hurricanes.

A highlight for students, staff, and scientists at the lab is the annual spawning of the coral. Discovered by HIMB coral scientists, on a the night of a particular phase of the moon, billions of tiny animals are spawned, creating the next generation of coral and the next thin layer of tropical reef.

These are some of the studies that have produced basic information required for the rational environmental management of tropical marine coastal ecosystems.[273] As a result, HIMB became a world leader in coral studies—just as Hiatt anticipated in 1948.

| Philip Helfrich, Laboratory Director (1980–1993)

Upon my return to HIMB in 1980, I saw my role as instilling a renewed sense of purpose in the staff by providing direction, support, encouragement, and resources for a strong research program in marine

| Dr. Philip Helfrich, Director, Hawaiʻi Institute of Marine Biology, 1980–1993. HIMB Collection

| *(above and opposite) The Edwin W. Pauley Marine Laboratory complex. Main laboratory building (left) containing four laboratory modules with support facilities and the William R. Pagen and Barbara Pauley Pagen Library. The adjacent Pauley classroom and lunch room (right). J. O'Reilly*

purchase the privately owned portion of Coconut Island as well. The grant covered the construction of three buildings including a modern state-of-the-art laboratory building, a classroom/lunchroom building, and a wet laboratory on the east lagoon dedicated to research facilities for the study of pelagic fish—the Edwin W. Pauley Marine Laboratory.

PAULEY FAMILY—THE NEXT GENERATION

When Edwin Pauley passed away in 1981, the family sold Coconut Island to Katsuhiro Kawaguchi and became less frequent visitors to Hawai'i, but continued to support programs at HIMB. The relationship was maintained through contact between Pauley's widow, Barbara Pauley Pagen, her new husband William Pagen, and me. During my tenure as director, when I presented the proposal to fund planning and construction of the Pauley Marine Laboratory, a continuing cordial relationship existed with Mrs. Pauley Pagen, with increased involvement of her son Dr. Stephen Pauley and his wife Marylyn.

Although the offer to support building the Edwin W. Pauley Marine Laboratory was clearly the decision of his mother, it was Stephen Pauley who solicited an offer to consider our proposal. He then facilitated the transaction that would result in the largest single grant from a private party made to the University of Hawai'i at that time. The Pauley family's generosity provided for the acquisition of a new marine laboratory, and, in anonymity, for purchase of the central part of the island from Kawaguchi.

The relationship that exists between the Pauley family and the Hawai'i Institute of Marine Biology was aptly expressed by Stephen Pauley in the eulogy for his illustrious mother at her funeral on 13 September 2002:

She often held receptions for the scientists and staff at the Hawai'i Institute of Marine Biology on Coconut Island. They were like second family to us all.

biology in areas that would take full advantage of the unique environment surrounding Coconut Island. In this I was again assisted by the Pauley family who agreed to the inauguration of the Pauley Summer Program. Encouraged by the frequent public interest in the island, I instituted a program of volunteer assistants. I placed high priority on the acquisition of new positions and the recruitment of excellent young faculty to invigorate HIMB's research programs and to initiate new research endeavors. I was fortunate in being able to recruit some outstanding researchers: E. Gordon Grau, Kim Holland, and Marlin and Shannon Atkinson in shared appointments with the Zoology, Oceanography, and Animal Science Departments.

With vibrant new staff and faculty on board the need for new laboratory facilities soon became evident. I prepared a proposal for the construction of a modern, new marine laboratory and applied to the federal government for support, to no avail. A surprise visit by Stephen Pauley left me encouraged to apply to the Edwin W. Pauley Foundation. And in another act of extraordinary generosity, the Pauley Foundation responded with funds, not only to construct the new lab, but to

| *The Pauley Pelagic Fish Laboratory with tanks capable of holding large pelagic species such as tunas and sharks. Coconut Island was the first place tunas were successfully kept in captivity in ponds constructed by Christian Holmes. J. O'Reilly*

Those friendships last to today. The gifts of Coconut Island to the University of Hawaiʻi, the new Edwin W. Pauley Marine Lab and the William R. Pagen Library on Coconut Island honor those close ties. Mom loved Coconut Island, and in my opinion was the person most responsible for preserving its natural beauty. I think the aloha spirit of Hawaiʻi made her own life much richer.

During his tenure as interim HIMB director, and to the present day as Sea Grant director, Gordon Grau has maintained excellent rapport with Stephen and Marylyn Pauley, as has current HIMB director, Dr. Jo-Ann Leong. Pauley, a medical doctor, credits his interest in science back to his youth, when he and his brother spent summers assisting HIMB researchers in fascinating scientific tasks around the laboratory.

| EDWIN W. PAULEY SUMMER PROGRAM IN MARINE BIOLOGY

Summer instructional and research programs for visitors and residents were initiated in 1967, 1968, and 1978 (then sponsored by the University of Hawaiʻi and the National Science Foundation), and from 1983 to the present (sponsored by the Edwin W. Pauley Foundation) as the Edwin W. Pauley Summer Program in Marine Biology. The first of this series of summer programs, similar to a type that traditionally had been offered at other U.S. marine laboratories, was proposed by myself in 1967 and 1968. The 1967 course was on coelenterate biology, and the instructors were Leonard Muscatine of UCLA, Howard Lenhoff of the University of Miami, and Larry Davis of the University of Hawaiʻi. The 1968 course was on molluscan biology and was directed by E. Alison Kay of the University of Hawaiʻi, Martin Wells of Oxford University, Vera Fretter of the University of Reading, and Alan Kohn of the University of Washington. John Caperon presented a summer course in 1978 on corals. After that time the program was not offered again until 1983,

Laboratory work in the first summer program (1967) with Larry Davis and students. HIMB Collection

when the continuous series sponsored by the Pauley Foundation began. (See Appendix, Table 4 for list of topics).

Topics chosen in the Pauley Summer Program reflect the research interests of an individual or group of researchers at HIMB, and one that could be addressed in the laboratory or in the field in Kāneʻohe Bay. This has been a remarkably productive program that has resulted in

countless collaborative relationships, as well as publications of significant advancements in marine biological research. It is a clear indication of the commitment of the Pauley family to marine education and research on Coconut Island that has continued from the first commitment of Edwin Pauley to Bob Hiatt—an assurance of support that has persisted to the present time.

| DISTINGUISHED FRIENDS OF HIMB

The long-standing interest of the Japanese imperial family in marine biology prompted an invitation to HIMB colleagues John E. Randall and me to visit Tokyo and have an audience with Crown Prince Akihito, son of the Emperor Hirohito, to discuss a mutual interest in marine fish. Subsequently, Ernst Reese of HIMB also had a private audience with the crown prince to discuss the common interests of the two marine biologists. All arrangements were made by the crown prince's mentor in marine biology, professor Tokiharu Abe of Tokyo University, a longtime friend of Randall, Reese, and myself. A few years later, while visiting Hawai'i, Akihito's brother, Prince Hitachi, honored the

| (left) Prince Hitachi, brother of the current emperor of Japan, examines specimens of living coral during a visit to Coconut Island. P. Helfrich

| (far left) HIM Emperor Akihito of Japan. He and his family are enthusiastic marine biologists and friends of HIMB. Japanese Consulate, Honolulu

University of Hawai'i and HIMB by visiting Coconut Island, where he was hosted by President and Mrs. Albert Simone and the staff at HIMB Crown Prince Akihito has now assumed the Japanese throne, but the emperor still retains an interest in marine biology, and occasionally contacts HIMB's Jack Randall to discuss fish and challenge him to a friendly game of tennis.

FISHERIES BIOLOGY RESEARCH PROGRAM —
DR. KIM HOLLAND AND ASSOCIATES

Fisheries biology is a long-standing component of the research program at HIMB.[274] As noted earlier, a major thrust of the program with Albert Tester was fisheries biology, and the twelve original positions provided to the Coconut Island laboratory in 1965 were all specifically allocated for a fisheries program. Current studies include investigation into the reproduction and development of fishes, trophic relationships within Kāne'ohe Bay ecosystems, population dynamics and ecology of baitfish, and the role of fish aggregation devices in the management of fisheries resources. The use of conservation zones as fisheries management tools and the bioenergetics and behavior of mobile species are being investigated by tagging of reef fish, sharks, turtles, and tunas.[275] Special emphasis has been placed on shark behavior by Holland and his associates, including an analysis of some of Tester's recently unearthed shark data.

| *(top right) Kim Holland completing the surgical implantation of an electronic tracking device in a 75-pound bigeye tuna. Holland has been a world leader in the use of telemetry technology to track the movements of tunas, marlin, and sharks. K. Holland*
| *(bottom right) Carl Meyer and Dean Grubbs preparing to attach an electronic tracking device to a large, uncooperative tiger shark. K. Holland*

Biogeochemistry and Remote Sensing of Coral Reefs — Dr. Marlin Atkinson and Associates

Marlin Atkinson's major research interest is in biogeochemistry of coral reefs. His approach is a broad scale examination of a coral reef ecosystem in contrast to focused studies by Jokiel and others at the Point Laboratory who have looked at individual components of coral

| *Marlin Atkinson conducts research on the biogeochemistry of coral reefs utilizing a device he constructed to observe the hydrodynamics and fate of nutrients in water flowing over a simulated coral reef community. M. Atkinson*

ecosystems. Atkinson's primary emphasis is on the uptake and cycling of inorganic nutrients and their relationship to carbon production and calcification. The cycling of nutrients on a coral reef is strongly influenced by hydrodynamics of water flowing over the reef and the distribution of different bottom communities. His research involved the design and maintenance of three flumes containing assemblages of reef animals and plants in the laboratory at HIMB, and conducting field research on the 16 sq. km barrier reef in Kāne'ohe Bay. He also experimented on the same scale on reefs throughout the Pacific, Atlantic, and Indian Oceans.

Atkinson and his colleagues have contributed to the solution of several problems in this area, and have clarified much about the dynamics of coral reefs that were unresolved in the past.[276] In 1995, Marlin Atkinson conducted the Edwin W. Pauley summer course in the biogeochemistry of coral reefs.

As envisioned during the laboratory's founding, Coconut Island and Kāne'ohe Bay are ideal sites for the study of nutrient and carbon dynamics, and the process of calcification on coral reefs and in coral microcosms. The concern is that this coral system and the associated laboratory, which are unparalleled in any research facility in the world, will be sustained.

Marlin Atkinson has proven himself as a researcher by his peer-reviewed publication record and his ability to attract major funding to support his research team. Atkinson's research can only be done on an unperturbed, living coral reef in the vicinity of a marine laboratory (HIMB–Coconut Island), and close to a major research university (UH-Mānoa). Through a better understanding of the biogeochemical dynamics of coral reef systems, and the careful monitoring of these systems by scientists like Atkinson and his fellow coral researchers, the status of HIMB as a renowned center for coral studies will be maintained.

| E. GORDON GRAU, INTERIM LABORATORY DIRECTOR (1993–2000)

Since arriving in Hawai'i, Grau has had an impressive record of achievement. He taught courses in the Zoology Department, and was rated an outstanding teacher. He has been mentor to numerous Ph.D. and Master's program students, most of whom have attained professional status in prestigious organizations. Grau organized a team of researchers and technicians, and has had a distinguished and highly productive research career, conducting pioneering investigations on osmoregulation (salt-water balance) in fishes and the role of the hormone, prolactin.

In addition to his academic and research achievements, Grau has served as associate director (1990–1993) and interim director (1994–2000) of the Hawai'i Institute of Marine Biology, and is currently the director of the University of Hawai'i Sea Grant College Program (2000 to present).

| *Dr. E. Gordon Grau, Interim Laboratory Director, Hawai'i Institute of Marine Biology, 1993–2000. E. Gordon Grau*

PAUL NACHTIGALL, INTERIM LABORATORY DIRECTOR (2000–2002)—MARINE MAMMAL RESEARCH— PAUL NACHTIGALL, WHITLOW AU, AND ASSOCIATES

Although marine mammals have often been housed on Coconut Island (early Sea Life Park dolphins resided for a time in the East Lagoon), they were never a strong research component of the early lab. The U.S. Navy had a large marine mammal training program on nearby Kaneohe Marine Corps Base, and in the early 1990s the program was slated for major personnel and animal cutbacks and a subsequent transfer to San Diego. Two of the scientists, Paul Nachtigall and Whitlow Au, approached me and asked if there was room for their basic, non-military mammal research on Coconut Island. Christian Holmes's former zoo area was made available to the program and the navy quickly provided engineering know-how and helicopter-assisted construction of offices on the former zoo site. Floating dolphin enclosures were constructed

| (above) A dolphin held in an enclosure at HIMB and used for research by Paul Nachtigall and Whitlow Au on the discriminating abilities and hearing processes in dolphins. HIMB Collection
| (right) Education at all levels has always been promoted by HIMB. A group of young students is in awe at the sight of live marine invertibrates being displayed by Joe O'Reilly, Coconut Island community education coordinator. J. O'Reilly

and moored in the waters off the west side of the island, providing enough natural current to comfortably contain dolphins and small whales. Research interests focus on taste reception, vision, auditory processes, signal processing and echolocation in bottlenose dolphins, Risso's dolphins, false killer whales, and melon-headed whales. Studies have been conducted on the effects of noise on these animals, their discriminating abilities, as well as the examination of the hearing processes while the animals echolocated. In 1993 the Marine Mammal Program became part of the HIMB family. They have since gained international respect by developing an understanding of basic hearing processes, cetacean ecology, and sonar signal processing.

When Grau transferred to the Sea Grant program, Paul Nachtigall stepped in to provide leadership during the continued search for a new laboratory director. Dr. Jo-Ann C. Leong was chosen as the HIMB director in 2002.

The Hawai'i Institute of Marine Biology in the 21st Century, by Dr. Jo-Ann C. Leong

Among the world's marine research institutes, the Hawai'i Institute of Marine Biology stands out with its modern research facilities within 30 feet of live coral reefs and ready access to the open ocean. It sits in the center of a bay with fringing and patch reefs, and the only barrier reef in the Hawaiian Archipelago. This unique facility has the potential and responsibility to excel in marine biology research. When I assumed the position as director, HIMB was viewed by the University of Hawai'i-Mānoa administration as a field station for the main campus. Its policies and support systems were designed to provide services for faculty whose locus of effort was on the main campus. Indeed, there were only seven tenured faculty lines at HIMB: Marlin Atkinson, Paul Jokiel, Kim Holland, Gordon Grau, George Losey, Arlo Fast, Ed Laws, and Robert Bidigare. Paul Nachtigall and Whitlow Au had moved their

Dr. Jo-Ann C. Leong, Director, Hawai'i Institute of Marine Biology, 2002–present. J. Leong

marine mammal and bioacoustics programs to HIMB from the Kaneohe Marine Corps Base, and their contributions were key components of the HIMB research effort, but they occupied non-tenure track positions. Robert Kinzie III, Timothy Tricas, and John Stimson had research laboratories at HIMB, but their tenure resided in the College of Natural Sciences, Department of Zoology. It was not a large group and since 2002, HIMB saw the retirement of Arlo Fast, a researcher who helped establish a vibrant aquaculture program in Hawai'i, and George Losey, whose program in UV sensory perceptions in fish opened a new field in fish behavior. HIMB was on the verge on being just a field station for the Oceanography Department in the School of Ocean and Earth Science and Technology.

Fortunately, the Edwin W. Pauley Foundation had donated funds for a Master Plan for HIMB and the construction of a modern research laboratory building. This new building as well as a promise of six new positions made it possible for HIMB to become a major research institute in coral reef biology. When I stepped on shore at Coconut Island on 1 October 2001, I was enthusiastic about the prospects of working with this faculty to develop HIMB. In the Boston Whaler, crossing the channel from the Lilipuna pier, I gazed at the spectacular backdrop of the Ko'olau Mountains and thought, "I must be the luckiest person in the world!" That day was memorable because the first student that I met had just fallen through one of the docks and needed the first aid kit in front of my office. All of the docks were in need of repair and the old buildings were showing signs of wear from the ocean environment. There was an amazing amount of old equipment, iron chains, discarded lumber, and equipment on island. HIMB was severely understaffed and, in the next five years, we used every opportunity we could find to increase our maintenance, fiscal, and security staff

We hired four young faculty members in the 2002 recruitment year: Brian Bowen, Ruth Gates, Michael Rappe, and Rob Toonen. Brian Bowen was the first to arrive from the University of Florida. He brought much needed expertise in the phylogenetic characterization of fishes. Rob Toonen from the University of California-Davis brought his expertise in invertebrate marine larval connectivity studies. Ruth Gates from the University of California-Los Angeles was an expert in the physiology and molecular biology of corals. Our last recruit from Oregon State University, Michael Rappe, had already published several papers in *Science* and *Nature* on the culture of the marine picoplankton, *Pelagibacter ubique*. He was the marine microbiologist in the group. These four young scientists formed a nucleus of new scholarly activity for HIMB and they brought cutting-edge technology and enthusiasm to the place. We obtained funding through an NSF-EPSCoR (Experimental Program to Stimulate Competitive Research) grant to equip a functional genomics facility, and these young scientists were quickly interacting with the research community to answer questions regarding the probability that fish larvae from the Northwestern Hawaiian Islands might re-populate an overfished main Hawaiian Islands.

In 2005, Steve Karl joined the HIMB faculty to fill an evolutionary genetics position that resulted from the chancellor's commitment to provide positions for the NSF-EPSCoR grant, Investing in Multidisciplinary University Activities (IMUA) through Hawai'i EPSCoR. Steve will be the last "molecular biologist" to join a core group of researchers in ecological and evolutionary genetics. This core group will begin work that should lead to the development of a science-based ecosystem management plan for the Northwestern Hawaiian Islands, a chain of small islands, atolls, and submerged reefs that extends northwest from the main Hawaiian Islands. These islands make up a unique marine ecosystem found nowhere else in the world. Former president Bill Clinton declared these islands as a coral reef reserve by executive order in December 2000 in order to conserve and protect this coral reef ecosystem and its cultural and natural resources. HIMB scientists have been engaged as the research arm for the Northwestern Hawaiian Islands Coral Reef Ecosystem Reserve. In the next decade, we will hire two faculty members to add to these strengths. A new building to house the new faculty is being designed by Ferraro & Choi, an architectural firm in Honolulu. The firm has been charged with designing a building that is energy efficient and sustainable from a water usage and waste disposal standpoint. The 2004 Hawai'i State Legislature approved $31 million in revenue bonds for the completion of this new building and the repair of the existing buildings at HIMB. The University of Hawai'i administration must now decide whether it will authorize the issuance of revenue bonds for the new building.

| *The planned new laboratory facility for Coconut Island. Ferraro Choi and Associates*

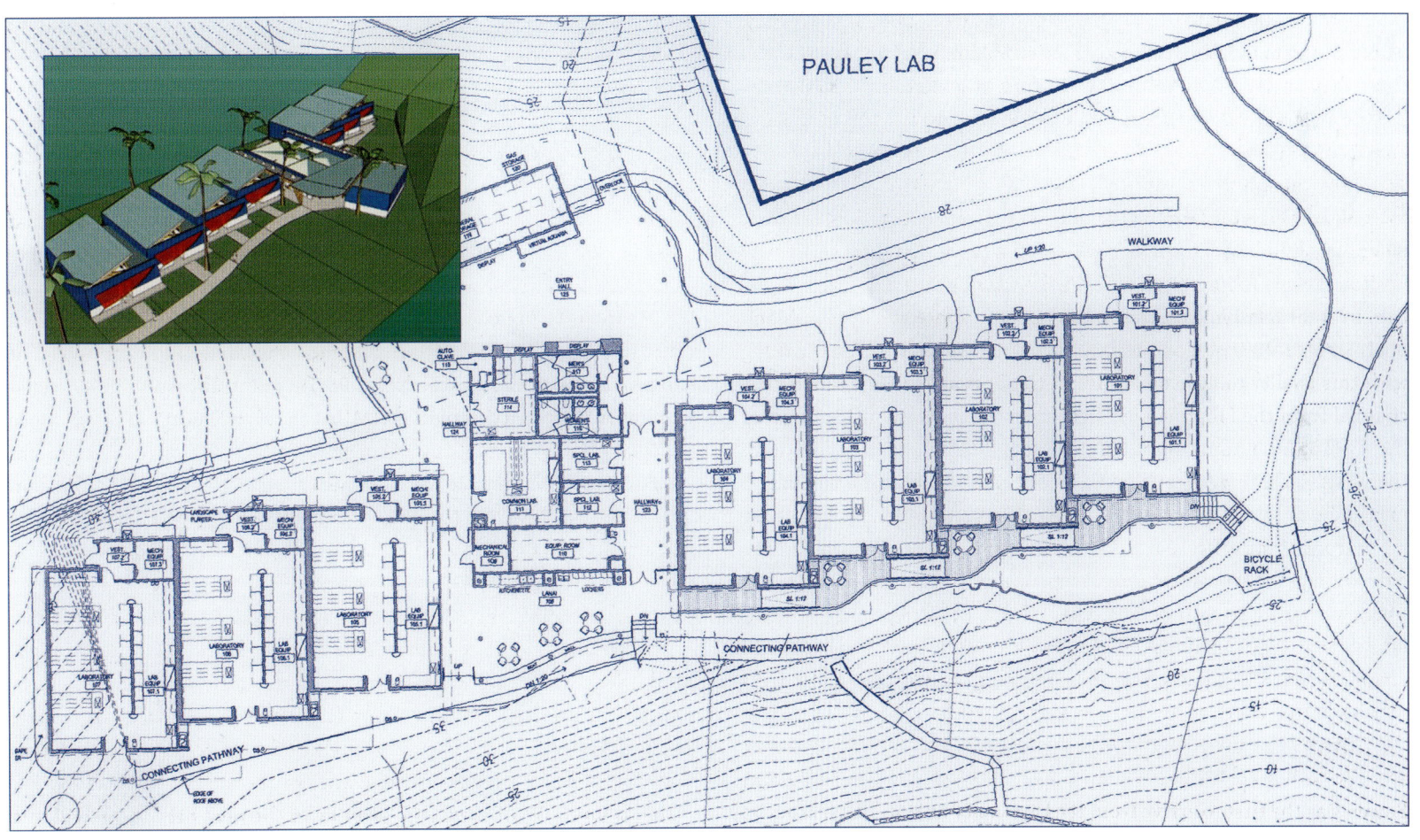

An aerial view of
Kāneʻohe Bay looking
north, Coconut Island
with its fringing reef
in the foreground,
numerous patch reefs
in the sheltered bay,
and the barrier reef
and sand bar reef
beyond make for an
ideal study site for
coral biologists.
Brian Daniel

Paradise Captured

I would linger awhile...

"On A Coconut Island"

*I*n late 1995, after 33 years of division, the private and public sections of Coconut Island were reunited. For the first time ever, the artificial and the natural realms were legally joined. The amalgamation was made possible by a $9.6 million cash grant from the Edwin W. Pauley Foundation to the University of Hawai'i Foundation—the largest gift in the latter institution's history.

The year before, University of Hawai'i president Ken Mortimer, HIMB director Philip Helfrich, and Kay Tamaribuchi from UH Foundation traveled to Los Angeles to meet with the board of the Edwin W. Pauley Foundation. They asked for a $7.6 million grant to build a new marine biology laboratory on Coconut Island. However, the Pauley Foundation trustees were leery of building extensive facilities on the private portion of the island with what appeared to be a less than cooperative owner, especially one who was in serious financial trouble.

At the 1994 meeting, Dr. Stephen Pauley suggested a plan that would deliver the whole island to the University of Hawai'i through fore-closures already in process against Hachidai-USA Corporation. This plan was successfully accomplished in stages: First, the island was appraised by Craig K. W. Leong, MAI of Appraisal Hawaii, Inc. The property in con-sideration was the original 12.5 acres of Coconut Island, and the 61,392 square feet of residentially zoned shoreside land on Lilipuna Road. The island was valued at $2 million. Hachidai's banks and Katsuhiro Kawa-guchi finally offered to sell the private portion of the island to the UH Foundation at that price. The law firm of Watanabe and Ing were retained to negotiate the sensitive sale.

The Pauley Foundation provided the $2 million as a grant to the UH Foundation. Under the terms of the grant, UH Foundation would lease the island for $1 a year to the University. The Pauley Foundation's requirement that the island be owned by the UH Foundation was done to allow for more flexibility in the area of future grants to scientific proj-ects on the island. A donor conceivably might shy away from giving money directly to a governing authority (the State), which could possibly divert some funds for other purposes. Non-profit charities are carefully regulated by the specifications of IRS tax laws, especially on restricted funds. The Pauley Foundation requirement also by-passed potential academic in-fighting and politics that always seem to go with the devel-opment of state budgets and allocations.

In the end, the University of Hawai'i received the largest philan-thropic gift in its history, totaling $9.6 million, $2 million for the island purchase, and $7.6 million for the new marine laboratory. But the gift came with a necessary price tag. The already over-burdened state trea-sury would now have to appropriate money for annual island upkeep and security—the symbolic "$1,000-a-day" maintenance cost paid by Holmes in Depression-era dollars, with its equivalent continuing through the Pauley tenure.

SUSTAINABLE FUTURES

After a prolonged environmental impact study (of which an ear-lier version of this manuscript and the archaeological reconnaissance of Klieger and Lebo were parts), construction of the new Edwin W. Pauley Marine Laboratory began. Many features of the past were still intact on Coconut Island, including the caretaker's house, the Retreat house, and other interesting fixtures. The state-of-the-art fixtures and innovations spun in Holmes's mind in the 1930s were now archaeological features.

In 1998, Mrs. Pauley Pagen and other dignitaries opened the new laboratory and library, among the finest facility of its kind in the world. The new center for marine biology will continue to underscore the uniqueness of Coconut Island and its coral setting in Kāne'ohe Bay.

In the late 1990s, Group 70 International, Inc., an architectural planning firm, was consulted by the University of Hawai'i to provide a long-range plan for the development of Coconut Island. They established the following:

| *The old cottage, original home of the Miranda family, 1996. P. Christiaan Klieger, Author's Collection*

*(above) Interior,
Retreat house, 1996.
P. Christiaan Klieger,
Author's Collection*

*(right) Holmes's old
shrimp tanks, 1996.
P. Christiaan Klieger,
Author's Collection*

*(far right) One of
Holmes's search lights
by the lagoon pool,
1996. P. Christiaan
Klieger, Author's
Collection*

The purpose of the Long Range Development Plan is to create new physical and operational space designed to accommodate the expansion of activities and uses while maintaining the natural beauty and casual atmosphere of the island. Furthermore, the intent of the plan is to integrate the vision and goals of the university, as it relates to its commitment of developing a world-class center for marine science research by creating a "planned community" on Coconut Island which will provide both educational and economic benefits for the greater local community. Four themes were identified to guide the future development of the island, which include the promotion of research, education, sustainability, and environmental stewardship.[277]

In 2005 the institute developed a five-year strategic plan. Noting that with its expanded scope and new facilities, HIMB stood "on the verge of unprecedented international leadership in Marine Biology" due to its unique combination of field access, advanced molecular biotechnology capabilities, comfortable housing for visiting scholars, and position as a leading scientific faculty.[278] A faculty retreat was held on 15 June 2004 to help draft mission and vision statements. The statement that was adopted states that HIMB

...is the flagship institution for the University of Hawaii, the State of Hawaii, and the Nation for the facilitation and support of multi-disciplinary research and education in all aspects of tropical marine biology. HIMB's unique location on Coconut Island (Moku O Lo'e) with ready access to estuarine, coastal

| *(top right) Dedication of the Edwin W. Pauley Marine Lab and library, 1998. (left to right): UH Regents Vice-Chair Clyde Kodani, Chair Donald Kim, President Kenneth Mortimer, Bobbe Pauley Pagen, Stephen Pauley, Susan Pauley Hillyer French. HIMB Collection / Honolulu Advertiser*
| *(bottom right) The William R. Pagen and Barbara Pauley Pagen Library. HIMB Collection*

| *Scalloped hammerhead shark, part of a high school research program under Kanesa Duncan. HIMB Collection*

and offshore environments promotes the integration of excellent laboratory sciences and rigorous field-work."[279]

Faculty at the planning session defined a research strategy to develop new technologies and methods for examining the interactions between marine organisms and their environment. In addition to their HIMB programs, institute faculty serve on graduate committees in zoology, oceanography, botany, geography, and microbiology at the main UH-Mānoa campus, and are members of graduate programs in ecology and conservation research training and marine biology. During the academic year, HIMB is the site of the marine biology intensive laboratory. It also offers K-12 education through a partnership with the Myron B. Thompson Academy, an online charter school of the Hawai'i Department of Education. Outreach is extended to high school summer interns through federally sponsored programs, and is facilitated with a significantly expanded volunteer docent program. HIMB serves as a resource for wildlife management agencies, helping to develop broad public stewardship of marine biodiversity. Outreach is greatly enhanced by the Pauley Summer Program and the Coral Molecular Biology Techniques Workshop that attract international scholars, graduate students, and working professionals.

The strategic plan envisions HIMB becoming the leading tropical marine biology research institution in the U.S. Presently the institute is pre-eminent in research on coastal and pelagic ecosystem processes upon coral reefs, as well as marine animal sensory processes and ecology, marine evolutionary genetics, and the physiology and diseases of fish and corals. These studies are all facilitated by the position of Coconut Island within living coral reefs, its proximity to open ocean, its location within an estuary bounded by a coastal watershed. Coconut Island has direct access to running seawater of very high quality, and the improvements initially designed by Holmes provides animal holding facilities, as well as sewer, electricity, and fresh water for sustained human activi-

ties. The new facilities and the supporting academic infrastructure of the University of Hawai'i contribute to make HIMB an almost unique research platform for the advanced study of marine biology. With current grant funds at $14 million per year, HIMB plans to increase this to $20 million by 2010. (HIMB grant funding has grown each year from $5 million in 2002). During the five-year period outlined in the strategic plan, the institute also hopes to hire two additional faculty members, achieve salary parity to within 80 percent of peer institutions, raise publication rates in peer-review journals by 20 percent, and motivate faculty to further develop international and national standings. HIMB is determined to expand its donor base and create partnerships within the regional community, in addition to expanding its funding from the National Science Foundation and the National Oceanic and Atmospheric Administration.

The new venture into molecular genetics at HIMB was recognized in 2005 by the NSF-funded Experimental Program to Stimulate Competitive Research, which noted that the research thrust was a world-class evolutionary program. Integrated within the traditional program of marine biology, it will further strengthen HIMB's international position.

New laboratories are being designed by Ferraro & Choi, in addition to the consideration of a general renovation of the marine wet labs. Budgetary self-reliance has nearly always been a facet of HIMB operations on Coconut Island. As such, efforts to reduce costs through energy efficiency are a priority.

Long-range plans call for a Center for a Sustainable Future, a nonprofit organization affiliated with the University of Hawai'i and the UH Foundation, which will address environmental problems associated with the Pacific Rim, serving as a kind of "think tank" in conjunction with HIMB. It is currently headed by Dr. Stephen Pauley. In many ways, the plan resembles one of the original ideas of Edwin Pauley—Coconut Island as a retreat to stimulate creative minds. In a pragmatic sense, the Center will attempt to reverse the effects of detrimental environmental

| Christian Holmes V on Coconut Island where he is studying aquatic biology. *Author's Collection*

impacts that have occurred throughout the Pacific Rim, including the damage done to Kāneʻohe Bay and Moku o Loʻe.

The plaintive story of the dredging of Kāneʻohe Bay to construct sea lanes and the use of coral rubble as fill for the landing fields at Mōkapu is examined in detail in Devaney et al.'s *Kāneʻohe, A History of Change*.[280] Briefly put, development in and around Kāneʻohe Bay has been rapid and severe. After World War II, more than a dozen walled fishponds along the bay were filled in and converted to residential lots. Discharge of mud from the construction of the Wilson vehicular tunnels through the Koʻolau Range above Kāneʻohe not only choked the streams but greatly damaged the delicate coral ecosystem of the bay. The founding and nurturing of marine biology research, first under Holmes then sustained and expanded by the Pauleys, have ensured that at least one section of a once pristine coral paradise will be preserved for the study of marine biology. The institutions on Coconut Island will directly encourage the restoration of the natural aquatic environment around Kāneʻohe Bay and elsewhere in the Pacific.

Stephen Pauley reflects upon the special nature of Coconut Island:

It would seem that the island has a kind of mana. *The fact that the island resisted the forces of progress, development, the military, religious zealots, morticians, nudists, and the lure of the dollar for 60 years, and because the Pauley Foundation believes its best end use really ought to be a peaceful setting where environmental issues of the Pacific Rim should be discussed, could make even the most cynical skeptic believe that there are forces acting on that paradise of which the previous owners were unaware.*

NATURE AND ARTIFACT

Encapsulated, self-sufficient, isolated—these are the common themes in this idealized desert island *topos*. Moku o Loʻe was really never isolated from the natural and cultural context of the surrounding bay and mainland of Oʻahu (even the sheep got to Heʻeia when they had enough of the rats). It was somehow envisioned to be such a place, the real world invisible, just beyond the horizon.

For Native Hawaiians, Moku o Loʻe was a place of exile for Loʻe, and a fortuitous lookout from which to watch the behavior of fish. What better place to manage the harvest of rich schools living among the coral heads in the bay? Moku o Loʻe was an ideal spot for Paul Beyer to establish the highly successful Hawaiian Tuna Packers and to raise his family of beautiful free spirits.

For Christian Holmes II, Coconut Island was an artificial pleasure dome from which to throw uninhibited Hollywood parties and watch the behavior of people among the palms and playful diversions. It was a self-contained cosmos of botanical gardens, zoo, and aquaria stocked with the myriad of biological species Holmes found amusing, beautiful, or rare. It was a Noah's Ark, detached and adrift without earthly cares, a self-imposed Gilligan's Island. For Holmes's family today, it remains an archive of the memory of their extraordinary ancestor and the achievements of the Fleischmann and Holmes legacies.

For retiring naval officers, Coconut Island was a sedate retreat from which to escape the horrors of war.

Allen Chase, Troy Post, Poncet Davis, Walter Child, and Katsuhiro Kawaguchi, conceived of ways to make the island a profitable investment. They were businessmen trying to optimize a difficult investment. For both the military and the entrepreneur, the island was in many ways a bit too detached from the economic realities of post-war Hawaiian life.

For Edwin Pauley, the outlier became simply a healthy, safe, wholesome place to raise his sports-loving family, and by extension a facility to encourage the development of science and young scientists.

For the faculty and students of the Hawaiʻi Institute of Marine Biology, Coconut Island is still an ideal place for the observation of fish and corals. With this continuing emphasis, the human story of the tiny rock has come full circle.

| *Aloha! Pauley Collection*

From what was left of the core of an ancient volcano, Moku o Loʻe has been a broad canvas upon which a wide spectrum of dreams have been painted. In the process, each has shown the historical record a different concept of Hawaiian paradise. Coconut Island is not a wholly natural place, nor is it entirely artificial. Over time, humans have modeled and shaped the tiny dot of land, often at great price, in order to reflect their particular vision of Shangri-La. In the process of creation and adaptation, art and nature are seen to influence and reinforce each other to the point that one often cannot separate the dream from the reality. Whether a place of geologic or contrived beauty, Coconut Island is perhaps best described as a place with an uncanny ability to inspire, generation after generation.

APPENDIX

TABLE I | TITLE HISTORY OF MOKU O LOʻE: COCONUT ISLAND

PRE-MAHELE LAND TENURE

OWNER	KONOHIKI	YEAR
Kamehameha I	?	1795–1819
Kamehameha II	Abner Pākī	1819–1824
Kamehameha III	Abner Pākī	1824–1848

POST-MAHELE LAND TENURE

OWNER	LEASEE	SUBLESSEE	YEAR
Abner Pākī			1848–1855
Laura Konia			1855–1858
Bernice Pauahi Bishop	Miscellaneous tenants in Heʻeia		1858–1884
Bernice Pauahi Bishop	John McKeague		1866–1869
Bernice Pauahi Bishop	Heeia Sugar Plantation Co.		1869–1884
Charles Reed Bishop	Heeia Sugar Plantation Co.		1884–1885
Charles Reed Bishop	Heeia Agricultural Co.		1885–1889
Charles Reed Bishop	Marcus Colburn		1889–1890

Owner	Leasee	Sublessee	Year
Bishop Estate	Heeia Agricultural Co.		1890–1899
Bishop Estate	Heeia Co.	Fred Bolte	1899–1904
Bishop Estate	Heeia Co.	John Sumner	1904–1908
Bishop Estate	James Castle		1908
Bishop Estate	Heeia Co.		1910–1933
Bishop Estatae	Heeia Co.	Paul Beyer	1921–1925
Bishop Estate	Heeia Co.	Chris Holmes II	1933–1936
Christian Holmes II			1936–1944
Holmes Estate			1944–1946
Holmes Estate	U.S. Government		1945
Moku-o-Loe Corp.	Coconut Island International		1946–1964
Moku-o-Loe Corp. .... Territory of Hawaii (HML)	Coconut Island International (added areas public)		 1947
Moku-o-Loe Corp. .... Territory of Hawaii (HML)	Coconut Island Hotel		1949
Moku-o-Loe Corp. .... State of Hawai'i (HML and HIMB)			.... 1962–present

Owner	Leasee	Sublessee	Year
Ed Pauley / American Life Insurance .... State of Hawaiʻi			1964–1974
Ed Pauley / Sheridan Ing .... State of Hawaiʻi			1973–1974
Ed Pauley .... State of Hawaiʻi			1974–1981
Barbara Pauley Pagen .... State of Hawaiʻi			1981–1987
Hachidai Corporaton .... State of Hawaiʻi			1987–1995
State of Hawaiʻi	Island Reunified		1995–present

TABLE 2 | STAFF AND ADMINISTRATION OF THE HAWAII MARINE LABORATORY — JUNE 1951

NAME	POSITION
Gregg M. Sinclair, L.L.D.	President of the University of Hawai'i
Robert W. Hiatt, Ph.D.	Professor of Zoology and Director, Hawaii Marine Lab
Albert H. Banner, Ph.D.	Associate Professor of Zoology
Vernon E. Brock, M.A.	Lecturer in Fishery Biology
Maxwell S. Doty, Ph.D.	Associate Professor of Botany
William A. Gosline III, Ph.D.	Associate Professor of Zoology
Sidney C. Hsiao, Ph.D.	Associate Professor of Zoology
John L. Kaask, Ph.D.	Lecturer in Fishery Biology
Donald C. Matthews, Ph.D.	Associate Professor of Zoology
Charles Nakamoto	Resident Caretaker
Oscar E. Sette, M.A.	Lecturer in Fishery Biology
Albert A. Tester, Ph.D.	Professor of Zoology
Lester Zukeran	Maintenance Supervisor

TABLE 3 | HAWAII MARINE LABORATORY | HAWAI'I INSTITUTE OF MARINE BIOLOGY
DIRECTORS: 1948 TO PRESENT

NAME	POSITION	DATES
Robert W. Hiatt, Ph.D.	Director	1948–1955
Albert H. Banner, Ph.D.	Director	1955–1963
Vernon E. Brock, M.A.	Director	1963–1969
Philip Helfrich, Ph.D.	Interim Director	1970–1971
John E. Bardach, Ph.D.	Director	1971–1977
Willam Coops, Ph.D.	Interim Director	1977–1978
John Caperon, Ph.D.	Director	1978–1980
Philip Helfrich, Ph.D.	Director	1980–1993
E. Gordon Grau, Ph.D.	Interim Director	1993–2000
Paul E. Nachtigall, Ph.D.	Interim Director	2000–2002
Jo-Ann C. Leong, Ph.D.	Director	2002–present

TABLE 3 | THE EDWIN W. PAULEY SUMMER PROGRAM IN MARINE BIOLOGY | PREVIOUS TOPICS (1983–2006)

YEAR	TOPIC
1983	Population Biology of Coral Reef Organisms
1984	Solar Radiation in the Sea
1985	Nutrient and Energy Cycles in Phytoplankton, Bacteria, Zooplankton
1986	Endocrinology of Tropical Marine Vertebrates
1987	The Biology of Sex Changes in Reef Fishes
1988	Marine Shrimp Biology and Production Technology
1989	Metabolism on Coral Reefs
1990	Behavioral Ecology and Ethology of Coral Reef Animals
1991	Diffusion Barriers and Carbon Limitation in Reef Corals
1992	Hormonal Control of Growth and Development in Fishes
1993	Application of Advanced Technologies to the Study of Fish Growth and Development
1994	Ultraviolet Radiation on Coral Reefs
1995	Biogeochemistry of Coral Reefs
1996	Marine Mammal Biology and Management
1997	Reproduction in Coral Reefs

Year	Topic
1998	Marine Shrimp Biology and Production Technology
1999	Gene Expression in Fish
2000	Elasmobranch Biology
2001	Cetacean Audiometrics
2002	Molecular Biology of Corals
2003	Assessing the Health of Pacific Corals
2004	The Search for Homeostasis
2005	Ecological Risk Characterization for Coral Reefs
2006	Aquatic Animal Health and Disease

Notes

Prologue

[1] Gorham Gilman, "Notes on a Tour of Oahu," Ms. in Hawaiian Historical Society Library, Honolulu, 7.

[2] Elvi Whittaker, *The Mainland Haole* (New York: Columbia University Press, 1986).

Chapter 1

[3] Norah Sterns, *An Island is Born* (Honolulu: Honolulu Star-Bulletin Publishers, 1935).

[4] Moku o Lo'e sits at the column of magma that hardened in the throat of the volcano. Being denser than the surface ejecta, the dike has remained long after the flanks of Mt. Ko'olau have eroded away. The tiny island shares this geological characteristic with two hills on the border of He'eia and Kāne'ohe, namely 194-ft. Pōhākea and 280-ft. Pu'u Pahu, located directly across the approx. 1500-ft. channel that separated Moko o Lo'e from the mainland of O'ahu. Moku o Lo'e is also geologically akin to the prominent dike Mt. Olomana. See Harold Sterns and Knute Vaksvik, *Geology and Ground-water Resources on the Island of Oahu, Hawaii,* U.S.G.S. Bulletin 1 (1938): 85.

[5] Ibid., 95, 99, 100, 121, 136; and Scott Henderson, "The Geology of Mokapu Peninsula, Oahu," 1994. Ms. on file, Environmental Compliance and Protection Department, Kaneohe Marine Corps Air Station, O'ahu.

[6] Patrick V. Kirch, *Feathered Gods and Fishhooks* (Honolulu: University of Hawai'i Press, 1985).

[7] S. S. Williams, "Early Inland Settlement Expansion and the Effect of Geomorphological Change in the Archaeological Record in Kane'ohe, O'ahu," *New Zealand Journal of Archaeology* 14 (1992): 67–78.

[8] m.=male; f.=female

[9] Hawaiian Ethnographic Notes, Bishop Museum, Honolulu. Translation in Elspeth P. Sterling and Catherine C. Summers, *Sites of Oahu* (Honolulu: Bishop Museum Press, 1978), 206.

[10] E. S. Craighill Handy and Elizabeth Green Handy, with Mary Kawena Pukui, *Native Planters in Old Hawaii*, Bishop Museum Bulletin 233 (Honolulu: Bishop Museum Press, 1972).

[11] Nathaniel Portlock, *Voyage Round the World 1785–88* (London: John Stockdale, 1789).

[12] Scott Henderson, "The Geology of Mokapu Peninsula, Oahu," 1994. Ms. on file, Environmental Compliance and Protection Department, Kaneohe Marine Corps Air Station, O'ahu.

[13] W. H. Easton, "The Geologic Relation of Reclaimed Land to Coconut Island, Hawaii," 1967. Ms. on file, Hawai'i Institute of Marine Biology, Coconut Island, 6.

[14] Marion Kelly, *Loko I'a o He'eia* (Honolulu, Bishop Museum Press, 1974), 74–78.

[15] Catherine Summers, *Hawaiian Fishponds*, Bishop Museum Special Publication 52 (Honolulu: Bishop Museum Press, 1964).

[16] J. G. McAllister, *Archaeology of Oahu*, Bishop Museum Bulletin 104 (Honolulu: Bishop Museum Press, 1933).

[17] Kelly, ibid.

[18] Richard Paglinawan, "Traditions of Waiahole Valley," *News from the Pacific* 15 (1964): 1–7.

[19] Ibid., 5.

[20] Pukui, Elbert, and Mookini.

[21] A. L. MacKay, "Where the Coral Blossoms Bloom," *Mid-Pacific Magazine* 11, no.2 (1916): 117–121.

[22] Hawaiian Studies Institute Map of O'ahu (Honolulu: University of Hawa'i-Mānoa, 1987).

[23] Handy, et al.

[24] Samuel Kamakau, "He Manawa Haowale a nei Keia, a Kaili a Pakawale?," *Kuokoa* (Honolulu: Bishop Museum, 1875).

[25] Handy, et al., 271–272.

[26] Ibid., 283.

[27] David Malo, *Hawaiian Antiquities*, Bishop Museum Special Publication 2 (Honolulu: Bishop Museum Press 1951), 189.

[28] Martha Beckwith, *Hawaiian Mythology* (Honolulu: University of Hawai'i Press, 1970).

[29] Malo, 209.

[30] Ibid.

[31] McAllister, 171–172.

[32] John Cobb, "The Commercial Fisheries of the Hawaiian Islands," *Bulletin of the United States Fishing Commission for 1903* (Washington, DC: Government Printing Office, 1905).

[33] "Kamaaina Tells of Kahuna Days on Coconut Isle," *The Honolulu Advertiser*, 23 January 1937.

[34] The tales of human burials were raised again in the 1990s and 2000s when long-range planners were considering options in the construction of new laboratory facilities on Moku o Lo'e. In conjunction with this need, Dr. Susan A. Lebo and myself from the Bishop Museum identified two possible burial sites on a 1997 archaeological reconnaissance of the island. One archaeological test excavation was subsequently dug by Helen Leidemann at one of the sites shortly thereafter. No human remains were found. In 2003, Group 70 International contracted Scientific Consultant Services to conduct a more extensive archaeological survey of the island. After 13 test pits located in the suspect area were excavated, no human remains were found either. The survey did discover traditional cultural materials, however. In a test pit located near the lagoon "swimming pool" on the north side of the island, flaked stone tools, possible hammerstone, wood charcoal, shell, and coral were found. This is reflective of human activity and demonstrates the occupation of the island by Native Hawaiians. While not specifically linked to fishing activities, these artifacts are the first material evidence of Native Hawaiian occupation to be documented at Moku o Lo'e. The wood charcoal collected yielded a reliable radiocarbon date of 540 years before the present, plus or minus 60 years. Moku o Lo'e had human activity on it at least as far back as the fifteenth century, a time of great expansion of population and intensification of production.

[35] Abraham Fornander, *Fornander Collection of Hawaiian Antiquities and Folk-Lore,* ed. Thomas G. Thrum, Memoirs of the Bernice Pauahi Bishop Museum Volume 5 (Honolulu: Bishop Museum Press, 1918–1919), 576–583.

[36] Ibid., 580.

[37] Beckwith, 155.

[38] Pilahi Paki, *Legends of Hawaii: Oahu's Yesterday* (Honolulu: Victoria, 1972).

[39] McAllister, 173.

[40] "Cristy Rules Coconut Isle Bishop Land," *The Honolulu Advertiser*, 13 January 1937.

[41] Mary K. Pukui and Samuel Elbert, *Hawaiian Dictionary* (Honolulu: University of Hawai'i Press, 1986).

[42] See Klieger, *Moku'ula: Maui's Sacred Island* (Honolulu: Bishop Museum Press, 1999) for a discussion of the meaning of Moku'ula, the royal residence at Lahaina, Maui.

[43] McAllister, 173.

Chapter 2

44 Kirch, 305.

45 P. Christiaan Klieger, *Nā Maka o Hālawa*, Bishop Museum Technical Report 7 (Honolulu: Bishop Museum Press, 1995), 20–21.

46 Ibid., 21–24.

47 John Papa Ii, *Fragments of Hawaiian History*, ed. by Dorothy B. Barrère, translated by Mary K. Pukui (Honolulu: Bishop Museum Press, 1959), 50.

48 Testimony of Miriam Kekauʻōnohi, Equity 200, Court Proceedings for 15 December 1047 (in Hawaiian), ʻIolani Hale, Ms. in Hawaii State Archives, Honolulu.

49 Kamakau, *Ruling Chiefs,* 292.

50 Ibid., 291.

51 Ibid., 303

52 Ibid., 197.

53 These include ʻili in Haʻikū (Land Commission Award [LCA] 3307, Book 6:541), Heʻeia Kea (LCA 6062, Book 6:531), Hoi (LCA 5816, Book 6:538), Kakualaukī (LCA 7736.2, Book 6:535), Kalimaloa (LCA 2162.3, Book 4:673), Kalimukele (LCA 3393, Book 6:536), Koaena (LCA 2562, Book 4:672), Kumupali (LCA 7514.2, Book 6:595), Mōkapu (LCA 6062 Native Register 5:225), Pahele (LCA 2162.1, Book 4:673), Pilaloa (LCA 8193, Native Register 5:506), Pūnāwai (LCA 8193, Native Register 5:506), Puʻulani (LCA 7539, Book 6:535), Waipao (LCA 3307.3, Book 6:541), Wawae (LCA 5755, Book 4:669), and undifferentiated *ahupuaʻa* lands (LCA 6062.3, Book 6:531), LCA and Native Register books on file, Hawaii State Archives, Honolulu.

54 Lilikalā Kameʻeleihiwa, *Native Land and Foreign Desires* (Honolulu: Bishop Museum Press, 1992), 267.

55 Ibid.

56 Land Court Application 1100, Territory of Hawaii Land Court, Honolulu (1933).

57 Patrick Bowland, *Saint Ann's Church & School* (Honolulu: Presentation Plus, 1991), 14.

58 "House of the Sun," perhaps from the name the dormant volcano on Maui.

59 Many *aliʻi* kept summer retreats on portions of their extensive properties. A good example of a Victorian-era resort was Queen Emma, who maintained a beach home at South Hālawa, Oʻahu. See Klieger, *Nā Maka o Hālawa* (Bishop Museum Press 1995), 48.

60 Marshall Sahlins, *Anahulu: The Anthropology of History in the Kingdom of Hawaii,* vol. 1 of *Historical Ethnography,* ed. Patrick V. Kirch and Marshall Sahlins (Chicago: University of Chicago Press, 1995).

61 Bowland, 19; Kamakau, *Ruling Chiefs*, 420–421.

62 Kāwika McKeague, "Coconut Island (Moko o Loʻe) Long Range Development Plan," 2003. Cultural Impact Assessment, prepared for Hawaiʻi Institute of Marine Biology by Group 70 International, Honolulu, 2–22.

63 Krout (1908), 204, cited in McKeague, 2–6.

64 Kamehameha I and Kamehameha III left several thriving lineages from different women. However, under the new Christian laws of the kingdom, these descendents were now considered "illegitimate." The traditional *aliʻi* of Hawaiʻi often maintained many spouses of both genders, which inflamed the strict Calvinist missionaries.

[65] George Kanahele, *Pauahi: The Kamehameha Legacy* (Honolulu: Kamehameha Schools Press, 1986), 84.

[66] Land Court Application 1100.

[67] Kanahele, 84.

[68] Dennis Devaney, Marion Kelly, Polly Jae Lee, and Lee S. Motteler, *Kāneʻohe: A History of Change* (Honolulu: Bess Press, 1982), 49–55.

[69] Land Court Application 1100.

[70] Mackay, 120. Princess Bernice Pauhi, as well as Queen Emma and other *aliʻi nui*, were famous for their coconut palm plantings in arid regions. This cultivation was done to provide food, water, and shade for human habitation. It is not known if coconuts existed on Moku o Loʻe before Bernice's action.

[71] Bernice was not the last descendent of Kamehameha I as mentioned previously. The "illegitimate" lines could not inherit the throne or dynastic property.

[72] Bernice was asked by childless King Kamehameha V to be his heir on the throne. She politely refused.

[73] Land Court Application 1100.

[74] Libers of Record, Bureau of Conveyances, Honolulu, 119:132.

[75] Ibid., 144:132.

[76] Abstract, Land Court Application 1134, Territory of Hawaii Land Court, Honolulu (1937).

[77] Libers of Record, Bureau of Conveyances, Honolulu, 185: 409.

[78] Ibid., 257: 186.

[79] Ibid., 298: 292.

[80] Ibid., 79, : 196.

[81] Black, Cobey. "Along the Miracle Mile," *Honolulu Star-Bulletin*, 11 August 1956, 11.

| CHAPTER 3

[82] From the newspaper article, "Major Fleischmann Invested in Community's Future," 17 October 1951.

[83] Early biographers usually claim that Charles was Hungarian, born near a suburb of Pest. Session Wheeler suggests that he was born at Jaegerdorf, allegedly in a suburb of Vienna. However, according to a website history of Krnov, Czech Republic, Charles's parents Abraham and Babette Fleischmann lived in that city. In the days of the Habsburg Empire, the town was known by the German name Jagerndorf, the "Hunters' Village," of the Silesian Mountains. The Fleischmanns are really Silesian. The Hungarian association most likely is due to Charles's early apprenticeship with the Hungarian distiller, and the fact that Charles emigrated to the United States from the Kingdom of Hungary.

[84] Sessions Wheeler, *Gentleman in the Outdoors: A Portrait of Max C. Fleischmann* (Reno: University of Nevada Press, 1985), 10.

[85] Lois E. Hughes, Hamilton County, Ohio, Citizenship Record Abstracts, 1837–1916 (Bowie, MD: Heritage Books, 1991), 107.

[86] William G. Panschar, *Baking in America: Economic Development*, Vol. 1 (Evanston, IL: Northwestern University Press, 1956), 36–37.

[87] Melvin Grayson, *42 Million a Day: The Story of Nabisco Brands* (East Hanover, NJ: Nabisco Brands, 1986), 8.

[88] Julius Bergen, "They Helped Make America," Ms. on file. 99-DVI/5/2/5 Max Fleischmann files, University of Nevada-Reno, 194.

89 Martin Fischer, *Christian R. Holmes: Man and Physician* (Springfield, IL: Charles C. Thomas, 1937), 2.

90 Ibid., 123.

91 Ibid., 149.

92 www.sybase.com/detail?id=1011654

93 Fischer, 225.

94 Roland Marchand, *Advertising the American Dream* (Berkeley: University of California Press, 1985), 39.

95 Ibid.

96 Ibid., 17.

97 Ibid., 39.

98 Standard Brands Inc., *Annual Report* (1929).

99 Jewish Community Center, Sands Point, L.I., New York; also www.commsyn.org/HTML/About.htm.

100 Monica Randall, *The Mansions of Long Island's Gold Coast* (Rizzoli, 1979).

101 Julius also had a private Pullman car, the *Cyprus*, renamed *Middleneck*. The Fleischmanns were fond of riding their private railroad cars to their summer resorts in the Catskill Mountains. The family outfitted the Fleischmann-Griffin Corners band with liveried uniforms, which greeted the family upon their arrival. See Fleischmanns' History, www.catskill.net/fleisch/museum.htm.

102 Wheeler, 45.

103 Fischer, 225

104 Ibid., 216

105 Eileen O'Brien, "The Saga of Chris Holmes," *Paradise of the Pacific* 56 (Honolulu, May 1944), 10–13. Holmes's cousin, Julius (Junkie) Fleischmann II also established a huge private zoo in Naples, Florida. See Klieger 2004.

106 Benjamin Hampton, *History of the American Film Industry* (New York: Dover, 1970), 235.

107 Daniel Blum, *A Pictoral History of the Silent Screen* (New York: Grosset & Dunlap, 1953).

108 DeSoto Brown, Anne Ellett, and Gary Giema, *Hawaii Recalls* (Honolulu: Editions Unlimited, 1982), 124.

109 Elvi Whittaker, 102–103.

110 Ibid., 103.

111 Mary Kawena Pukui, et al., 207.

112 O'Brien, 13.

113 The fish market is still in operation in downtown Honolulu.

114 *Polk-Hustead City Directory of Honolulu, 1919–1936* (Honolulu: Polk-Hustead, 1936).

115 "Suit Reminder of Old Plague," *Honolulu Star-Bulletin*, 26 January 1937, 7.

116 Libers of Record, 1325: 92.

117 Only after Holmes secured the lease did a few Native Hawaiian families come forth with claims to the property.

118 Devaney, et al., 241.

119 Gertrude Moller, "Remembrances of Eleuthera," www.jaxshells.org/remb.htm.

120 O'Brien.

121 The razor sharp memory of some of my informants recalled this special treasure of Holmes. During the "military occupation" of the island during World War II, the dagger disappeared. Rumor had it that it found its way to no less a person as Admiral Nimitz. However, when I related the story to Holmes's daughter, Ann, at her home in Santa Barbara, she disappeared for a few minutes and returned, bearing the jeweled Venetian dagger with the "NB" monogram. It was one of the few objects that she had inherited from her father.

122 The zebra was confirmed by Mona herself in conversation with step-grandson Christian Holmes IV.

123 Coconut Island, *Paradise of the Pacific*, December 1947, 73.

124 G. G. Penn, "Introductions of American Crawfish into Foreign Lands," *Ecology* 35 (February 1954), 296.

125 V. E. Brock, "The Introduction of Aquatic Animals into Hawaiian Waters," *International Revue Ges. Hydrobiology* 45, no. 4 (1960).

126 Board of Commissioners for Agriculture and Forestry, Territory of Hawaii, *Reports for the Biennial Periods ending Dec. 31, 1918 to 1952* (Honolulu: New Freedom, 1945), 8–9.

127 Devaney, et al.

128 Joseph Brennan, *The Parker Ranch of Hawaii*, (New York: John Day, 1974), 208–211.

129 Obituary of Mona Hind Holmes, *Sunday Star Bulletin & Advertiser*, 31 May 1987.

130 In fact, many WWII-era Hawaiian cookbooks mention using Coral Brand tuna by name, to capture that "authentic flavor."

131 Frank Taylor, Earl Welty, and David Eyre, *From Land and Sea* (San Francisco: Chronicle Books, 1976).

132 "Seth Parker," *The Honolulu Advertiser*, 23 April 1961, 3.

133 www.offshore-radio.de/fleet/sethparker.htm.

134 Frigidaire Coporation, *Seth Parker* booklet, 1934.

135 "Schooner Seth Parker Awaits Warship's Aid," *Honolulu Star-Bulletin*, 11 February 1935, 3.

136 McKeague, 2–31.

137 Obituary of C. R. Holmes, *New York Times*, 6 February 1944.

138 Accession record in Administrative Offices of the Steinhart Aquarium, California Academy of Sciences, San Francisco.

139 "Christian R. Holmes Dies in New York Hotel," *Honolulu Star-Bulletin*, 5 February 1944.

140 Cobey Black, "Along the Miracle Mile," *Honolulu Star-Bulletin*, 11 August 1956, 11.

141 "Personal Estate of C. R. Holmes Near 3 Million," *The Honolulu Advertiser*, 8 May 1945, 5.

142 "Rare Holmes' Antiques to be Offered at Sale," *The Honolulu Advertiser*, 21 April 1946, 3.

143 Obituary of Mona Hind Holmes.

144 "Empress Put to Sleep," *Honolulu Star-Bulletin*, 15 April 1986.

145 www.dole.com/Company Info/About/Timeline/3.jsp

146 Ibid.

147 Ibid.

148 In November of 1944, Davis placed Coconut Island and all its improvements on the auction block. As adequate bids failed to materialize, the property was leased to the army.

INTERLUDE

149 The Pagliottis subsequently were hired by Ann Holmes in Santa Barbara.

150 In Holmes's day, drinks were ordered by telephone that ran to the bartender in the Main House, and were delivered at the Observatory, or anywhere else for that matter.

151 Philip Helfrich, personal communication

152 Charles Langlais, *There Was a Ship* (San Francisco: Charles Langlais, 1948), 52.

CHAPTER 4

153 "Pauley Confirms Purchase of Island, Names Partners," *The Honolulu Advertiser*, 8 May 1946, 6.

154 "Coconut Island Owners Here to Start Building," *Honolulu Star-Bulletin*, 5 June 1946, 4.

155 "Coconut Island Club to Cater to Select, World-wide Members," *Honolulu Star-Bulletin*, 2 November 1946, 4.

156 Coconut Island Owners.

157 "Coconut Island International Club," *Paradise of the Pacific*, January 1947, 19–21.

158 "Coconut Island Looms as Robinson Crusoe Site," *The Honolulu Advertiser*, 11 June 1946, 6.

159 Brochure, Coconut Island Club International, on file, Hawai'i Institute of Marine Biology.

160 "Coconut Island Owners Are Hosts at Cocktail, Dinner Party on Isle," *Honolulu Star-Bulletin*, 22 January 1947, 13.

161 Coconut Island Looms

162 "Coconut Isle Club May Be Converted into Deluxe Hotel," *Honolulu Star-Bulletin*, 20 May 1947, 1.

163 "Red McQueen, Coconut Island Impresses Ram Party," *The Honolulu Advertiser*, 11 September 1948, 8.

164 "James W. Carey, Coconut Island Could Be Bought for $1,000,000, Says Pauley," *Honolulu Star-Bulletin*, 10 July 1948, 5.

165 "Group Seeks Use of Coconut Island," *The Honolulu Advertiser*, 11 March 1958, A1.

166 McKeague, 2–32.

167 "Coconut Island Hotel Will Open Next Saturday," *Honolulu Star-Bulletin*, 7 February 1950, 6.

168 Jane Ellen Wayne, *Gable's Women* (New York: Prentice Hall, 1987), 206–207, 215.

169 Wedding announcement, Mr. and Mrs. Gilbert Clark, *Oregon Journal*, 1 March 1950.

170 It would be more than a generation before the country resort concept would be a successful formula in the Hawaiian visitor industry.

171 "Windward Development Plan May Turn It into Paradi$e," *Honolulu Star-Bulletin*, 30 January 1957, 11.

172 Harold Pauley had died from a heart attack while horseback riding.

173 Ray Coll, Jr., "'Father' Divine Cult Seeks to Purchase Coconut Island," *The Honolulu Advertiser*, 3 July 1952, A1, A6.

174 "Sam Frear, Coconut Island, DeRussy Swap Offered," *The Honolulu Advertiser*, 31 May 1957, A1, A10.

175 Ibid., A6.

176 Millard Purdy, "Tax Office Raises Problem of Coconut Isle Ownership," *Honolulu Star-Bulletin*, 16 December 1955, 1.

177 One of the lingering questions was why Holmes, with resources to hire the best legal advice, did not realize the potential ramifications of this rather common law. I speculate that it may have had something to do with traditional Hawaiian land tenure, and the still common practice of looking upon the fisheries as part of the adjacent *ahupua'a*. Moku o Lo'e belonged to He'eia, complete with all the fishponds and underwater reef resources surrounding the tiny island. Furthermore, "citizens" of each *ahupua'a* had access rights to all of the various resource areas. This privilege was guaranteed in the Great Mahale, and has come down to us under present state law. This is why today all Hawaiian beaches, and even Coconut Island, must maintain some public access.

178 Windward Development Plan.

179 Price was married to Mamaloa Price, a Native Hawaiian chanter. They had two children with cerebral palsy.

180 Group Seeks Use.

181 "Firm Buys Fifth of Coconut Isle," *The Honolulu Advertiser*, 1 April 1958, A3.

182 Sam Mosher, like Max Fleischmann and Christian Holmes, invested in Santa Barbara real estate. Mosher owned a huge ranch near Gaviota where he raised orchids.

183 James Cunningham, "Coconut Isle: For Execs Only?," *The Honolulu Advertiser*, 27 July 1964, A2.

184 Helen Altonn, "State, 2 Financiers Own Coconut Island," *Honolulu Star-Bulletin*, 30 April 1964, A1.

185 "Coconut Island Resists Commercialism," *Honolulu Star-Bulletin*, 1964, B3.

186 Hawai'i became a state in 1959.

187 Letter from Shiro Kashima to James Dunn, 28 March 1962, on file, HIMB, Coconut Island.

188 Easton, 1.

189 Ibid.

190 Bob Jones and George Marshall, "$1-Million Nudist Camp: What Are the Bare Facts?," *The Honolulu Advertiser*, 12 April 1963, A1, A2.

191 Cunningham.

192 Stanley H. Brown, "The Golden Castles of Troy V. Post," *Fortune*, January 1965, 155.

193 Geza Szurovy, *Classic American Airlines* (MBI Publishing, Osceola, WI, 2000), 164

194 Ibid., 156.

195 Cunningham.

196 "Troy V. Post Redeploys His Money," *Business Week*, 20 October 1973, 90.

197 Ibid.

198 "Coconut Isle Land Purchased," *The Honolulu Advertiser*, 4 December 1973, D8.

CHAPTER 5

199 Pauley Family notes, on file, Special Collections, UCLA Archives.

200 Douglas Shuit, "Edwin W. Pauley, Oilman and Political Figure, Dies," *Los Angeles Times*, 29 July 1981, Part 1.

201 Elbert L. Pauley, *Pasadena Community Book*, 1947.

202 Ibid.

203 Herb Childs interview with EW Pauley. On file, UCLA Special Collections.

204 Colleen Stanley Bare, "Catching Up with the McHenrys: Meet Bobbe Jean McHenry Pauley Pagen," *About the House*, December 1994.

205 Shuit.

206 Letter from Pauley to Truman, on file in Truman Library, Independence, Missouri.

207 Shuit.

208 http://en.wikipedia.org/wiki/Free_Speech_Movement. See also Seth Rosenfeld's interview of Clark Kerr, 10 June 2002, *San Francisco Chronicle*, www.commondreams.org/headlines02/0610-05.htm.

209 Herb Childs indicates in his manuscript on file at UCLA Archives that Elbert Pauley also invested in the corporation. This author has found no evidence that he did.

210 H. S. Truman, cited in David McCullough, *Truman* (New York: Simon and Shuster), 932.

211 John Brosnan, "Coconut Isle Will Offer Rare Vacation to Trumans," *Honolulu Star-Bulletin*, 25 March 1953, 8.

212 Ibid.

213 McCullough, 932.

214 A play, no doubt, on "Kitchen Cabinet," a press term for the Truman style of administration.

215 Robert Ferrell, *Harry S. Truman and the Modern American Presidency* (Boston: Little, Brown, 1983), 154.

216 Years later the author had the pleasure of seating Mrs. Johnson at a luncheon at Glacier National Park Hotel dining room. Seconds later an interloper burst through a service door from the bar and ran past Mrs. Johnson's table, prompting a flurry of activity from the Secret Service agents. Perhaps it was something about luncheons.

217 Edward Carter became chair of the Board of Trustees from 1964–1968. He is fondly remembered for bequeathing his Japanese Garden to UCLA.

218 Bare.

219 "1st Culture-rock Fest a Success," *The Honolulu Advertiser*, 13 October 1969, A4.

220 "Volunteers to Clean Up Coconut Isle," *The Honolulu Advertiser*, 13 October 1970, C5.

221 As a young instructor teaching an anthropology class at the base, I vividly recall competing with jet afterburners during my lectures.

222 Rick Carroll, "For Sale-One Island," *The Honolulu Advertiser*, 31 October 1985, B1.

223 James Dooley, "Coconut Island Sale Stymied," *The Honolulu Advertiser*, 23 May 1995, A1, A2.

224 Ibid., A5.

225 Rick Daysog, "Coconut Island, Eaton Square Sales OK'd," *Honolulu Star-Bulletin*, 4 August 1995, B1.

226 Darren Pai, "$9 Million Gift Uplifts Coconut Isle Lab Status," *The Honolulu Advertiser*, 7 September 1995, A5.

227 Dooley, A2.

228 Daysog.

229 Ibid.

230 It was during this time that the author began research on the Coconut Island project. Due to the sensitivity of the negotiations, it was a difficult time to interview the parties involved, or even be present on the island. Fortunately, that epoch passed quickly.

231 Bare.

[232] D. M. Karl, "UH and the Sea. The Emergence of Marine Expeditionary Research and Oceanography as a field of Study at the University of Hawaii." Unpublished ms., May 2004, 3–31.

Chapter 6

[233] E. A. Kay in R. Kamins and R. Potter, *Malamalama: A History of the University of Hawaii* (Honolulu: University of Hawai'i Press, 1998), 196.

[234] O. A. Bushnell, "Forward" in *Malamalama: A History of the University of Hawaii* (Honolulu: University of Hawai'i Press, 1998), viii.

[235] Karl.

[236] Ibid.

[237] Ibid.

[238] Ibid.

[239] Kay in R. Kamins and R. Potter, 200.

[240] Frederick Potter, Jr., personal communication.

[241] Robert Weyeneth, *Kapiolani Park: a history* (Honolulu: Kapiolani Park Preservation Soc., 2002), 105.

[242] R. Kamins and R. Potter, *Malamalama*, 319.

[243] P. Jokiel, "Ultraviolet Radiation and Coral Reefs," Report on the E.W. Pauley Summer Program in Marine Biology, 15 June 1994 to 15 August 1994. Ms. on file, HIMB, Coconut Island, Hawai'i.

[244] R. W. Hiatt, personal communication.

[245] R. W. Hiatt. As told to R. Potter. "Organized Research Units" in *Malamalama: A History of the University of Hawaii* (Honolulu: University of Hawai'i Press, 1998), 190–191.

[246] Ibid.

[247] Karl, 3–37.

[248] R. W. Hiatt, personal communication.

[249] Karl, 3–41.

[250] Ibid., 3–43.

[251] Hawaiian for "house."

[252] A. L. Tester and S. Hsiao, "Reaction of Tuna to Stimuli-1952-1953. Part II Response of tuna to visual and visual-chemical stimuli," U.S. Fish & Wildlife Service, Spec. Sci. Report Fisheries, no. 130: 63–76.

[253] A. L. Tester, "Olfaction, gestation, and the common chemical sense in sharks," in *Sharks and Survival* (Boston: D. C. Heath, 1968), 255–282.

[254] Karl, 3–43.

[255] P. Helfrich and R. Ray in *The Natural History of Enewetak Atoll: Vol. I–The Ecosystem: Environments, Biotos, and Processes* (Office of Scientific and Technical Information, US Department of Energy, 1987).

[256] R. E. Johannes et. al. with Chris D'Elia, "The metabolism of some coral reef communities: A team study of nutrient and energy flux at Eniwetok," *BioScience* 22: 541–543.

[257] A. H. Banner, P. Helfrich, P. J. Scheuer, and T. Yoshida, "Research on Ciguatera in the Tropical Pacific." (Proc. Gulf & Caribbean Fisheries Institute, 1963), 84–98.

[258] A. H. Banner, P. Scheuer, S. Sasaki, P. Helfrich, and C. B. Alender, "Observations of ciguatera-type toxin in fish." *Annals N.Y. Acad. Sci* 90(3): 770–778.

[259] Karl 3–39

[260] Les Nouvelles, Papeete, Tahiti 17.8, 1968.

261 P. J. Scheuer, "Ciguatera and it off shoots—Chance encounters en route to a molecular structure," *Tetrahedron* 50(1): 3–18.

262 T. Yasumoto, I. Nakajima, E. Chungue, R. Bagnis, *Bull. Japan Soc. Sci. Fish,* 43: 69–74.

263 Y. Hokama, A. H. Banner, D. Boylan, *Toxicon* 15: 321–325.

264 N. Palafox, L. Jain, A. Pinano, T, Gulick, R. Williams, I. Schatz, *J. Am. Med. Assoc.* 259: 2740–2742.

265 V. E. Brock, "A Proposed Program for Hawaiian Fisheries," Hawaii Marine Laboratory, 1965.

266 J. Bardach, J. Ryther, and W. O. McLarney. *Aquaculture: The Farming and Husbandry of Freshwater and Marine Organisms* (Hoboken, NJ: John Wiley, Inc., 1972).

267 J. V. Bryne, Byrne Report on UH Marine Programs, 21 November 1977.

268 P. L. Jokiel and S. L. Coles, "Effects of temperature on the mortality and growth of Hawaiian reef corals," *Mar. Biol.* 43: 201–208.

269 P. L. Jokiel, "Temperature Stress and Coral Bleaching," in *Coral Health and Disease* (Heidelberg: Springer-Verlag, 2004), 401–425.

270 In another great irony in the family, Christian Holmes IV, grandson of Christian II who mined the coral reefs and sandbars to create Coconut Island, rose to become Chief Operating Officer of the U.S. Environmental Protection Agency.

271 S. V. Smith, W. J. Kimmerer, E. A. Laws, R. E. Brock, and T. W. Walsh, "Kaneohe Bay sewage diversion experiment: perspectives on ecosystem response to nutritional perturbation," *Pac. Sci.* 35: 279–395.

272 Ludwig Franzisket, "The Atrophy of Hermatypic Reef Corals Maintained in Darkness and their Subsequent Regeneration of Light," *Int. Revue ges Hydrobiol.*, 1970.

273 P. L. Jokiel, S. P. Kolinski, J. Naughton and J. E. Maragos, "Review of coral reef restoration and mitigation in Hawaii and the U. S. Affiliated Pacific Islands," in *Coral Reef Restoration Handbook* (Boca Raton, FL: CRC Press, 2006).

274 Coconut Island Long Range Development Plan, prepared by Group 70 International, Inc., June 1998.

275 Ibid.

276 M. J. Atkinson and J. L Falter, "Coral Reefs," in *Biogeochemistry of Marine Systems* (Boca Raton, FL: CRC Press, 2003), 40–64.

277 Group 70 International, Inc., Coconut Island (Moku o Lo'e) Long Range Development Plan, prepared for Hawaii Institute of Marine Biology, September 2003, 1-1.

Epilogue

278 Hawai'i Institute of Marine Biology, Strategic Plan, 2005, 1. Ms in author's collection.

279 Ibid.

280 Devaney, et al.

Index

Roosevelt, Eleanor, 165, 167
Roosevelt, Franklin Delano, 124, 157, 161–162
Roosevelt, Theodore, Jr., 61
RV *Salpa*, 4, 213, 217

| S

Sakamoto, Soichi, 4, 186–187
Seth Parker, SS, 33, 80, 83, 90, 101, 104, 106–113, 127, 129, 135, 149, 202, 217
Sharkey Bill, 157
sharks, 31, 33, 77, 80, 83, 88, 96–97, 98, 188, 219, 221, 236, 239, 252, n253
Signal Hill oilfields, 154, 157
Signal Oil and Gas Company, 132
Skelton, Red, 183, 184
Standard Brands, 65–67, n98
Steinhart Aquarium, 116
sugarcane, cultivation of, 23, 28, 31, 42–46, 257
Sumner George, 2, 90, 104, 105
Sunshine & Health Club, 146-147, n189

| T

taro, cultivation of, 21–23, 26, 28–29, 33, 42–44, 92
tax, claims on Coconut Island, 143–144, 146, n176
Temple, Shirley, 98, 100–101
Terrell, Ann Holmes, 1, 101, 103, 118, n149
Tester, Albert, 211, 215, 219–221, 239, 260
Thompson advertising agency, J. Walter, 63–64

Tito, Marshall Joseph, 165, 169
Truman, Bess, 174–177
Truman, Harry S., 5, 9, 16, 132, 138, 161–163, 172–177, 180, 196, n206, n210, n211, n214, n215

tuna: captivity, 216, 217, 236; fishing, 7, 16, 33, 74–77, 97–98, 111, 121, 208, 219, 220

| U

University of Hawai'i Foundation, 16, 206–207, 210
Uyehara, Ethel, 2, 87, 105, 115

| W

Waikalua pier, 105, 138, 213, 217
Waikiki Aquarium, 210-211, 212
Wailehua, Rose, 4, 181, 187
Wake of the Red Witch, The, 111
Walker, Henry, 2, 67, 184
Whittaker, Elvi, 13, 15, 72
Woolman, Marge, 131, 190, 191

| Y

yeast, 54, 55, 61, 63–64, 67, 77

| Z

Zukeran, Lester, 1, 4, 9, 10, 30, 90, 91–93, 97, 103, 121, 202, 213, 216–218, 224, 230, 260